When Everything Beyond the Walls Is Wild

THE SEVENTH GENERATION
Survival, Sustainability, Sustenance in a New Nature

A WARDLAW BOOK

WHEN EVERYTHING BEYOND THE WALLS IS WILD

BEING A WOMAN OUTDOORS IN AMERICA

LILACE MELLIN GUIGNARD

Foreword by M. Jimmie Killingsworth

TEXAS A&M UNIVERSITY PRESS • COLLEGE STATION, TEXAS

This paper meets the requirements of
ANSI/NISO Z39.48–1992 (Permanence of Paper).
Binding materials have been chosen for durability.
Manufactured in the United States of America

Library of Congress Cataloging-in-Publication Data

Names: Guignard, Lilace Mellin, author.
Title: When everything beyond the walls is wild: being a woman outdoors in
    America / Lilace Mellin Guignard; foreword by M. Jimmie Killingsworth.
Description: First edition. | College Station: Texas A&M University Press,
    [2019] | Series: The seventh generation: survival, sustainability, sustenance in
    a new nature | Series: A Wardlaw book |
Identifiers: LCCN 2018045370 (print) | LCCN 2018046390 (ebook) | ISBN
    9781623497651 (ebook) | ISBN 9781623497644 | ISBN 9781623497644
    (pbk. : alk. paper)
Subjects: LCSH: Outdoorsmen—United States—Biography. | Women
    naturalists—United States—Biography. | Naturalists—United
    States—Biography. | Outdoor life—United States. | Outdoor recreation for
    women—United States.
Classification: LCC GV191.52.G85 (ebook) | LCC GV191.52.G85 W54 2019
    (print) | DDC 796.082—dc23
LC record available at https://lccn.loc.gov/2018045370

Contents

Foreword

In this provocative memoir, Lilace Mellin Guignard chronicles her quest to find a satisfying representation of outdoor experience beyond the stereotype of nature as wild and dangerous for women. From girlhood to motherhood, she measures the received wisdom against her own life as a rock climber, river guide, professor of outdoor recreation leadership and women's studies, poet, and environmental activist. Onto the story of her own experience, she grafts episodes from the lives of other women she has studied, including such colorful characters as Grandma Gatewood, the first woman to thru-hike the Appalachian Trail (at age sixty-seven), and other women adventurers whom history has largely ignored. This broadening of context, never pedantic and always relevant to her own personal narrative, places the adventuresome author in a sisterhood of brilliant and energetic women whom the wilderness has attracted with a fierce and undeniable power. These women ("wild" in many ways but rarely in the ways that the stereotype of the wild woman might suggest) must overcome not only the external barriers of culture, conventional morality, and even fashion but also the internal barriers of having grown up being told of the danger they face outside the home. Guignard draws deeply upon her scholarship in natural history, human history, literary ecology, and women's writing but resists the clichés and catchwords of academic scholarship to keep her own writing readable and suitable for a wide audience. Her prose style draws more upon her work as a poet than upon her status as a professor. In fact, she inserts among the narrative chapters prose poems that seek the deeper edges of her emotions and desires. And yet the prose is never overwritten or pretentious. It fits the subject matter like a good, tight climbing harness. The writing never detracts from the forward momentum of the story, which flows like a river unimpeded by obstructions and self-consciousness.

Her message is that while all individuals approach the wild in different ways, women are capable of taking control of their choices and enriching their overall experience through a meaningful encounter with the natural world, even if it's sometimes a complicated business. "Both women and nature are protected, restricted, and made passive," she writes, and she aims to set the world aright with new possibilities.

In addition to the elements of memoir and women's history, the book offers some fine travel writing and adventure tales. From the Cascades to the Great Smokies, from the swift rivers and high mountains of California to the forested hills of Pennsylvania and North Carolina, the narrative follows the risk-taking adventurer through half a lifetime of encounters with nature, humanity (highly gendered as it is), and herself. The very concept of risk comes under analysis in an interesting way, drawing on Paul Slovic's suggestive distinction between risk and danger, the former a problem of perception, the latter a problem of experience. What's wonderful about Guignard's writing is that the story never suffers from excursions into philosophy, history, and poetry. It just keeps flowing along, carrying the reader on a reliably smooth current.

For the Seventh Generation series at Texas A&M University Press, the book offers a much-needed feminist perspective on the New Nature. It reveals the assumptions and attitudes that stand in the way of an outdoor experience for women (and for people of color and others beyond the range of the straight white male stereotype that still dominates the model of the heroic adventurer), and it reveals the rewards and insights that come to the woman who risks defiance and seeks adventure. It is a book that will open the eyes of male readers, even those who thought they understood the plight of women in the wild, and for women readers, it offers both an invitation to take matters in hand and an encouraging model for exploring the world beyond the walls.

—M. Jimmie Killingsworth
Series Editor

When Everything Beyond the Walls Is Wild

With brother Tom on Champlain Mountain, Acadia National Park

Setting Out

It was 1976, the nation's bicentennial. Stretched out on my belly in the cab-over of the small motor home, my nine-year-old body couldn't sit up, but that was fine. For once I didn't have to share my space. My tall teenage brothers took turns below in the shotgun seat beside Dad where they could stretch their legs and get the best view. Above them, with the curtain pulled between me and the kitchen and dining area where Mom rode, I watched the short-wide panorama change from strip malls and the occasional mixed hardwood forest to wide rivers, flat plains with intimidating skies, the orange-raspberry desert, and finally the fairy-tale spires of Bryce Canyon rising from unlikely gouges in the earth. Dad's calls of what we were passing were followed at meals with stories of when he, his brothers, and parents took their version of this trip in a Model T.

I didn't realize how much more there was to see beyond the Maryland suburbs until my family of five piled into the Shasta motor home Dad bought thirdhand and set out for two weeks cross-country. Our route was planned around visiting major national parks. Oh, I'd been to the Smithsonian museums many times on school trips, but the historical parks seemed like a slightly more interesting schoolwork assignment. I preferred going to Greenbelt National Park only ten miles away to walk the mere 1,176 acres of familiar trees and creeks. On the outer trails I could hear the highway's rumble over the wind's rush. The size and silence of western parks and their looming landforms changed my frame of reference forever.

The visitor center walls plastered with images of wild land and people revealed a secret to us kids once we reached California. There, in the exhibits for Sequoia and Kings Canyon

National Parks, Grampa's face stared at us. Not Grampa, Dad explained, but Grampa's uncle, William E. Colby, secretary of the Sierra Club from 1900 to 1946, who camped and crusaded alongside none other than John Muir. Maybe my brothers knew who John Muir, founder of the Sierra Club, was. For me, I met him in that visitor center.

This was the most exciting of the exhibits, the only one as exciting to me as the gift shops. Once, I was allowed to buy a toy bison whose pelt was rabbit fur glued over a plastic frame. The incongruity of that didn't sink in then, and neither did the fact that I rarely saw women highlighted in the displays, gift shop books, or even ranger uniforms. I'd long been accustomed to inserting myself into the male hero's role in any narrative.

The following year, we explored New England, culminating in Acadia National Park. My fantasies of adventure and exploration were aided by my father's decision to let me come on the hike up Champlain Mountain—which included metal rungs bolted into the rock—despite my mother's concern and my brother's arguments that I'd slow him down. It was one of the few excursions that went beyond the quick trails off the parking lot, and I reveled in how the space opened up beneath and behind us, how no railing or mother was there to corral me.

For most American women, culture has defined anything beyond walls and social protections as wild and dangerous. Yet many women have found it exciting and freeing to step into the wild where gender expectations can be easier to shed, the way nineteenth-century female mountaineers often shucked their skirts at the base of a mountain climb. Not all women have the same experiences or perceptions, but women all face the same forces to different extents and must make—or demand the right to make—our own choices.

This book charts my struggles as a girl and young woman to access the outdoor spaces and activities that sustained me, and the quest to understand the forces that still inhibit many women's participation in outdoor recreation and their connection to nature. I found that my struggles were shaped by American history and cultural assumptions. Looking back on my experiences outdoors, I can see how my academic pursuits, the courses I've taught, and my environmental activism have helped me take control of my choices, learn to assess risk for myself, and enjoy adventure and challenge outdoors—with men, on my own, and in groups of women. Now when thinking of nine-year-old me, I am more grateful than ever that my father made a place for me in those early adventures.

My experiences have exposed me to a variety of American women's perceptions of outdoor spaces. I have known theoretical feminists who were afraid to crack their windows, let alone venture beyond the shrubbery in the way of Jane Austen's Elizabeth Bennet. I have also known female raft guides who didn't consider themselves feminists and were confused by how some male guests and coworkers treated them, by the mixed messages and impossible expectations. Many women are terrified of nature (especially the dark), while others wish to live a life in pure nature without all the cultural muck dragging them down; and there are women everywhere in between. And not just women. Recently the stories of many whose identity is not as simple as male or female have claimed an important place in our understanding of nature and gender. After all, ecology teaches us that diversity equals strength and greater adaptation.

This book braids my stories together with what I've learned from varied disciplines, including cultural geography, American history, literary criticism, recreation and leisure studies, and feminist theory. It explores how the American theoretical and metaphorical understanding of women and nature is more tangled than a laurel hell in the Blue Ridge Mountains. It asks: Why does it matter that everyone have the opportunity for experiences that often lead to increased self-reliance and a greater sense of connection to the natural world? What do we risk by perpetuating messages that keep women afraid in spaces beyond the public protections we are told we need? Why is our culture, which encourages women to overshop and loathe our bodies, so threatened by women who step outside that conditioning? Can playing outdoors become a way to help achieve social change, rather than retreat from responsibility?

As in other areas of inquiry, women who want to advance the understanding of how gender affects people's interaction with outdoor spaces must hunt harder to find their path. It doesn't help that the paths women have pioneered outdoors have been ignored and rarely marked, unlike those of their white male counterparts. Or that women have been told we *are* nature and therefore do not need to venture *into* nature. This is in contrast to what men are told: they are animals—wild and uncontrolled—while simultaneously being at risk of becoming overcivilized. Men, American culture tells us, *need* risk and wildness. Men *belong* in rugged outdoor spaces. And even as women are conflated with nature, we are warned away from it, because of the potential danger of both nature itself and the men that inhabit those wild spaces. American culture separates women from nature in the same way it separates nature from routine human experience. Both women and nature are protected, restricted, objectified, idealized, and made passive.

Walking in the wilds, women and members of the LGBT+ communities carry the warnings and threats from society in our heads—that by venturing into wild spaces we are asking for it. That we are possibly *more* sexualized and objectified in such spaces, even as we attempt to escape such cultural labels and restraints. Our doubts and fears are a constant reminder of the bodies we cannot transcend. Yet, for this reason, we might spend less time than straight white males mourning the loss of "old nature," romantic and unadulterated by culture. Fact is, most of us have rarely experienced nature divorced from culture. For this reason, we may be less paralyzed and more creative in the face of environmental and climate threats. If fully included in the conversation and expedition, those of us "others" who have been denied easy cultural access to wild spaces can be important trailblazers in understanding and bonding with the planet we've altered.

For us, it's always been an imperfect world.

With Junior on first road trip, Wyoming

Independence, Road Trips, and Backpacking

LARGE AS LAND

As a teenage girl, there were many things I never questioned, such as how in cheap romances even the *strong* women get rescued at least once. Seems I was savvier in grade school, before being blinded by purple eye shadow, when I'd hated Valentine's Day—all those invitations to BE MINE sealed in envelopes with my name misspelled. But as an adolescent, my daydreams were filled with catastrophes, any excuse to be held by someone. At seventeen I decided I'd leave the cookie-cutter town I grew up in and went to college in the Blue Ridge Mountains. After college I drove far enough that none of my high school's suburban expectations could reach me. I had no address. Mother couldn't send any more letters folded around "Dear Abby" clippings on date rape or how to walk home after dark if you're a woman.

I want to tell you a story about one night when I finally learned something really important, something never covered in any class or advice column. Like you, I'd been told by parents and teachers there were things that couldn't be taught, but it seemed they always tried to teach you anyway. Human sexuality class, for instance. Certain obvious homework assignments were never given. Even worse was when my friends who'd lost their virginity the night before gave me advice on when and how to do it, and when and how not to. But when you're young it can be hard to tell assumptions from wisdom born of experience, and some assumptions hang like burs to your cuffs as you grow older. And you go on, unaware that they're slowing you down.

I've tried to tell this story before. It never worked because

I told it for the wrong reasons. This time I'm going to tell it differently.

♣♣♣

Before grad school, I drove cross-country. It was an adventure I'd studied for. My dog sat in the passenger seat of my truck—she liked to ride with her nose pressed against the windshield—and everything else I owned was piled in the back or tied down. We were headed west. (If I told you any more, you might expect the destination to be an important part of the story, which it's not. Which it rarely is.) On the afternoon before the night in question, we were in New Mexico. I drove into Elephant Butte Lake State Park—there are dams all along that section of the Rio Grande—and paid the ranger for one night's camping. First, he came up to the passenger window. My dog, who'd been lying out of sight, jumped up and barked at him. She isn't a barker. They were both startled, but she stopped when the ranger came to my side of the car and we started talking.

I took the road the man pointed to. It was over flat stones that had been loved too well by water, and these stones looked just like the stones around them so that there wasn't really a road at all, just someone's expectation of where others should go. My truck made noises unlike those it made driving the gravel roads I'd explored in the Appalachians, noises that said this experience was the same in some ways, but I wouldn't understand what made it different until later. It was more than that the rocks were bigger and had milder surfaces.

There were two lakes connected by a channel. Speedboats zoomed back and forth, skiers on the end of the line at the boater's mercy. It reminded me of playing tug-of-war with small dogs, the yippy kind that no one likes because they're weak and hardly real dogs at all. I headed for the area farthest from the boat ramp.

There weren't campsites in the usual sense. The picnic tables were randomly spaced and far apart, each accompanied by a fire ring. I chose my spot because it was well within sight of a family's Winnebago while still being pretty much on its own, and there was a space big enough for my tent that someone before me had cleared of rocks. This was one of the rare days I stopped early enough to play. At the time, I thought I was experiencing the land, when really I never left my own head.

Once, while I was telling the story, an older male friend asked, "What do you think it is you're running from?" I had no answer. I didn't understand the question.

First, I hooked my dog's chain to the picnic table and set out her bowls. I set the pink cooler on the table and threw my tent, still in its bag, on the ground nearby. I didn't set it up right then because the breeze was strong, and even if I weighted down the corners with rocks, the tent could still be blown around and rip. I was proud of myself for averting that disaster.

I didn't want to worry about anything; I just wanted to let the lake water bathe me at no extra charge. I'd driven four days without air conditioning, my dog sweating through her tongue and me through everything. I took her to the water's edge, not far from where I'd stationed my stuff, and tossed stones in scattered directions so she could chase their splashes. When she was wet full-through her oily outer coat, I left her on the chain to curl in the shade beneath the table. From a box of clothes, I grabbed an old orange bikini and towel. Barefoot, I walked across warm stones to change in the Porta-John, which stood out with commanding awkwardness—like a priestless confession booth—forty yards away. I headed toward the lake. My dog picked up her head when I passed. I looked back over my shoulder, the water rising higher on my thighs, waist, to see whether she'd bark, to see how long she'd watch me. I dove in and surfaced. She was still watching. I swam away.

Dripping, I found the cord I'd stashed in case what I'd strapped on the truck started slipping, and I made a clothesline that stretched from the roof rack at a long slant to where I tied it to the table. After changing into shorts and a cleaner T-shirt, I hung my two-piece and towel on the line where they flapped sometimes, the way the flags outside motor homes across the lake flapped. It was the fifth of July and a Friday. On the other, sandier side of the reservoir, RVs lined up like tanks. I pitched my tent, leaving the fly off since it was hot and rain unlikely. Inside I laid a thin foam pad, faded sheets, and pillow. For the next couple of hours I studied the map or sunbathed or read a dime-store romance. No one came by to offer me a beer (not that I'd take it), and I didn't go for a walk or look for company. I knew better. It wasn't the 1970s, when sisters looked out for sisters. It was the early 1990s, and I'd seen only guys and families as I traveled.

Later I ate refried beans from the can. Using a spoon kept in the glove compartment, I alternated bites with my dog, loving how her head twisted to allow her tongue into the curve. I didn't own a camp stove and never bothered with a fire because I traveled alone and who would I sit up and talk to?

> At this point a boyfriend (who did have a camp stove) said, "Well, at least you don't have to travel alone anymore."
> What I said back isn't part of this story.

I listened to the distant sounds of the family closest to me as the parents called their children to bed. I could hear them, but not well enough to make out names or to be sure whether they spoke Spanish or just had heavy accents. As the sun left,

I put the cooler back in the car and dumped my trash in the barrel by the Porta-John, where I made one more stop before bed. When I came out, only the front cab light was on where the mother and father had pulled the curtain behind them and sat close together, probably whispering. In the darkness, the Winnebago had shrunk as small as stars.

I left the truck unlocked, still tied to the table, but unchained my dog. We settled in, and I could see out the mesh, the breeze moving through it like a ghost. This wasn't one of those campgrounds that put streetlights up everywhere; I was grateful I didn't have to hide my head to sleep.

When I woke up at 2:30 a.m. it was because of the noise. A pickup with its headlights jerking through the darkness stumbled over the rocks, radio playing. Figuring they'd shirked the fee by arriving late, I hoped they'd pick a spot, set up quickly, and go to sleep. They drove around the far side of the Winnebago (I didn't look but could tell from the movement of the music) and stopped near the water. I heard young male voices shout in Spanish before they turned the radio up. I couldn't tell what they were saying, but drunk is drunk in any language.

This is the part where my mother said, "Now don't you wish you'd stuck with your Spanish?"

I didn't tell her they were drunk, just obnoxious. I didn't tell her the rest of the story.

It was easy to figure that even Truth or Consequences (the nearest large town) had nothing for teenagers to do on a Friday night, let alone a holiday weekend. All I wanted was for them to turn the music down. At some point one guy did, but I guess the others didn't like his decision. Bottles knocked. The comparative quiet lasted five minutes at most.

Of course, now that I was awake, I had to go to the

bathroom. The guys were far enough away to suit me (though nearer to me than the family, whose walls, I hoped, were thick enough to buffer them). I propped up on my elbows. The Porta-John looked tiny; no way was I going to tramp out in the open like that. I unzipped the flap, got out, and zipped it up again. My truck stood between me and where their pickup hunkered, headlights swimming in the lake. I crouched by my back tire to pee.

    This is where a friend's sister who'd been listening said, "Gross" and left the room.

Because part of me was straining to hear them over the music, it was kind of hard to get started. It sounded like the guys were sitting in the back of their truck, sometimes jumping out and running to the edge to chuck rocks in the water and at each other. I was almost done peeing when I heard their engine start. They turned in my direction and slowly followed the bank. I didn't think, I just climbed in the front seat and lay across it, pleased that I'd turned off the dome light earlier when the door was open. I pushed the lock down now.

    Here's where my friend laughed at me and said, "You're so paranoid! No wonder you never meet anyone on your trips."

The music's beat fought to match the tires' rhythm. Headlights swung toward my stuff and stopped in my windshield. The smudges from my dog's nose shone like greasy hieroglyphics. All at once I could picture my orange bikini glowing on the line, hanging like telltale scraps snagged by a branch when someone had run by. I'd left the keys on my seat; they were digging into my hip. The rope would break easily. I thought of my dog, probably snoring. If I were in the tent I could wake her up and get her barking. I wondered what would have to happen, how bad it would have to get, before I'd leave her behind.

> When I told my brother, he scowled and was probably thinking what good is a dog who'd sleep through this anyway, but he knows me and said nothing.

I lay with my face in the passenger seat a long time, not knowing what I'd do if one or more of them came up to the window and saw me. I couldn't hear very well with the windows up. There was no way to be sure what was happening out there. That was the worst, wondering whether I'd be found cowering before anything had even happened. When maybe nothing would. But they didn't see me, and after they'd driven off— not out the same road but on around the lake—I decided I wouldn't hide that way again if they came back.

I got out of my truck and looked around. The lake was still beautiful, and I didn't want to be scared off. Though dark, the sky managed to shine enough that I knew it was no threat. Alone I was safe.

> At this, the guy at the Christmas party moved closer and said, "I find strong women very attractive."

In the tent, my dog was awake. I pulled her against me. If they came back, I thought (not knowing what the chances were), and if they came over to where I was camped, I would fake sleep unless someone got out of the truck. Then I'd step out of my tent and confront them, only mentioning the noise and would they please turn their radio down. My pepper spray in the tent pocket had seemed practical once. How come I'd never imagined there'd be a group of guys? I could yell to the people in the Winnebago—but, given what had just happened, what were the odds of them hearing? That was the first time it occurred to me that even if they woke up they might not help.

When I told my father this (having made him promise not to tell Mother), he nodded and looked away. I wondered whether he was thinking of the phenomenon of bystander noninterference he'd once told me about but never explained. Then he started in on his own story of how he'd often had to hitchhike home from college in the rain, and though each time he'd thought no one would give him a ride, someone always did. I never finished telling him mine.

This part is an experiment.

I haven't had much practice telling the rest of this story. In place of describing everything that went through my head as I tried to fall back asleep, I'll tell you instead how I used to trick myself into falling asleep as a little girl. I made up a game to keep my mind occupied in a way that required my body stay relaxed and still. I created monsters. First, I dreamed up a story of a great and dangerous contest, which involved eleven rooms in the hall of a far-away and legendary building. No one lived there anymore, but the owner made money by offering a huge reward to the person who could stay in one of the rooms all night and wake up alive the next morning. The participants would pay a fee and then, when eleven had signed up (it could take years), the contest would be held. At dark, so the story went, all sorts of nasty flesh-hungry creatures emerged. Over the centuries only one person was rumored to have survived. And that had been long ago.

Many parts of the story didn't make sense, but I'd gloss over those details. What I was sure about was that somehow I had discovered the secret to surviving one night with the beasts. Maybe I'd found it in an old book, or maybe a great-grandson of the first and only winner—grateful after I'd saved him from certain death elsewhere—had passed it on to me. The "how" changed each night. What mattered was that the monsters would eat only *live* humans. By itself, this information wasn't helpful, but when combined with the knowledge that the monsters of room number six were not at the head of their class— they thought steady in-and-out breathing was a sign of death rather than life—well! The hurdles of adulthood that would now keep me from believing such a secret didn't faze the girl who, back then, could leap impossibly high without wishing for someone to catch her.

While the evening would turn to dusk and the dusk to something that grown-up words had painted black, I'd lie motionless under the covers, eyelids unflickering, and concentrate on breathing evenly. Then I'd imagine the monsters, none of them alike, pushing the door open and slogging with all varieties of monster feet over to my bed. I'd purposefully picture them leaning so close to my body that the green nameless things hanging from the big one's face would graze my flowered bedspread. I'd busy my mind with conjuring the scene in new and greater detail than the night before. I was so very careful not to move at all (while pretending they poked and prodded at my shoulders, belly, hips) that eventually I'd fall asleep.

Always waking up alive the next morning.

I wasn't scared to go to bed as a little girl. I was simply playing with fear and found it useful in this way. This is not what I did in the tent with the night moving in and out of my mesh-and-nylon bedroom. That night I *was* scared, and there were no secrets. I knew I'd set myself up to be a sidebar in the local papers, the ones mothers everywhere laid by their daughter's juice glass each morning. I was ashamed and angry, but I knew how to breathe

in and out. How to lie still. And when the pickup's noise woke
me up at 4:00 a.m. and again at 4:30, that's what I did.

As the truck idled nearby, I feigned sleep and occupied my
brain by developing new strategies for future camping trips.
With my eyes shut against the headlights pointed in the back
of my tent from forty feet away, I listened to the strange voices
while listing the things I should get: a used pair of men's briefs
for the clothesline and maybe a pair of my brother's old boots to
set outside where they'd be seen. I listened for truck doors or feet
landing on stones. I could carry one of those small tape players
with my brother's voice saying something like "Who the hell is
out there? Honey, hand me my gun." Of course, then I'd have to
put the fly on the tent so no one could see inside, which would
mean I wouldn't be able to see out, either. Damn, I'd hate to lose
the stars. At the very least, I'd never hang my bikini up again.

No matter how much noise they made, I didn't move. They
never got out of the truck. In the end the guys circled a few times
before heading for a nearby picnic table. From the noise they
made, I gathered they tied it to their bumper and dragged it off.

> This is the end of my story, the part where a woman I
> work with asked, "Why do you do it, travel alone, camp
> by yourself? It's stupid. Don't you read the papers? You're
> asking for it, you know."

You will believe what you want. That I was stupid, or brave, or
ordinary. But how can getting surprised by a bear in the woods
be more stupid than crying at home over someone who doesn't
call for weeks, or over what he says when he does? I'd rather five
guys stomp around my campsite at night, speaking a language I
don't understand, shining their lights through my screen. I don't
know what I would've done if they hadn't left, only what I'd have
missed by not going. What is the world if not a body as much

mine as others'? What is this life but a gift I may sigh away or
risk for something large as land, heartbreaking as an open sky?

MEN AND TENTS

I turned twenty in a small, rural liberal-arts college full of
peace activists, environmentalists, vegetarians, and streakers.
Lured south from the suburbs of DC by the space, green hills,
lush trees—and did I say space?—I chose the school of five
hundred students because it was in the Blue Ridge Mountains
of Western North Carolina. Even though I was carless, there
were over 1,100 acres of creeks, cow-dotted fields, thick rhodo-
dendrons, and muddy root-threaded trails I could roam when

Camping by the Colorado River, Grand Canyon National Park

not in class. The air smelled of pine and freedom. I wasn't a feminist; I was a tomboy whose mother had stayed at home and whose father had encouraged me in all my escapades. I'd kept up with my older brothers, spoke up for myself, and felt that if anything I was an individualist. Feminists were victims. They hated men. Nope, not me.

This was the late 1980s and already young women were starting to forget the recent struggles of the women's libbers. I wince now at how averse I was to being associated with anything that had the prefix "fem." Apparently I'd bought the cultural message that women were somehow less than men. I wanted to be associated with masculine traits of independence and strength, and I wanted to be in the places where guys were doing the things guys did: hanging out with my uncles on the porch rather than in the kitchen with my aunts; managing the men's soccer team rather than playing on the women's team; paddling rapids rather than learning the names of wildflowers.

I didn't know then that women's ability to move about freely in outdoor spaces had been declining since the ancestors of Western civilization shifted from hunter-gatherers to nomadic herders to settled farmers. "It is only with the coming of agriculture," writes eco-philosopher Paul Shepard, "that [women] were sentenced to confinement." I'd felt confined in the suburbs, certainly, especially by my overprotective mother, whose fears for me I interpreted as her own timidity. But on the banks of the Swannanoa River, sunning on flat rocks to catch the first heat of spring, dangling a foot in the cold water as long as I could stand it, I finally let down my walls. If I'd read Paul Shepard's quote then, I probably would've shrugged it off as easily as my shirt.

My freshman year at Warren Wilson College, I took a white-water canoeing class on a whim, developing strength and good technique. It turned out that as an English major, I could read rivers as well as I could read poetry. The canoeing instructor got several of us summer jobs at Nantahala Outdoor Center, and when I wasn't washing dishes in the restaurant I was learning about kayaking, skinny-dipping, rock climbing, and the Grateful Dead. A road trip to Georgia for a day of multipitch climbing at Mount Yonah was the first time I'd sat on a midcliff ledge alone, attached by a rope to people I could no longer see, watching vultures and hang gliders trade graceful arcs below my feet.

But it wasn't until spring break of my senior year that I tried backpacking. Some friends were planning a trip to Cumberland Island off the Georgia coast, reachable only by boat. They had a permit to hike in past the campground on the national seashore and camp in the wilderness area—a place where feral horses, nine-banded armadillos, and American alligators roamed free and people were scarce. I had no gear, but boosted by their confidence in me (perhaps spurred by their need for another vehicle and my owning a pickup with a cap), I found myself with new boots, a cheap backpack bought on sale, a borrowed sleeping bag, and space in Mike's two-person tent.

There were six of us on the trip and three tents: one for a boy-girl couple, one for a pair of girls, and one for Mike and me. Mike was a good friend I'd known all four years of college, a stand-up guy. We'd even had our senior picture taken together one day when we were both wearing overalls and looked damn cute. But I'd never felt more than friendship for him, and it never occurred to me that he might feel more. I still don't know whether he did. What I know is that on the third day, as I was sunbathing with the girls, I vaguely recalled Mike getting amorous the night before and my pushing away, rolling over, and ignoring him. So dream fogged was this memory, I doubted whether it had happened. I wasn't sleeping well on the foam mat. But the next night, with my subconscious on alert, I woke up to kisses and sweet murmurs. Sitting up, I told him to stop. Mike apologized and said I was tossing, turning, and whimpering, clearly uncomfortable, and he was trying to soothe me so I'd sleep better. I let him know I'd sleep better being left alone and never had to mention it again.

This had happened before. The summer I was eighteen a group of us had stealth camped illegally in rest areas on the drive from North Carolina to Ohio to see the Grateful Dead. I'd had to shove a male friend away in the middle of those nights too. Friends now tell me I was naive, and I know I was in so many ways. Yet the people I lived with in dorms and river outposts sunbathed naked, skinny-dipped, and stripped by the side of the road to change into dry clothes. We weren't modest or proper. None of this stripping was seen as sexual invitation, and by comparison sharing a tent seemed tame to me. Besides, I wasn't a hottie. But now when I think of how women must often rely on men to gain entrance into outdoor activities and places, it's not surprising that this misunderstanding happens so frequently. As someone who'd always been one of the guys, I never thought to clarify my tent intentions before such trips.

Isn't this partly the message of culture? Men have provided the shelter, the protection, and women have historically paid with their bodies. Not that either guy was thinking this so calculatingly, but I know from other women's stories that my experience is not unusual. Oh, I'd wished for the boyfriend who had his own gear—maybe even a VW bus—and would take me on trips and teach me all I needed to know (wink wink). I had my eye on one but he had a girlfriend, who I had to admit was earthy and beautiful and competent in the out-doors—all the things I wanted to be. It never occurred to me that she might have been all of those before she met him. Luck-ily, I wasn't willing to settle for any guy just so I could take a shortcut to the wilds. I did learn my skills mostly from male friends, and I continued to dread that uncomfortable moment when I needed to clarify that my willingness to share a tent did not extend to zipping our sleeping bags together.

The Dark Side of Outdoor Recreation

Back then, before gear became so commercialized that even those who didn't climb or paddle or camp knew the high-end brands such as North Face and Patagonia, there was still a wide variety of tents: three- or four-season, backpacking or car camping. When picking one out, you must consider whether you want a color that helps you blend into your surroundings or one that can be spotted from a helicopter. What's more important—merging with the natural world or being rescued from it? No purchase has been more exciting than my first tent, though the rusty red was not my favorite color. Bought right after college, it was small enough to carry by myself, and big enough to sit up in. The main reason I chose it was that without the rainfly, I could lie inside and look through mesh at the stars, falling asleep as black-winged spruce swayed against the Milky Way. I could feel the wind while I dreamed.

I could've slept out in the open on clear nights, and it wasn't simply the possibility of bugs that made me prefer the tent. A tent was my small space staked out amid the vast darkness. It made the wild homey. Intimate. I didn't need to claim some land for myself so much as I wanted to feel I belonged. Walls—even soft ones—helped me feel that way. The thin membrane between me and whatever might be out there made me feel safe.

Women have long been told that we're safe only behind walls. At least familiar walls. The Victorian era with its idea of separate spheres indoctrinated us in the concept of gendered spaces. As cities during the industrial revolution turned more chaotic and crowded, homes became the domestic and feminine realm where a man had a chair all his own (the largest and most comfortable) in the parlor, a space managed by his wife as a sanctuary from his work. Here was privacy, where the family could relax tucked away from the rabble of the streets. A place they needn't leave except to shop or go to the park because the man would handle all other necessary aspects of public life such as working, banking, and voting. Essentially, a lady in the city needed either a gentleman companion or a socially acceptable purpose that was immediately evident to anyone who saw her. Except for parties and the theater, for which she would have an escort, a proper lady never left home after dark.

In the 1800s, cities themselves were considered wildernesses—dangerous, full of uncivilized creatures. If a woman ventured out into the wrong area at the wrong time, such as after men had gotten off work, she risked walking the gantlet where groups gathered outside gentlemen's clubs. Rude comments and leers would be thrown her way. But there were places women could walk in public. Large department stores were designed to mimic the Victorian parlor and offered women escape from the home. There they'd stroll, admiring the shop windows, knowing they were as much on display as anything the shops exhibited. Women's acceptable role in public spaces came to be about consumption. No surprise that middle-class (mostly white) women today make up the largest consumer group in the United States. Even in the 1980s, when I was in high school, the enclosed shopping mall was where I'd go after school. It was considered safe (though we still encountered gantlets and creeps). Besides, hanging out in the parks didn't help us keep up with fashion.

But other than parks and city streets, outdoor spaces were not clearly classified in Victorian times. My feelings about tents reflect this cultural confusion. Tents create a domestic patch in the wild beyond the walls. They give privacy to some extent (visually, that is, but the modest should undress with the flashlight off). Being small homes, tents can feel like perfectly acceptable places for women outdoors. They grow more complicated when a woman chooses to tent camp by herself. Mobility has never been a gift freely given to women, and a tent is the ultimate symbol of independence: a house she can take anywhere and provide for herself. So, is a tent a place of protection from the elements and unwanted creatures—thwarting bugs and other visitors who either do not have thumbs to work zippers or are conditioned to understand that even nylon doors shall not be entered uninvited? Or is it an announcement of your vulnerability—flimsy walls and bright colors calling attention to your presence in a space without police or phones or doors that lock? Do we get to choose, or is it always both and more?

Dealing with darkness is the reason I think any activity in which you sleep in tents away from buildings, cars, and toilets is one of the most extreme forms of outdoor recreation for a woman. Before backpacking, I'd hiked alone, paddled Class III rapids, and climbed multipitch rock faces, but none of those activities required me to spend the night in a tent away from the protections women are taught to rely on, especially women like me raised in suburban and urban environments. When I was growing up, walking alone after dark was a big no-no. In "Walking after Midnight," Rebecca Solnit reveals how "legal measures, social mores subscribed to by both men and women, the threat implicit in sexual harassment, and rape itself" have historically limited women's movement in the public sphere. Our language, she points out, reflects condemnation of women's mobility—streetwalkers, women on the town, women of the night, tramps (note the sexual overtone of this term when applied to women, which doesn't occur when applied to men). Walking and sleeping outdoors after sundown require women to transgress this gendered boundary in a way many other outdoor activities do not because it's really hard to go backpacking and not be out after dark, unless you're somewhere like Alaska or Iceland in June.

When shining a headlamp on the barriers to Americans' participation in outdoor recreation, I wish the effect such social codes have on women received more consideration from researchers. These are influences so deeply absorbed that we don't recognize them, and of course the effect is different for different women. Victorian ideas have carried over into our habit of judging a woman by where she is, when, and with whom. Consequently, women have internalized this spatial patriarchy, voluntarily limiting their mobility without conscious consideration of which spaces are really the most dangerous. For centuries we have been told not to go out in public, especially alone and after dark. Despite what the media portrays, the trail far from the parking lot is statistically less dangerous than a woman's home. Still we make choices based on the concept of separate, gendered spheres, assuming that feminine spaces are safer for females (when they could be, uh, traps for them).

The 2014 *Outdoor Recreation Participation Report* shows that "among females ages 21 to 25, indoor fitness overtakes outdoor recreation as the preferred physical activity, and it remains the most popular form of activity throughout life." It's easy to understand a fitness center as public space sanctioned for females, complete with appropriate clothing marketed to women. That is, the machines area and exercise classes are female spaces; my female and male students report that the free-weight area is still decidedly masculine space. For males, indoor exercise doesn't overtake outdoor recreation until after age sixty. Though male youth participate in outdoor recreation at a higher rate than female youth, rates of boys and male teens have been falling even as there has been a 2–3 percent rise among young American females engaging in outdoor recreation. The report shows that parents are getting children out more, and adults with children in the house participate over 10 percent more than adults without children in the house. But it raises the question of why, if girls as well as boys are exposed to outdoor activities as children, only boys remain steadfastly outdoors throughout their lives.

The top reason nonparticipants give is lack of interest, a reason so broad as to suggest many possibilities, including those buried social messages about separate spheres and safety. Many other things could influence females' lack of interest, including how girls don't know to be curious about what they aren't exposed to. If you grow up in Boulder, Colorado, you'll encounter women in the mountains at any time or season. In rural Pennsylvania, where I live now, females of all ages can be seen out in the woods hunting and fishing. But most women live in areas where such role models are much less common.

The next five reasons for not participating, in decreasing order, are lack of time, lack of skills/abilities, too busy with family responsibilities, no one to participate with, and too expensive. These are the reasons for all ages and genders over six years, but it's clear that many of these reasons doubly affect women, who still have the majority of family care-giving duties, are less likely to have developed outdoor skills, and feel more pressure not to be active outdoors alone. And the cost of proper clothing and gear to keep children comfortable and safe can quickly become prohibitive.

Even back when no one cared what logo was on my fleece jacket, it cost money to get started. In college, when I had free time, my family responsibilities were fewest and I could borrow boats, life jackets, climbing shoes, backpacks, and tents; I still made do with poor-fitting gear. The cheap boots I bought for my first backpack trip restricted the flex of my ankle, inflaming my Achilles tendon so painfully that I tied them to my pack and hiked barefoot. Thank goodness I was on a southern island! (Truthfully, much of our other clothing became optional after a day or two anyway.) The backpack did not fit my long torso and lacked a suspension system. Miserable gear that hurts or doesn't protect new participants from the elements can make an early experience so unpleasant as to keep them from attempting another. Luckily, I was surrounded by people who loved the outdoors, and even more than I wanted to paddle or climb or backpack, I wanted to be like them: happy, unrestricted by social expectations, beautiful in a way not shown on TV and in magazines—strong, tan with no makeup, with wide friendly smiles.

Even then it wasn't easy to find people to do things with since I was a beginner and had little to offer (other than a truck). And not just any people—people I trusted. My course in whitewater canoeing was fantastic. It gave me skills, a network of people whom I knew to have good judgment as well as good character, and a mentor who became one of the most important figures in my struggle to belong in these groups and places. Windy Gordon, whose constant smile made his eyes squint, was both a professor of psychology and an expert paddler. We came to Warren Wilson College the same year and met when I took his Intro to Psych course. He was one of the cool young profs and a great teacher, which I'm sure made me more willing to step out of my comfort zone. I wasn't one of his majors, but he patiently taught me paddling technique, helped me develop my judgment, and encouraged but never pushed me even as less-skilled males ran rapids I wouldn't. And he was responsible for introducing me to many female role models who eventually became mentors after college.

Going from hiking to backpacking spring break of my senior year brought new anxieties. I wished I could learn bit by bit about camp stoves, fitting a pack, carrying a load, choosing the right clothes and food to pack—the way I'd first learned paddle strokes in a pool. For that first backpack trip, I had to rely on others. Christy told me what clothes to take. Mike planned the food and showed me how to make Logan bread, a dense, dairy-free brick that wouldn't mold. I didn't feel self-reliant. I had to tamp down the voice in my head that wondered whether I could keep up, would be strong enough to carry everything, or would get enough to eat. In the midst of all that, I never thought to worry about the mixed messages of sharing a tent. I was just glad not to add the weight to my load.

I had little experience testing myself physically. I wasn't a nature girl or adventure girl—I was an artsy-fartsy girl. After all these years, I've gained confidence in my abilities when trying something new (and no longer pigeonhole myself into one identity). I trust my physical ability and judgment. Back then I was learning to trust others with making choices about risks while also learning to trust my body and instincts for the first time. It was stressful and emotionally draining in ways I hid. No one else around me appeared to have these issues, so I kept them to myself. Wanting to belong kept me from showing the chinks in my Gore-Tex armor, and this made me feel like a poser. An imposter. Fake.

Stepping Out

Many people have described the pull to be in wild spaces, though the most familiar quotes are from men. While I too find that "going out is really going in," as John Muir writes, I relate more to this 1909 quote from mountaineer Mary Crawford:

> Take the woman whose usual occupation is a sedentary one. . . . Put her on the train and send her to the mountains. . . . She is going to know herself as never before—physically, mentally, emotionally. And so she starts out, gains confidence with every step, finds the dangers she has imagined far greater than those she encounters and arrives at last upon the summit to gaze out upon a new world. Surely not the same earth she has seen all her life?

I wanted to know, *Who was I when released from the hang-ups of my daily life?* Stacy Alaimo, in *Undomesticated Ground: Recasting Nature as Feminist Space*, raises "the possibility that women often enter the wilderness, literally or imaginatively, precisely in order to throw off—or complement, subvert, or bracket—their domestic roles." I didn't want to take my gender expectations with me into the wild (even though I now see they can't be completely left behind because I carry them in my mind). I didn't want to tame or conquer the spaces I explored; instead I longed to become a stronger, wilder self in communion with the natural world.

Women have been running to the woods for a long time, for play as well as escape. Emma Gatewood's husband regularly beat her (broken ribs, broken teeth) and forced himself on her several times a day, resulting in eleven children. When things got really bad she'd escape into the woods. Her husband threatened to have her committed if she left him, but after nearly twenty years of abuse, she divorced him in 1941. Soon the woods became a refuge again. In 1950, at age sixty-seven, this grandmother was the first woman to thru-hike the two-thousand-mile Appalachian Trail, and only the fifth person to do so. Being poor, she didn't have a tent. She carried a plastic shower curtain and twelve pounds of food and clothing in a denim bag she'd sewn. Instead of boots she trekked in canvas Keds sneakers. She told her now-grown kids only that she was going for a walk.

Thinking back to when I packed for Cumberland Island, both excited and anxious, I wish I'd known about Grandma Gatewood. Perhaps I'd have seen her as exceptional and rare in terms of her courage, perseverance, physical strength, and stamina. Still, I think having her as a role model would've made it easier for me to imagine myself dealing with the challenges my first trek presented. My week of backpacking on flat land at the age of twenty would've seemed less intimidating compared to Gatewood's amazing accomplishments. But the superwoman myth that gets attached to women like her who finally get noticed isn't helpful either. The media promotes women accomplishing awesome feats in masculine arenas in such a way that they seem outliers, freaks of nature. To many of us their achievements are wonderful, but to a society still mired in old-fashioned notions, they are also seen as threatening the social order. When they are made to seem unusual, women can admire them without easily thinking, "I can do that too!" They can wonder, "Why on earth would Grandma Gatewood want to do that?" rather than asking, "What do I want to do?"

Yes, Grandma Gatewood was strong, brave, and badass. But she was also a woman in her late sixties with no experience long-distance hiking, no guidance or advice, no special training, who had spent a large part of her life more tangled up in domestic roles and gender expectations than I can begin to coil a rope around. For years she stayed in an abusive situation that her community knew about but offered no help escaping from. What this part of her story tells me is that there are not strong women and weak women, average women and superwomen. We're all capable of getting into bad situations and getting ourselves out of them, though some have more hurdles than others. Walking the Appalachian Trail or climbing a mountain is not the answer for every woman dealing with abuse, addiction, or whatever life's thrown at her, but every woman should feel as if these are options.

Strolling in English gardens and parks, showing off dresses and hairstyles, was one of the few outdoor pastimes ladies were allowed long ago. And damned if we didn't bring that over the ocean to American cities. (Women on the American frontier escaped a lot of that out of necessity; men needed women to pitch in equally. It's no surprise that Wyoming, Utah, Colorado, and Idaho were the first states to grant women the right to vote.) Solnit explains: "The implication [is] that women walk not to see but to be seen, not for their own experience but for a male audience, which means they're asking for whatever attention they receive." Even as gender roles and society have modernized, a female's visibility is still equated with sexual accessibility, especially if she is out after dark. We may not feel as strongly that she is loose, but the message that she is "asking for it" is still repeated by those who wish to protect as well as those who wish to take advantage.

Back then I didn't know why I felt so self-conscious, so under a microscope. I had no feminist theory or women's history in my rucksack. As a teenager in the suburbs I walked to get places, and I endured (and early on, sought) whistles and catcalls. But in my twenties I craved a tent of my own so I could get far away from those eyes.

Maybe in some ways it's easier to be in one's sixties, past the time society thinks of women as sexual objects, as Grandma Gatewood was when she went out for her long walk. I'm not there yet, but I'm not too far from that age either, and many of my friends feel they're becoming invisible as they grow older. Some enjoy this, and others are enraged. But it's all part of the way a woman's public presence is linked with her value as a sexual object.

On our spring break backpack trip, I tasted that falling away of inhibitions and quieting of my inner critic. We quickly left behind the ferry landing and campground—full of parents, little kids, and restrooms—and entered the maritime forest. Live oaks flaunted their frocks of Spanish moss. Palmettos poked teasingly from the understory. Horse droppings dappled the pale sand path, so different from the dark earth I was used to. Driving from the early spring chill of the Appalachian Mountains, we'd arrived in a balmy, warm paradise. Gone were the dorms packed with loud peers. Space and birdsong, sunshine and stars defined our days. We had only the food we brought in and were allowed no fires in the backcountry. We collected water from the sulfur springs, treated it with a filter or iodine tablets, and then added whatever flavor powder we brought. It tasted nasty, but that was also exotic.

The island was sixteen miles long by three miles at its widest, no more than three hundred people were allowed at a time, and most stayed along the southern tip, where the ferry came and went twice a day. No paved roads. I had no watch, no mirror, and no cares. I wore the same clothes for days and nights in a row. I hadn't thought to bring a ball cap, and when I got annoyed with my dirty shoulder-length hair, one of the other girls braided it into tight cornrows. My skin grew dark from sun and dirt. I ate summer sausage, hard cheese, and Logan bread. Gorp, rice and beans, and tequila are the other staples I recall now. Life was stunningly simple.

Once I got through the first day and found I could keep up with Mike (who had short legs but a notoriously fast pace), my anxiety about everything except accidentally running into an armadillo melted into the sun and sand. The ranger told us armadillos carried leprosy, so any rustle in the palmettos at night when I was peeing caused me to clench. That same ranger appeared at least twice to remind us that we weren't allowed to sunbathe topless and that even if hikers did not find our secret sand garden in the dunes, helicopters did fly over. It seemed he gave this reminder a lot and didn't think it was an issue of any significance. Just doing his job. If Mike had sunbathed with Christy, Kristen, and me, he wouldn't have been told he couldn't be topless. In any case, after five days of Kool Aid–flavored sulfur water and nonconforming bliss, we all decided to hike out naked via the beach rather than the trail. Bootless, this suited me, and we squeezed on the last of our sunscreen, donned our large packs, and snapped our waist belts.

Luckily, we didn't run into the ranger, and we put our

clothes on before reaching the campground. He apparently had the day off. When our ferry landed and we walked to my truck, loading our packs and two passengers into the covered bed, I saw the ranger out of uniform loading groceries into his pickup.

"Hey, your truck is topless!" I yelled, pointing at mine to show I was covered for once. We drove away laughing and waving. The others were talking about where they wanted to pitch their tents next, and I knew what I was spending my graduation money on.

Escape from Indoors

The Cumberland Island trip didn't involve significant hiking except for the first and last days, and the terrain was pretty flat (though walking on sand is hard on the calves). It was a good introduction to backpacking and getting beyond the crowds. I'm aware of how lucky I was that Mike was a person of character; I never worried about my safety and we remained friends. But somewhere deep in my subconscious I grew more hesitant to collaborate on big trips with a guy. So when I thought about my next adventure and the places I wanted to go, I chose a road trip, my dog (which my father had kept while I was in college), and my truck. I asked my parents for a good sleeping bag as a graduation present. At the last minute, I decided to cut off my hair, which I'd spent all year growing past my shoulders, so I'd look like a boy from a distance.

I swear, I wasn't a fly-by-the-seat-of-my-pants risk taker. I was painfully responsible, almost canceling my plans to drive cross-country when it occurred to me I wouldn't have health insurance. I had a job waiting for me in North Carolina in the fall if I chose to come back East. I also had a position as a nanny waiting for me in Oregon whenever I showed up midsummer. There were no cell phones, no GPS, and no internet access on the road. I'd always wanted to be like William Least Heat-Moon and travel blue highways, waking up and deciding the next day's route. I spread my sleeping bag over a thick pad on a wooden platform just high enough to slide milk crates under. My last semester in college, when I'd shown up with my two-wheel-drive Toyota long-bed, a friend of mine took one look in the back of my truck with platform, pad, and pillows and said, "My father warned me never to get in a vehicle like this." We laughed, knowing her father had assumed it would be a guy's pickup.

In the crates I stashed shoes, jackets, clothes, books, camera, flashlight, lighter, dog food, and an extra leash. I slid my guitar case beside the platform. In a large cardboard box and small cooler, I packed my food, a few dishes, and utensils. I had gallon jugs of water. I had a road atlas, travel mug, and lots of cassette tapes up front. I had an extra key in a magnetic box hidden in the undercarriage. I had a jack and a spare, and I knew how to change a tire because my father had taught me immediately after I got the truck. That man made me feel that if I used good sense I could do anything.

Dad enjoyed smoking a cigar or a pipe when he walked outside, claiming it kept the insects away. I didn't know how to build fires well and didn't plan to cook, but I wished for the smoke in case it was buggy. So Dad took me to pick out cigars, pointing me toward Swisher Sweets cigarillos with the plastic tip. "You probably won't want to smoke a whole one at a time," he said, "so just put it out and reuse it." The plastic tip meant I wouldn't have to deal with the sensation of decomposing leaves between my lips.

But while Dad was supportive, Mom grew more anxious. Over the dinner table she froze up when I mentioned I'd bought a two-person tent. (Actually a one woman–one dog tent.) She wanted to know what I was planning to do with it, which I thought was fairly obvious.

"But that's why you got a truck, to have a vehicle you can sleep in." She'd bought me the truck after years of hoping I'd change my mind and want a sedan. Her face grew more and more pursed as I explained that I liked to look at the stars through the mesh roof, and if it was hot I'd be cooler than inside the fiberglass cap.

"Well, I'm going to say a really good goodbye," she blurted, her voice cracking. I sat there, stunned to realize she thought I might not come back safely. I left soon after that, moving my departure up, sensing my resolve might weaken if I didn't get out of there fast.

My plan was to get west as quickly as possible. I had this sense of Montana being the Holy Grail, specifically Glacier National Park. My family hadn't gone to that one and it seemed romantic, both in a Thoreauvian back-to-nature way, and in an I-might-meet-the-kind-of-guy-I'm-looking-for way. Maybe I'd offer to share *my* tent. I'd learned that national forests had the cheapest and most rustic camping, but until I got past the Mississippi River there weren't that many on my path. I stayed the first night in a private campground in Ohio, glad to be inside the truck when it squalled all night. The owner posted signs in the cement bathhouse to head there if you heard the tornado siren. Two young men in the next site tried to cook outside despite the storm. It looked as if they eventually gave up and settled for drinking beer.

The irony of Mom's concern about my sleeping in a tent was that there was no way to lock the back of my truck cap from inside. A couple of years later, in graduate school, after I'd already twice driven cross-country solo, two male friends solved that problem. They both bought me cleats (the kind used on boat decks) and nylon cord. Once a cleat was bolted to the tail-gate and the cord tied to the inside handle, I could "lock" the door—at least long enough to discourage someone or buy me a little time. But during that first trip, I was realizing such vulnerabilities as I went. Such as how small my thirty-pound dog really was. I admit I practiced sliding through the windows of the truck cab and cap, seeing how quickly I could get into the driver's seat. I decided headfirst was best because I could reach the horn faster even if someone grabbed my ankle. I locked the cab doors at night and kept the keys by my head. So much for being able to turn my radar off. Still, it felt safer than the tent, which stayed in its stuff sack.

The Midwest was one big tornado watch, but when I got to Wisconsin and the Upper Mississippi River I was surprised by its beauty. The river braided around lush islands as I looked down from limestone bluffs. There were so many landscapes left to learn about. I headed for visitor centers, scenic routes, and green blotches on the map. The Badlands were just like I remembered them when my family drove through South Dakota going east. I never walked far from a parking lot or overlook. Early on I didn't question this, maybe because my family trips as a kid had been more focused on how many parks we could visit rather than how immersive our experience was. And maybe because I had a dog, which always had to be on a leash and wasn't allowed on many trails. It wasn't until I found myself in Wyoming's Bighorn National Forest that I decided to stay more than one night. I pitched my tent, moved the pad and sleeping bag inside, and sat at the picnic table playing my guitar and smoking a cigarillo. The smell reminded me of Dad, which comforted me at the same time as it made me more aware of how alone I was.

No, that's not right. It made me realize how vulnerable I felt. I liked being alone. I loved not having anyone else to think about—their feelings or plans. I was thrilled to find a small primitive camping area that no one else was in. What I didn't like was not being able to control whether I'd remain alone. Anytime I heard a car on the road, I prayed it wouldn't turn in. In the few days I'd been traveling I'd stopped looking for people to talk to. There were no women or mixed groups my age, and—awful as it is to think about now—I thought most people over forty were boring.

There was a trail that went behind my tent. I didn't have a map for the area but planned to hike it the next morning, coming back the same way I went out. The night had been restless, with me rousing every time a vehicle drove by, or so it seemed. But in the morning, I was still alone, and the sun was making quick work of the frost that glittered like fairy dust (the kind enabling you to fly and never grow up). Looking forward to exerting myself, I locked up, took Junior off his leash, and watched him run up and back along the creek, his reddish-brown tail a charging plume among the sparse grasses. The evergreens and dry-needled forest floor were so different from the deciduous hardwoods of the Southeast. I don't know how far I'd gone before I started to worry, but it didn't take long. What if someone took my tent while I was gone? What if someone saw the tent and waited for me to come back? What if someone saw the tent and followed me on the trail? What if I twisted my ankle? Or broke a leg?

I'm almost sick remembering how the cultural pressures came on, sudden and relentless, like a flash flood. And I'm embarrassed, imagining readers rolling their eyes at my neurotic episode. But I figure I'm not the only woman this has happened to, and it's time we admit how damn hard it is to tell which fears are legitimate and which aren't when so many have been shoved into our brains ever since some doctor looked between our legs and said, "It's a girl!"

Getting in Touch with My Inner Pit Bull

So I called Junior and turned around. When I got back to the truck (and felt silly because it was fine and no one was there), I packed and hit the road again. I also started thinking a lot about the voices I heard in my head. It was easy to do, since there were no other voices. Over the next week of driving I noticed what these voices were saying and tried to pinpoint where they came from. It was King Culture whispering relentlessly. I practiced resting bitch face when getting gas, especially in Oregon where they have to pump it for you. (They should warn you better. I nearly jumped through the windshield when the young man leaned on my window to ask what I wanted.) Now I recognized all sorts of messages I'd internalized about how anything I said could be seen as an invitation—so don't look directly at the guy who wanders to your campsite asking to borrow a can opener. I realized how much the fact that rape was historically a crime against property (a husband's or father's) shaped such messages. Here I was alone, unclaimed and therefore up for grabs. My anxiety and confusion over making decisions about where to go, and knowing when it was okay to relax and enjoy the beauty and peace, started a transformation as monumental as when eastern red-spotted newts lose their gills, turn orange, and walk out of the pond to wander over land for years as red efts. Almost overnight, I'd become a feminist, though I wouldn't actually use that word out loud until graduate school.

Suddenly I realized two things: one, that my truck and dog were substitutes for a male companion—lover, brother, father—on this trip; and two, that I was learning a ton about myself by having to go solo, discovering the deep, satisfying comfort that comes from not needing someone else to validate my decisions or witness my experiences.

Oh, and I realized something else—I wanted a younger, bigger dog.

After six months in Oregon, getting my first mountain bike, and exploring the Siskiyou Mountains and Cascade Range, I returned to Western North Carolina, where I gave Junior back to my father so both could grow old together in comfort. My next dog was half pit bull (mixed with Lab and blue heeler), mostly black with white socks, a speckled white belly, and a white swoosh down her forehead to her nose. While Allie was a medium pit bull, her bark was large, low, and loud. When she pulled her head back, her thick neck merged with wide shoulders and made her look intimidating. She was social but also independent and loved it when we lived in the truck. She didn't look for altercations and didn't invite attention from strangers. She was an altered bitch, as stated by her vet records, while some might argue I still had some work to do in that area. We were a perfect match.

While I worked for my alma mater coordinating public relations and news services, I also consciously cultivated outdoor mentors, especially women in their thirties. Kristy Walters had long hippie hair, a laugh that held nothing back, and a cool little house on a pond. She taught me how to roll a kayak and talked to me about choices she'd made in her life, ones that usually meant less money and more freedom. While I learned from Kristy and other women how to choose proper clothing layers for the season and activity, and keep the right level of calories and hydration, I also watched them in their relationships. The men in their lives enjoyed doing things with them outdoors, were comfortable with their girlfriends and wives handling tasks that required strength or mechanical competence, and laughed with them a lot. Though I dated, and my dates were as likely to be hikes as movies, I was not interested in settling down. But when I did, I'd have an idea of what to look for.

The next time I moved cross-country in my truck was to go to graduate school in Southern California at UC–Irvine. The movie *Thelma and Louise* came out just before I left. In this rare female road buddy movie, the premise is that two friends—one young and in an awful marriage and one older who is reluctant to marry her man—go on an adventure. On their way, they stop at a honky-tonk and get a little loose, dancing and drinking. There's a wannabe cowboy hot for naive Thelma who maneuvers her outside when, tipsy, she needs some air. Pressing her against a car hood as she struggles and says no, he attempts to rape her, but Louise shows up behind him, gun in hand, and stops him. Dead. Now on the run from the law, they decide to head to Mexico but can't drive through Texas because Louise had a bad experience there (presumably the type of thing she saved Thelma from).

Knowing I was about to drive cross-country by the southern route, taking I-10, I signed up for a one-day women's self-defense class. I couldn't stop thinking about how I'd be driving through Texas. Several points made in that session have stuck with me. First, the instructor referred to the aggressors in the scenarios she gave us as "varmints," not "men." I didn't realize then how important that was, but knowing now that it's repeat offenders who are responsible for the majority of the violent crimes against women, I appreciate her care with not lumping all men together. Trusting my instincts was a huge lesson, as well as being willing to make a scene if I felt threatened. Of course, if no one is around, there's no point making a scene. If worse came to worst, she suggested that we each think about whether our main goal was to stop the rape at all costs or to live through it. And not to blame ourselves if we couldn't stop it but to mark the perpetrator so it'd be easier for cops to track him down. "Go to the grocery store and get some radishes," she advised us when describing what to do when a varmint was at his most vulnerable. "Squeeze radishes to build grip strength. If you can pop a radish, ladies, you can pop a testis." Then she demonstrated the two-finger hook twist-pull.

I didn't feel invincible, but I was less clueless than before. And armed with more sense and a can of pepper spray, I went out months before the semester started to find a place to live south of Los Angeles that I could afford and would take dogs.

This time I was more confident exploring farther from the truck. Allie and I were a well-tuned team, and she heeled easily as we walked through the French Quarter in New Orleans and shared beignets at Café du Monde, the powdered sugar coating her black muzzle. She'd hike all day without complaining as long as there was occasional shade and water. We both went swimming in the Rio Grande in Big Bend National Park in Texas on July Fourth. And while camping by a big desert lake, I took advantage of a half-day class to learn about windsurfing, having left Allie happily watching the parking area activity from her perch on top of the truck cab. We'd established this routine in North Carolina when I'd kayaked the Nantahala and Green Rivers. Rather than stay at home, she waited, tied to the front bumper, so she could lounge in the grass by the water bowl, crawl under the truck for shade, or—her usual preference—climb onto the hood and then up top to watch the world from her throne.

Back in North Carolina the places I parked her were familiar and safe, and we ran into people we knew. This parking area, filled with windsurfers instead of paddlers, had a similar vibe. When I returned after a humbling experience of trying to get a feel for the new sport (the physics of wind elude me), there she was, smiling her weird, wide grin by pulling back her upper lip. Leaning down, she licked my face in greeting as I stripped off the wet shirt over my suit.

"She wasn't that friendly when I said 'Hi' earlier," a cute young man said to me from in front of the pickup. Allie ignored him now with an invisible dog shrug. "She barked when *I* came up to her."

Like a mother pleased to hear a report of her children acting appropriately when not observed by a parent, I smiled and said, "Good!" The guy's face darkened. Angry, he walked away without saying another word. I was taken aback. Did he think I was trying to insult him? Had he ever considered what it was like to be a woman traveling alone? Couldn't he understand there was more at stake here than him getting his feelings hurt? For my part I was happy to hear Allie set boundaries clearly. Communicating directly was something I was still learning, especially with men I didn't know.

Near the end of my first road trip, I'd let down my guard a bit to talk with a man a few years older in a neighboring campsite. I'd missed conversation after weeks alone and couldn't help noticing he had a cast on his right arm. When he invited me to share his fire, I took my cold dinner and small dog over, thinking I could handle a one-armed man. Turns out he had gone to college where I was headed and told me about places to go in and out of town. He made no overtures either physical or verbal; didn't suggest we hike together the next day or meet up next time he passed through. No personal queries about my life or status. Never tried to sit near me. I relaxed. As night came he pulled out some pot, which I declined. While he smoked, we investigated by flashlight noises that turned out to be little raccoons in a nearby tree. How cute. Then he commented on what a big tent he had compared to mine. How much more room there was. How maybe I could come share it. In the dark, he couldn't see me freeze. Out loud I laughed, high and false, about how I didn't need much room. How that was nice of him, but my dog and I were cozy enough. How it was time for me to turn in now. He sat on his picnic table finishing his joint.

Later that night when I'd warmed up the inside of my sleeping bag, I did what I usually did. I took off my fleece, unzipped the tent flap, and tossed my pullover outside. Small tent, remember? But this night the zipper unzipping seemed to split the silence as surely as it split the fabric. Oh crap. I immediately wondered if he'd heard it. Would he think I'd changed my mind? Would he come over, knowing I was awake? Would he call out to me? Maybe he was sound asleep, or maybe he was up with the munchies. There was no way for me to know. As I eased the zipper closed again as quietly as I could, I heard my responses to him play back in my head: *Oh, I don't need much room, tee-hee. I like snuggling with my dog.* Not once had I said clearly: No, I don't want to share your tent. No, I want to be alone. No. No. No.

Peaks, Valleys, and Not Making the Summit

Once I reached Irvine, California, the English Department secretary helped me find an apartment to share with another graduate student and her German shepherd, but it wouldn't be available for another month. So I headed north to hang out with my cousin and her husband. He was a radiologist and was just about to meet up with some buddies from his residency days to windsurf in Hood River, Oregon, in the Columbia River Gorge. I went along to camp, hike, and hang out, already knowing windsurfing didn't interest me. Besides, I was too poor for such an expensive hobby. In the campground we met Sue, who was older and traveled alone with her rottweiler. I enjoyed not being the only female when she became part of our group. She was there to windsurf, but we also went on some hikes with our dogs, and she had tales to tell of outdoor adventures. Living just north of LA, she was a couple of hours from where I'd be going to school. We quickly became good friends. She invited me to visit her and hike in the San Gabriel Mountains in Angeles National Forest. She also asked whether I would climb Mount Whitney with her in early fall.

This was the first time a female had asked me to join her on an adventure. I knew that it wasn't just men who could have ulterior motives in asking me to share a tent, and if I hadn't known how much Sue liked Ratty, one of the doctors in our group, I'd have made sure we were clear about that. But Sue's motives were up front and ones I shared—to have easy, capable companionship on a trek she'd been wanting to do. Two women, two dogs—four friends. It sounded perfect to me, but Whitney is the tallest peak in the contiguous United States at 14,494 feet, and I'd never hiked at high elevations. Sue had gotten a day-use permit and planned on going light in early fall during the full moon, so we could get up and down in one long twenty-one-mile push. We'd camp in the Portal Campground at 8,350 feet to acclimate overnight.

"I have no idea if I can do this," I told her, "but I'm willing to try. You've hiked with me. If you think I can do it, then I'm game."

Unlike at previous times in my life, I wasn't anxious about this trip. I could read a map and gauge my physical limitations. I'd been jogging regularly that summer, so I was in decent shape. We'd be going up and down on the same trail, and there would be other people. In fact, it was the busy time for hiking Whitney, when snow had most likely melted at the peak and temperatures would probably stay warm enough for comfort. But it wasn't only my greater knowledge of myself and competence outdoors that made the preparation and anticipation less stressful. The possibility of feeling sick or weak when out with Sue didn't carry the same emotional risk for me as when I went with male companions. I trusted Sue not to push me into situations in which I felt uncomfortable; I knew she'd really listen to me. Other than with Windy Gordon, my male paddling mentor who was well versed in sports psychology, I'd often been worried about being labeled a stereotypical female if I felt weak or anxious or didn't want to take the same risks as the guys I was with. I'm not saying that all the guys I paddled, biked, and hiked with would have thought this. My anxiety was culturally induced. I'd been in situations where my fears were confirmed and in others where I was pleasantly surprised. But testing myself with Sue felt more freeing.

When we spent the night at the Portal Campground, I felt as if I was walking in slow motion. My legs moved as though the air was thick, when in fact it was thinner than I was used to. We got up before sunrise and hit the trail. Though we were doing fine and having fun, by the time the sun had risen Sue had a dull headache. We rested and drank water. I kept reminding her to drink more as we hiked slowly the next several hours, and her headache backed off some. After filling up water bottles again at Trail Camp, we started up the infamous ninety-nine switchbacks that rise over 1,700 feet through granite ledges, leaving the manzanita and Jeffrey pines behind. My right groin muscle felt pulled, but we were so close. Then we saw the cables. We got a good look because we had to wait for all the backpackers to come single file down the narrow path, made narrower because it was north facing and partly covered with snow that rarely melted. On the thin strip was a smattering of ice.

I'm not bothered by heights, but I looked at the dogs and thought how they'd slip right under the cables if they lost traction. Turning to Sue, I said, "Maybe we should head back now."

At first, she balked. We *were* awfully close. But with my pulled groin muscle and Sue's head still hurting (an indication of mild altitude sickness), a great hike could turn into an epic one. It was getting late—we hadn't been setting any speed records. I watched Sue wrestle with her emotions.

"I agree with everything you're saying but can't help feeling like we'll have failed," Sue explained. Still, she acknowledged that getting seriously injured, or God forbid losing one of the dogs over the edge, would be a true failure. "Maybe this is my real challenge on this hike," she stated, "learning not to judge myself or worry what others will think." The peak-bagger mentality is so prevalent in outdoor recreation, I could understand why she felt that way. As we headed down, our uphill muscles got a break and the views of the valley and purpling sky helped carry us back to the campground. The dogs seemed happy with our decision, and a handsome park ranger offered to wrap my groin pull with an ACE bandage from his first aid kit. Who was I to stand in the way of him doing his job?

As it turned out, both Sue and I liked to sing the same songs when it was just the two of us on the trail, exhausted and trying to keep our spirits up. Carly Simon's "You're So Vain," got us down under the moon's watchful eye.

Back in Irvine, as I read for my graduate classes and spent many weekends hiking with Sue, I looked for books about women outdoors. I'd never read accounts of women doing what I wanted to do. I knew there were books on solo women travelers and explorers, but the ones I'd heard of were about white women traveling in other countries. I was lured by the geographies of my home—the wilder the better. At the time, American nature and outdoor writing was almost all by men. I'd get glimpses that other women were similarly drawn to wild spaces. However, the surge to publish new and reclaimed women writers in combined and women-only anthologies had barely started in the early 1990s with Lorraine Anderson's *Sisters of the Earth.* It would be ten years before the second edition of *The Norton Book of Nature Writing* was updated to include more women and people of color. Before then, popular nature writing anthologies had erased most females from the outdoors the way Edward Abbey had edited his wife out of his essays.

One day in 1992 in a Laguna Beach bookstore, I spotted a book of short stories that had a great cover and an even better title. *Cowboys Are My Weakness* by Pam Houston showed off a turquoise-blue sky blazed with a purple-orange sunset over a vast western horizon. I flipped through stories called "How to Talk to a Hunter," "Highwater," "Jackson Is Only One of My Dogs," and "Sometimes You Talk about Idaho." I bought it on the spot. Sometimes you meet a friend at just the right time, like

Sue, and this book was one of those friends. The stories were full of wit, wry wisdom, and women who love men, dogs, and the outdoors. These were young women caught in the same web of cultural constructions and gender expectations as I was when trying to gain outdoor skills and experiences. Unlike me, these characters didn't avoid the easy sex and empty relationships with men who made them feel wilder and less alone for a while.

Why did these stories speak to me? Houston has been criticized for being a bad feminist because her characters make bad choices with men, but I didn't need more of the victorious, empowered woman story that almost always took place indoors. I craved these examples of the ways a strong, smart woman could get the balance between self and relationships wrong and why, as in the title story when the main character says, "When he asked me to come with him I knew it would be me or somebody else and I'd heard good things about Montana so I went." Houston admits her narrators are loosely autobiographical. "In fiction, my narrator is still me, but she's a much more naive me, more vulnerable, more uncertain. I am always asking her to walk into situations I have already walked into." Speaking at the Billings Family YMCA in Montana, Houston described the trajectory of *Cowboys*: "She learns how to have her own relationship with the wilderness without necessarily having that relationship translated by a man. . . . She confuses her love of the man with her love of the wilderness."

There is personal growth in the collection of stories, just not perfect resolution. Good. The last thing I wanted was a perfect protagonist. I was looking for insights into other women's struggles. I didn't want to read about anyone who had it all figured out. Houston's speakers are women I could relate to, even if I usually ended up making the opposite, responsible decision. *Usually.* In my two years in Southern California, as I wrote poems and studied literature, I also went on my most ambitious backpacking trips, always in male-female pairs, and always planned by men. These trips were often meant to woo. I also found my best road trip buddy, a friend's ex-boyfriend. These two years were educational—and only some of that had to do with my master's degree.

My first close friend at school was also in the English program, but she studied literature rather than creative writing so we didn't have classes together. Carol and I got to know each other when we both took a one-credit undergraduate course in martial arts, something the students in our programs thought we were odd for doing. She also loved hiking and was a feminist interested in freeing herself from the self-limiting habits she'd picked up as a girl. We both started training at the Tang Soo Do studio in town and had our first relationships with Southern California men. Carol was from the East Coast too, and we'd discuss geography and men in between grading freshman composition papers. When my romance with a black belt stoner fell apart, I started hanging out with Carol and her friends more. Her relationship with Alan, an older philosophy PhD student, was still going strong. Carol thought there was a student in the physics department I should meet, broken heart notwithstanding.

I'd felt so out of place in Irvine, a top-ranked planned community south of LA. When I'd gone for a short jog during my first week in the new apartment, I'd gotten lost in the housing complex. The streets were named San Jose, San Leon, San Juan, so I couldn't keep them straight. And all the buildings were off-pink. My trips to Sue's place every month or so helped keep me sane early on. On those visits, we'd hike, cook, and drink wine while talking about guys. She'd tell me how things were going with her and Ratty, and I'd complain that the few straight men in graduate school were married. The other men were gay, and many of the women were too. This was all fine as far as socializing was concerned, and I had wonderful friends, but it made me look outside the English Department for romance. Carol told me the best places to find straight guys who liked the outdoors were the science programs and the trailer park on campus.

There, on a beautiful wooden deck built off an old fifth-wheel RV, Carol introduced me to Brian, surfer of waves, paddler of seas, and builder of decks. He liked that I was strong and did things for myself. Several of us went on a two-night backpack trip, where I kept to my own tent but let Brian court me with food. That was easy to do. I still packed light and skipped the stove. I was wholly uninterested in the domestic aspects of camping, other than pitching a tent. But Brian served me marinated asparagus he'd made at home and cooled in the creek. He enjoyed hearing my road trip stories. I was getting over that black belt faster and faster. Carol smirked from across the campfire.

If Pam Houston were writing the story of our romance, she'd make it funny and worth reading. I will spare you the details, mostly because they aren't noteworthy. He was a good enough man with a penchant for never fully cutting ties with former girlfriends. One reason he liked me, I discovered, was that he could take me to family functions and his mother would approve. Turns out his previous girlfriends were Asian and African American, and his mother loved that I was white. *Ew.* At the start, he loved showing me off to his buddies—which meant demonstrating my fingertip push-ups. Then he started complaining that my martial arts training was taking too much time when I should be going to his family functions. When he said I didn't need him enough, I agreed and called it quits.

Later that summer, Alan, Carol's boyfriend, planned a backpacking trip in the Sierras through Kearsarge Pass to Kings Canyon National Park. He was older and wanted to show Carol

some of the places he loved. We were all hanging out at the
trailer park, where I'd recently moved in across from Brian. The
four of us drank beer and looked at maps as Alan told us about
the high mountain lakes and sequoias on the route. Oh, how I
remembered the sequoias from my childhood trips! Their height
and presence felt medieval. The chance to leave vehicles and
campgrounds behind to experience this landscape called to me.
Looking up and catching Brian's gaze, I could see that it—or
something—was calling to him too. By the end of the evening
the two-person trip had become a four-person trip. You might
think Alan would've preferred to have Carol all to himself, but
having an extra vehicle to run the shuttle simplified logistics.

We'd have full packs over rough terrain, and I knew it'd be
hard. But martial arts had me in good shape, and though Brian
and I bickered constantly, I trusted everyone. I still had my
crappy backpack, but I had nothing to prove. We worked as a
group to plan our food and equipment. Brian and I hiked faster
and spent our days together, joining Carol and Alan at camp.
We kept asserting we weren't together again, to which Alan
replied, "Suuuure you aren't. Only couples argue that much."

Granite dazzled underfoot and high above. The high alpine
lakes were tiny cups of intense blue Easter-egg dye from afar,
and up close our personal paradise. This landscape gave way
eventually to rivers and thick forests as we crossed the pass and
headed toward the sequoias. Granite still peeked out along the
rivers and jutted out of the brown forest floor and mountain-
sides. Where previously the trees had been only visitors in the
land of rocks, now the trees were in charge, reaching their full
height and power as if to put the granite firmly in its place.

My feelings for Brian hadn't changed, but I did enjoy him
as a hiking partner. Carol and Alan walked more slowly but
would go for hours without stopping. Brian and I preferred
to hustle to some spot we wanted to explore or hang out. I

remember one time passing a Boy Scout troop and racing ahead so we could skinny-dip in the creek before they reached us. The last day on the trail Alan asked me to take a picture of him and Carol on a rustic bridge over a creek with the setting sun beaming down on them. After I did, he told Brian to stand beside me and shot several of us.

In the title story, "Cowboys Are My Weakness," the speaker describes a picture in her mind of a ranch with pine trees and horses. "There's a woman standing in the doorway in cutoffs and a blue chambray work shirt and she's just kissed her tall, bearded, and soft-spoken husband goodbye." This story is partly about the pictures we have of how our ideal life would look, and how that can shape our choices. When we were back home getting ready for classes to start, Alan came over to the trailer park one night with the photos he'd gotten printed. We sighed over the landscapes and praised his composition skills. This was before digital cameras, and luckily for us, Alan had been a professional photographer. Toward the end of the last stack, there were the photos of Brian and me. The sun had been going down behind the camera, making our skin glow. The tawny highlights in his brown hair matched the lighter color of my own. Amazingly enough, my hair, which had been scrubbed in the creek but never styled or cared for, waved to my shoulders the way I'd always wished it would. Our smiles were relaxed and warm. My arm rested on his shoulder, his head tilted slightly toward me. Though he didn't have a beard (just some stubble) and I was probably in quick-dry paddling shorts, we fit the picture in my mind, which was pretty close to the picture Houston's character had. I got back together with Brian.

I was almost twenty-three and felt that my life was passing by. (I know, try to stop laughing.) This time, because of that photo and my desire to show it to our children someday, because I wanted to secure a future of being loved and feeling content, and because I loved having someone to do outdoor activities with, I decided to take seriously the words he'd said flatly when we first broke up: "You never sacrifice for someone else. You never need anyone very much. You're impossible to have a relationship with."

Okay, I thought, *here goes.*

The problem was, we didn't have a relationship based on mutual commitment and love. We had one based on mutual hobbies and a mutual dream. We wanted to be that couple in the photo. I'd been wise for so long, and it hadn't gotten me anywhere. The one man I'd loved, Charlie, my open-minded North Carolina redneck, had stayed with me less than three months. I worried I'd end up lonely, so I threw myself into the traditional role of girlfriend. You won't be surprised to learn that it didn't work at all. The more I put Brian's needs above mine, the more he demanded I change. No more fingertip push-ups. I stopped going on solo trips, just me and Allie. Amazingly enough, I didn't end it this time. One night we went to see the movie *The Last of the Mohicans*, which took place in New York State but I knew had been filmed in my old North Carolina stomping grounds. When the movie started, the screen filled with the Blue Ridge Mountains. I gazed at the misty ridges and started crying softly. This was home. I didn't miss only the landscape, I missed who I'd been when I lived there. It was as if the movie camera had turned its lens on the emptiness in me, and as I watched I cried harder. At the end, I was still crying when Brian broke up with me.

All this is to say, I understood the mixed-up women in Houston's stories. Though I wasn't physically abused like the main character in the short story "Dall," my staying with Brian was similarly motivated by the places we went and outdoor activities I could do so much more easily with him, just like the character who used her boyfriend to spend summers in the

Alaska Range stalking bighorn sheep. And Brian didn't cheat on me as openly as men in many of Houston's stories do. But like the woman who wanted to have that ranch and those pine trees and that soft-spoken bearded husband, I'd gotten trapped in a picture.

One reason I admire Houston's stories is that there is often a male character who possesses the adventurous, masculine traits the character's shitty boyfriend has, while also demonstrating a love of family and domestic life and a respect for so-called feminine qualities in general. Even though Houston's women often bemoan the way they can't seem to fall for the good men, the reader is aware that the choice is not between tame men and wild men. I'd finally stuck it out in a relationship until it exploded messily. If you count both times we were together, Brian was the only man I'd dated for more than three months. That record would stand for seven years, until I met my husband. After Brian, I began to think there was a missing parable that someone would find, like the Dead Sea Scrolls. The example of the Good Samaritan who cared for others selflessly had been pounded into me. But surely somewhere there was the Parable of the Sucker, and when it was found, women everywhere would have a clearer idea of where to draw boundaries. Now dumped out of that ideal picture, I went about finishing my degree and planning my last escapades before returning East. Sue had moved to Washington State with Ratty, and I missed our adventures.

Meanwhile, Alan and Carol had split up. One day Alan was petting Allie and talking to her about going on road trips. Alan's idea of a road trip was hitting the desert, High Sierras, and Pacific Ocean in twenty-four hours before coming home. We packed our tents, guitars, his camp stove, my dog, and a map. Sometimes he drove his car, sometimes I drove my truck. These trips were always platonic and soothed the graduate school stress, leaving only laugh lines around our eyes. How I loved having a laid-back companion whose aim was to find the darkest place in the middle of the desert, pull over, and turn off the headlights. Sometimes we stayed a few minutes. Sometimes we sang folk songs with the coyotes for hours.

I went backpacking in the Grand Canyon with Carol and two guys during the spring break of my last year in the program. I met Tim when I moved into the trailer park. His aluminum box was the smallest and so he slept on the picnic table, his coopless chickens roosting in the trees above him. He was friends with Brian, brilliant and quite eccentric. He had even gone backpacking in Joshua Tree with Brian and me once, but that was when Brian and I had been together. Tim was leaving California soon but seemed interested in more than friendship.

Meanwhile, Dave, a doctoral student in artificial intelligence, also lived in the trailer park and, unbeknownst to me, had a crush on Carol. Dave planned the trip. Carol and I shared a tent. The South Rim of the canyon was under snow, and fog socked the Tanner Trail in for the first mile. Soon scrub pines and sage were all that the snow clung to, set off against ground the color of crushed brick. As we looked behind and up, it was as if the top of the world had disappeared like Brigadoon, the bewitched Irish town in the musical. Fog blurred the rim. The steep, colorful cliffs showed their layers shamelessly. There was no water for ten miles, until we reached the Colorado River, and we were glad it was March because once the snow disappeared the temperature rose with no shade in sight. Eventually, temples made of pink, green, and red sand rose beside the river, which ran brown as if it were done trying to impress people. In the canyon, we wore shorts and went braless. The space taken up by warm clothes used so briefly annoyed me. That first night, Tim and I sat on some well-rounded rocks at the edge of the river, from which he pulled two Guinness he'd carried down and chilled. The woo was on.

As long as I was dating different men in order to figure out how relationships did and did not work, choosing the ones who took me places like Joshua Tree and the Grand Canyon and fed me marinated asparagus and stout was a good way to go. But, like Houston's characters, I started distinguishing my desire to go to wild places from my desire to be with those men. Rather than assume I'd always be with them, I treated these trips as opportunities to learn how to use different camp stoves, hang bear bags, filter water, read trail guides, and plan trips. I discovered that a couple of days before I got my period, my energy dropped to 70 percent. Poor Tim took a lot of weight from my pack when we hiked out Grandview Trail as thunder rumbled and lightning threatened. I couldn't accelerate as usual, and I couldn't explain it. Though I beat up on myself for a long time after that, hating that I'd shown weakness, Tim forgave me.

Throughout my experiences backpacking and road tripping in my early twenties, I learned to negotiate the sexual politics of outdoor spaces. I began to chart a course I hoped would lead me to self-reliance and competence, and with a few wrong turns, I did. I was never assaulted, despite many people's fears for me. Maybe I beat the odds. I went on adventures with men I knew well and trusted when I went with men at all. I chose a dog because I had no experience with guns, and companionship was as important as protection.

Nothing I learned to do was a guarantee of safety, but as soon as I stopped expecting any such guarantee, the better I prepared to deal with the risks I faced. It would be great if the world weren't more dangerous for women than for men, but the truth is, the world isn't safe for anyone. Many of us are drawn to outdoor recreation of different types in order to leave the fake safety of civilization and test ourselves against limits. To learn how to adapt. To become comfortable with not being in control.

Yes, the pretty views and healthy body are aspects I also love, but I can drive to views and exercise indoors. As I learned not to wait for a man to be a gateway to a new outdoor experience, I discovered that I was okay with long periods of being alone. That I like myself. That a good dog is better than an okay lover any day.

Even if I have to carry my own tent.

TO REACH GREEN BEFORE DARK

She hadn't realized how quiet America could be, even with the radio's squall and windows scrolled to nothing. After four years of higher ed, watching the wilderness on TV, reading about it in white men's journals, it was reassuring to discover stretches of such contented silence. Like Lewis and Clark, she would make her mark, slash southeast to northwest across the territory. The common ground visible outside the truck cab and in the small slabs of mirror soothed, like a good book found at a party where your ride's in the back room with the host's best buddy, her purse full of condoms and the car keys.

On those gray ribbons that bind this odd-shaped package of democracy, politics takes a back seat to geography, capitalism scoots over for capitals. Only the land's loose embrace can reach her here. No stopping, she promises herself (and her mother), for men hitching free rides. This trip is all hers, a tour down the future's memory lane. She'll take snapshots of mule deer and prairie dogs, bison and bears. Maps are puzzles, games she can't lose.

Driving for days, she observes how the sky changes along with state lines, ecosystems, accents, and roadkill. When you are used to the gradual bleeding of blue into the many ridges of home and their cloud-mist meetings, the Midwest's horizon seems as flat as a mother's scowl when you thought never to pry her lips apart. In Minnesota, the tornadoes make the world's sleeve all but vanish. The only evidence: rain heaved at the windshield. She thinks it could be possible with practice to identify a place just from a photo of the sky—the way surfers know the coast from where and how a wave breaks, and how farmers know a field.

Texaco attendants provide the little conversation needed. They clean the glass and ask where she's going. She practices not answering, as if there were an answer she could offer were his smile just right and the world a safer place. Never gives her name. This is real . . . is real . . . is real . . . thrumming mantra of her telephone-pole road trance, backdrop to other thoughts the way the buttes lounging on the curved horizon frame the fresh-thrown tumbleweed.

Late May. An RV owner says Montana snowed fourteen inches, so she goes north only to Missoula. If it weren't for her small dog and two-wheel drive, she'd have dared the cold. Glacier, a mammoth dream, the park that makes the Sierras seem common, must remain on the border's fence unreckoned. The one place she'd planned to stop. It'd been snug in front when she'd left the Smokies' fog-smudged dogwoods and endured North Dakota's blitz of billboards promising three-hundred-foot prairie dogs and WALL (just 93 miles ahead) DRUG. Always recalling those calendar photos of iced lakes and wildflowers sliding off steep grades, as close to Europe's fjords and Alps as she could drive.

In Idaho, browsing in a lodge gift shop while her cinnamon twist is heated, she strums the fringes of bandannas and jackets with hand-painted state emblems. But who to give them to? She tries to picture her college friends wearing such things and thinking about her here. Not as she is now, not as it really happened. They'd see her at the bar with old hunters, learning the local lies, casting bullshit and winks to the bartender bringing a drink from the fella who invites her to hike the gorge at dawn. She takes the warm roll and coffee to go, silently passing the men under animals stuffed and staring. A series of hairpins clung to with sticky fingers and she's in another state.

In the Central Washington desert it hits her: in her freedom she's fabricating reasons. A purpose for doing one thing and not another, something to hang emotions on rather than just letting them flutter in the sage scent and exhaust. She's going eighty trying to reach green before dark, aiming for a peninsula surrounded by cartographers' blue ink. Soon she'll stand on the other coast, actually touch the second bookend, which, like God, she'd always accepted was there without any real proof.

Camped in Olympic National Park, the rainforest is a companionable misfit. Her tent tucked under the unbreakable boughs of ancient trees, she dreams she'll die in a field in Montana one night when the stars blind like sun on ice. Rain will have shrunk her blanket to a square barely large enough for one. Somewhere it's dry, and friends crawl in bed with friends.

Up at 3:00 a.m., she shivers and imagines being held by the man in site 32 who'd borrowed a can opener before dinner and to whom she'd said only what was necessary. The stars poise their frozen tips above her head. Part of her wishes for the world of introductions, where she can meet people and not be afraid to linger or walk away. But out here she loves how there's no one to say, "I've never seen this side of you before." Tonight silence simmers. On a log by the unused firepit, she leans toward the ambiguous warmth of his tent next door, tracing the long zipper with her eyes. She doesn't mean to tease herself, is already thinking how teeth meet and part predictably, like finding an end to a once-endless Montana road that wouldn't have been enough, anyway.

Canoeing with brother Steve, Potomac River, West Virginia (photo credit: D. Joe Smith)

Whitewater Twenties

MARKING MY TERRITORY
Allegheny River, Pennsylvania

From my truck, I dragged the old, patched whitewater kayak a professor had sold me for fifteen dollars. I pulled on scratchy, secondhand polypropylene pants and top and then a purple windbreaker. Gray wool hat with a hole in the top for my ponytail. Zip up my PFD. No helmet needed.

I was home for the holidays, but not my home. The home where my father was raised, where my parents resided after my grandmother died. Nothing there was my territory, except maybe the river across the lane. I'd always been drawn to rivers though never lived on one. After Mom's Thanksgiving meal with no-fat gravy for Dad and the first turkey the whole family had shared since one brother became unvegetarian, every couch was claimed and I escaped outside.

I passed the empty porch and worked my way down the slick bank, remembering what Walter, who'd been my grandmother's neighbor, had said that morning as he'd tightened some bolts on my roof rack. *Too bad you weren't born a boy.* My neoprene socks made my steps down to the water sound like a seal's.

Dad watched me from the dock as I ferried across his river to determine the current's strength. His care was sweet, but I knew more about the risks here than he did. A river so flat and wide can deceive you. A big wind blowing upstream can make water appear to flow in the opposite direction. You might expect something serene and accommodating, something that won't put up a struggle. But it's your fault for making assumptions.

I slipped into the pattern of alternating paddle blades, my torso twisting side to side, feet pushing against pegs, knees pressed to the hull, water dripping from the airborne paddles to wet my hands and drip down my forearms. The chill made me happily aware I was outdoors. This was my trick, steering this boat and staying upright. This set me apart from those who were snoozing and warm inside, where I could return when the reality of what was outside lost its romance and became strictly cold. Even my father standing sentinel on the dock was separate from me, though less so. I paddled away.

I set out against the current. It's in my nature and makes coming home easier. Walter rode his bike on the lane, keeping pace with me until the river turned and he had to give up. Oh, Walter, too bad you weren't born a twenty-something female in the 1990s. I'd been focusing long and loosely on the arched bridge ahead. I wasn't sure when the reflection became clear enough to join its reality in one continuous ring. Suddenly the hills at the river bend beyond doubled below like paper cutouts with the bottoms attached, and the whole view went flat, swallowing the horizon. The scene loomed before me, an early American landscape painter's impression of my future, and I stared, wondering about boundaries, currents, and winds that seem to contradict what we're taught, until I was almost in the frame.

Too far, I thought, backpaddling as my bow pierced the bridge's reflection, blades slapped water like confused wings, and crying geese flew below my boat.

French Broad River, North Carolina

Rivers often get gendered, usually female. Maybe because they epitomize a strength that yields, each a sister to our monthly flows—who knows how they feel about these associations? With such an overwrought name, the French Broad couldn't escape being feminized. Visions of a heavily lipsticked dame with flamboyant airs swirled together with the reality of our rough and lowbrow lifestyle at the rafting outpost.

Named because its width allowed easy trade by water in the

otherwise difficult terrain and because it was controlled by the French. Still, it'd outlasted their claim and was going strong when I showed up, my pickup packed with kayak, laptop, and pit bull, to learn from the river as I tried to make a home, at least for a while.

The Cherokee name for it was "Long Man." I can hear the French Broad's throaty chuckle as it rumbles by. It has been defying labels for longer than the mountains that think their granite can contain it. "It's the third oldest river in the world," I told rafts of people who had come to gawk and be entertained.

"I like her style," wives would say when they learned the river flowed north instead of south, defying tradition.

"Prepare to meet a real man," called guys on leave from Fort Bragg as we entered a rapid too close to another raft because they ignored my commands of "All back." I'd be forced to hang my draw stroke out, attempting to shift us to the side, biting my tongue at their calls of "We showed the river who's boss."

Not the roughest river, with only one Class IV rapid, the French Broad suited me fine because the small outpost was enough of a settlement that I could keep my dog. The wildest river with a macho reputation was the Chattooga, on which the movie *Deliverance* had been filmed. When I'd visit Ken on my days off and tag along down the Class V rapids, the talk among guests and guides was different. There were still visitors who treated the river that transected a wilderness area as if it were a Disney World ride, only colder and with more trees. But the Chattooga earned respect, not just because it was remote and lots could go wrong, but because a threat hung over rafts of men when one started humming the opening notes from "Dueling Banjos." Accustomed to the cloud cover of fear that was a familiar part of growing up female, I enjoyed it when men started to squirm and comment on how they'd never be caught in these mountains alone. The scene of the outdoorsman being sodomized by a mountain man had a long life in those hills. I wondered how many of the guys imagined hillbillies with guns hiding behind the trees, waiting to penetrate their wilderness. Whether they did or not, the Chattooga was treated as masculine, powerful, and for the hours these guests spent on the river, even the men felt at the mercy of it and the guides.

Including female guides. At meals and around the campfire, the teasing seemed friendly and relaxed. The respect the guides had for each other's skill and the necessity of relying on each other daily took the edge off the gendered joking I heard at other outposts. Of course, I had only glimpses of what went on there, but a big part of my attraction to Ken was how, when we met at wilderness first aid training, he was neither intimidated nor weirdly titillated by strong women. He was used to them.

A bit older, cute, unambitious, and unreliable in terms of making plans, Ken would surprise me by showing up where I worked. I wasn't the only woman he liked visiting there—Gretchen made our outpost domestically inviting with her amazing meals, and guides would be drawn to the French Broad for the opposite reason they were drawn to the Chattooga. When newbies fresh from college rotated there, they often gaped at my serving sizes. I'd been loading, tying, unloading, hauling, and guiding alongside the teenage boys all day—did they really think I'd eat small portions? Once when Ken was there (he'd shown up right before dinner), he looked across the table at them and said, "She's a healthy girl." Then he grinned and waggled his eyebrows.

For me, the French Broad is a role model, encompassing qualities both masculine and feminine, tame and wild, commercial and natural, ancient yet new each day. Practically devoid of fossils, the French Broad knows its place and shapes its place. Not fickle like the Chattooga, which once flowed into the Gulf and now runs to the Atlantic. Call her or him or them

or it what you will—the French Broad remains my best guide
of how to settle in, how to resist interpretation.

River of Money, Georgia

Ken drove our assigned RV over the curb and onto the grass
beside the menthol-blue porta-potty in the parking lot across
from the new Publix grocery store. I followed, pulling my truck
covered with bumper stickers up beside the big red tent. This
would be our home for five weeks. Ken's Jeep was broken down
again, so I'd had to pick him up—hours out of my way. We'd
decided, even though we'd broken up, to share the main bed.
It'd save room, and pulling down the bed over the captain's
chairs every night was too much hassle. When the trees arrived,
our suburban campsite was complete.

Question: Where do Nantahala Outdoor Center raft guides
go in the winter? Answer: If they aren't working ski patrol, then
they're probably selling Christmas trees: Fraser fir, Colorado
spruce, and Scotch pine from Western North Carolina, trucked
in fresh weekly to parking lots encircling Atlanta, Georgia.
Five weeks of hard, nonstop work and your pockets would
be full enough to head to Chile, where the winter paddling's
good. In my case, it meant I could make more in five weeks
than teaching two sixteen-week composition courses. The flyer
for new staff emphasized how much oxygen was created and
carbon absorbed by the growing of these trees. I noticed lower
down it said Frasers were more expensive because they required
more care, which I assumed meant more chemicals. "Male-
female teams work best," our trainer said. "Women and men
sell differently and buy differently. And ladies, a little makeup
can compensate for all your hauling and sawing and loading, if
you know what I mean."

Ken and I worked well together because we trusted the other's competence. We hung lights from pole to pole and in the

tent, drilled holes straight up the trunk so they would stand tall on spikes we had set in rows, cut low branches with the same knives we used for our lunch, the smell of orange rind mixing with pine resin. I foraged the least-annoying holiday tapes from discount bins and played big band, crooners, jazz, and "You're a Mean One, Mr. Grinch" over and over. We wore our Santa hats religiously during business hours, unless it got very cold. We schmoozed with sincerity. At this new location in this new strip mall, management wanted the tree lot to be seen from the freeway, so they brought us a big Santa balloon. One night as I turned the blower off and Santa melted in a pool of red, a banshee child's voice came from somewhere across the dark highway: *Hey you, put Santa back up now. Put him up RIGHT NOW!* I weighted the fabric down, turned off the Christmas lights, and went inside to another supper of noodle packets. Sorry, Virginia, this Santa ain't real.

When I'd go to Publix for a snack run or to use the bathroom, it felt like being off the reservation even though our tree lot was completely Euro-American, a pure product of capitalism. People were friendly in a way that showed that a female dressed like me was a novelty there. "You're so cute," the woman at the register said once, clapping her hands together. Thank goodness the handicap stall had its own sink so I could inconspicuously shampoo my hair. Washing my hands one day, I caught a perfectly coifed woman's eye in the mirror. Gesturing to my too-big Carhartt overalls (they'd had only men's sizes), long underwear, and rabbit-fur mad-bomber hat, she drawled, "I love your outfit." I paused a moment while applying mascara and lipstick to thank her.

When a family tumbled out of their SUV, two or more kids scattering before the parents could corral them, I'd perk up. These were the customers I loved, especially when the dad was as excited as the rest. A little boy ran around claiming every other tree was his favorite, as the parents smiled and waited for his energy to settle. One girl, about six years old, wandered about making sounds as if she were in a grove of redwoods. *Ooo. Ohhhh.* I wondered as she wandered: Had she ever been to the mountains a couple of hours north? There was a three-foot spruce she kept going back to, asking whether she could have it in her room. Maybe she imagined the book *Where the Wild Things Are.* As a child, I'd thought the bedroom turning into the forest had been the best part of the story. After her parents chose a seven-foot Fraser fir for $69.95, I told the mother she could have the spruce for five bucks. After the baled Fraser and Charlie Brown tree were loaded, the mother ran back to thank me again and tell me what her daughter had said: *If someone else had bought this tree before I got there, I would be very sad and pregnant.* We laughed. Another virgin birth narrowly averted.

Money flowed one way, and it was our job to keep that river at the highest water level we could. Over a certain amount we got commission—and bragging points, since this was our first year. A new item for the wreath tent was the Swivel Straight Tree Stand. I spent more time in the tent than Ken because my bows were better, and we had lots of wreath orders. When that type of husband who couldn't be bothered to look at trees, but had a wife who looked at every tree twice, came in the tent to wait and mutter, I knew how to reel him in. Looking around, he'd perk up and say, "That tree's crooked!" As if I didn't know. As if I hadn't put hundreds of trees up straight already that season.

"Oh my goodness, you're right!" Walking to where the tree stood at a precarious angle in the Swivel Straight, I'd grab the tree trunk, put my foot on the hidden pedal, and swirl that conifer several times before stopping with its tip tentward and releasing the pedal. "Is it straight now?" I'd ask, all 1950s innocence, my mascara working overtime. Every husband I tried this with bought one, sure that this Christmas would be miraculously stress-free (assuming his wife ever made up her mind). Management wondered what our trick was and brought stands over from other lots. They sold for $89.95, more than all but our tallest Fraser firs.

Gadgets for the guys, wreaths for the women. Get them talking in the tent, tell stories of summers on the river, make buying a tree from us seem like an adventure. That's where the payoff was. Everyone comes for a tree, and most leave with one. The extras send your bottom line over the top. But there were even better extras. Bottles of wine dropped off for the poor raft guides away from family. Homemade spaghetti and venison meatballs. I could see the fantasies of what they thought Ken and I were to each other, our thrilling romance bopping from place to place. We let them conjure what they would, our gift to strangers.

A man who drove and repaired U-Haul trucks came in late. Ken was already in the RV, and I was about to close. Tired as this guy was, he glowed with hope, a single strand of white lights on an unpruned tree. We talked about choosing our jobs by what they offered—ones where we weren't stuck indoors and got to meet lots of people. "In my job, I meet many folks but not under good circumstances. Usually something is wrong, there's a problem. But y'know," he said, looking at me with such gentle eyes, "people are good mostly. Yep, folks are mostly good."

The next day I kept thinking about him. Had he sensed my weariness and uncertainty? His message repeated in my head like a familiar carol while I tried not to snap at Ken. I wondered whether the U-Haul driver meant that each of us individually is mostly good, or that out of the whole population of humans, most are good. After his taillights had contracted to nothing, swallowed by the highway, I'd stood in the parking lot both more and less alone than I'd been before.

From Thanksgiving through Christmas Eve, we sold trees.

Then they'd all go into the chipper and be spread on the ground—management's orders because there are always those who want something for free. By late on Christmas Day, the faux forest would revert to empty space. Right before closing one night the last week, when Ken was busy with a customer, Jackass walked in with his woman. I showed them around, but he found flaws in every tree and wanted to dicker. Now, I wasn't above lowering prices on occasion, and glowing with the coming of sweet baby Jesus, I'd done so several times that day for folks who seemed down on their luck. Ken said they sought me out because I was a pushover, easy to con. Said I was losing us money. It had all become about money, and I didn't care anymore, already knew I wasn't coming back next year. Jackass's strutting display of studliness, during which he'd scorn his woman for any tree she dared speak in favor of, had me lowering my antlers to charge. I offered to show him the budget bin he could afford. His face got red. He found a six-foot spruce with a broken bough and a hole in one side that should have been culled. "Ten dollars," he said, starting to grab it.

I shook my head, smiling beatifically.

"It's an ugly tree!" he yelled at me.

"It *is* an ugly tree," I agreed, "and if you want this ugly tree, it will cost you $19.95."

The woman and I exchanged apologetic looks as he stomped off.

At the end of the five weeks, every little thing we did got on each other's nerves, as if we were a real couple. But of all Ken's habits, it was the way he had of referring to the tree lot as *his* instead of *ours* that pushed me over the edge. How I bristled when he referred to the tent, in which I spent more time than he, that way. "Go get me the scissors from my tent," he'd say to one of the high school workers. "Just going to deflate my Santa and have a beer," he'd tell the last customer. I'd put in as much work and effort on the place, had been as much a part of settling this strip-mall frontier as he had. The day he referred to the RV as his, I exploded. His response was, "What's the big deal?"

On Christmas Eve, a few high schoolers stayed to help as Ken, against management's orders, burned the pines in a barrel. With hay and wood chips everywhere—a pile I, the rule follower, was making bigger and bigger—a stray spark would've caused an inferno. I walked over to where Ken was telling stories to Erik, who liked to be called Lard.

"What are you doing? Are you trying to burn my tree lot down?" I asked Ken, talking in the singular possessive for the first time. He sputtered, but before he could say anything I added, "Lard, would you set this crate outside my front door please?" Ken fumed as Lard disappeared in the dark toward the RV. "Why is it a big deal when I do it and not when you do it?" I asked.

He had no answer, at least none he wanted to admit. For hours, I tore down my wonderland while he tore down his, storing the lights, dropping the tent, and pulling up the stakes. We didn't speak. I could hardly wait until we met the others at the Indian restaurant the next day for Christmas goat. I would not sit near him. Too bad we had to ride together in the truck. Then it hit me.

Not *the* truck. He had to ride in *my* truck.

BABES IN THE WOODS AND ON THE RIVERS

At age twenty-five, I left the climate-controlled halls of higher ed; I walked outside and decided to stay there. My last semester in graduate school, a fellow poet asked Carol Muske-Dukes what the average career track for an MFA was. The student looked at me as she said, "Because I'm not going to be working in an outdoor gear store when I finish *my* degree." True, that

Guiding on the French Broad River, North Carolina (photo credit: Nantahala Outdoor Center)

was my only guaranteed job back in Western North Carolina, where I was headed, and it was only part time.

"Drive a taxi," Carol told her.

The message was clear, and I smirked. How could anyone be foolish enough to think that studying and writing poetry for two years had significant commercial value? And wasn't that the point?

I got a second job writing and doing photography for a non-profit monthly publication in Asheville and soon was handling their fund-raising and marketing. The job sounded great on my résumé, but a nonprofit paycheck is small. After six months of working two jobs and falling behind on my bills (even with the heat kept at fifty), I jumped at an opportunity to break my lease, throw all I owned into the truck, and become the outdoor recreation equivalent of a taxi driver—a raft guide.

It'd always been a dream of mine when in college, but I never got up the nerve to try. I conferred with Allie, my pit bull companion, and she agreed. She'd been named for a river, after all; Allie was short for Allegheny, the river my parents lived on.

This decision worried my mother almost as much as my decision to drive and camp cross-country at twenty-one. But it fell into place with the seeming inevitability of a fairy tale, and I followed the bread crumbs. My roommate Steve, whom I'd known in college, would be leaving to work again at Nantahala Outdoor Center (NOC) for the rafting season. He was my age but was training with my first paddling mentor for a spot on the Olympic whitewater slalom team. Windy Gordon had left his job at the college to manage the NOC outpost on the French Broad River, which would allow him to train. It was a relatively healthy kind of midlife crisis, and he was lucky to have a wife who supported this.

When I called Windy, he agreed to hire me. The French Broad was one of the few NOC outposts where I could stay put and keep a dog. With no official contract or notice of duties and pay, I headed to a life where my rent was sixteen dollars a month and food was five dollars a day. I didn't have my own phone, bathroom, or heat, but my room had real cinderblock walls and privacy, unlike the screen walls of the summer shacks used by roaming raft guides. I could stack my milk crates full of books and know they wouldn't get rained on. I put some plywood on two small filing cabinets and made a desk. Maybe not what Virginia Woolf had in mind, but it was a room of my own.

I arrived in April, well before any rafting trips began and

before Windy, the only person I knew there, arrived. He'd be away a lot for training and wanted to spend as many nights at home as he could before the schedule got crazy. The few folks around gave me sideways looks. They knew the new manager had hired me, that I was freshly dropped into their world. They wondered whether I'd be any good or a pain in the butt. Those chilly spring nights huddled with Allie in my sleeping bag, I wondered, *Am I avoiding growing up, as Mom fears?* One night I reread an old journal from my backpack trip in the Grand Canyon where I'd copied a quote from Sam Keen's book *To a Dancing God*: "Warning: Be careful what you spend your day touching because it will shape your mind, your body and your heart." I grew calm inside and trusted my instincts.

In those early days I hoped for R&M work—repair and maintenance—to earn a little money. Training would come in May, but for now I learned how to nail shingles and mow the lawn. I decided the overall experience was what I'd signed up for. *Be free-flowing like the river*, I told myself.

When I wasn't working odd jobs or driving back to Asheville to get some hours in at Black Dome Mountain Sports, I'd walk with Allie on the Appalachian Trail, which ran through the outpost. Or I'd take Allie and my guitar to the top step of the river take-out. The steps marked water levels with white numbers painted on the sides. Every morning after a hard rain, guides would run there like kids on Christmas to see what the gauge said.

Raft guides love rain. If you're only running dam-controlled rivers like the Nantahala or Ocoee, it's not as significant an issue on a weekly basis. But paddlers watch the weather hoping for rain as much as climbers and backpackers watch the weather hoping for none of it. Good rains all spring and summer make the river more interesting and maybe even extend the commercial season. Plus, higher water required guides in every

raft—more employment. The river at flood stage demanded
new routes and safety plans because rocks when covered with
water became holes. Our dependence and focus on rain made
me feel kinship with farmers. We were fully aware of and
focused on the elements beyond our control. This wasn't the
wilderness, of course, but I was living without money as my
focus, I spent most of my time outside, and the walls I did have
were not confining. It was a wild life, with plumbing.

The small settlement consisted of the Outback's screened-in
housing, the Block House with several rooms including mine,
the small wooden cabins that housed those with the most
seniority, the cinder-block bathhouse, and the Main House
across the road. It was luxurious compared to the accom-
modations at the rafting company next door. Most guides
there camped across the street in the meadow dubbed Hippie
Holler, and when the river flooded, so did they. This is what
I was touching every day: Dirt. Water. Boats. Bugs. People.
Paddles. Pit Bull. Pen. Paper. I reveled in it but still felt out of
place. The guys were fun to talk to and do odd jobs with, but
I felt that some of them watched me as if every new task was a
chance for me to mess up and amuse them. Anytime I did, it
was recounted at the dinner table over Gretchen's great food.
Some guys were easy to talk to and I could be myself, but some
looked at me warily as if I, the overeducated feminist poet, had
wandered like a coyote into their yard. Would I cause trouble
or suddenly disappear? Could I hack this? Would I latch on
to one guy or many? Or prove their suspicions of feminists by
turning out to be a lesbian? How much of this was in my mind
and how much of this was in theirs?

There were two other women around, both older than me.
Gretchen, with hair in a brown braid down her back, lived
nearby in Hot Springs with Shasta, her German shepherd, and
came daily to cook. Her meals were well known, and other

outposts were envious, especially of Saturday morning blueberry turnovers. But NOC was her job, not her life. Fritz, the assistant manager, had blonde hair, glasses, and years of experience. She seemed comfortable in her niche, and I wished I was as thick skinned and confident. She guided Grand Canyon trips in the off-season, and her life of adventure travel sounded amazing. She seemed a bit standoffish to me, and I got the sense Fritz thought I might be a spy for Windy. She may have wanted the manager job. As of yet, there'd been no females of my age or experience around. The next week was staff training, and I wondered whether that would make me feel more or less as if I belonged.

The night before guide training started, I drove to the main outpost on the Nantahala. Most new guides start on the Nanny and, as they prove themselves, get sent out temporarily or permanently to the French Broad, Chattooga, Ocoee, or Nolichucky. I figured my training group, called a pod, would probably all know each other because they lived in staff housing there. I left Allie chained to the truck, lying on the cab roof, sniffing the air and surveying her ever-changing territory as I walked to the get-to-know-you cookout. Over dinner I met our trainers: Angus, a redhead with a Neanderthal build and leprechaun smile; and Joy, a tall, strong, short-haired Amazon who radiated her name. My pod included a couple of other females. I hit it off with Barbara, who was older than I was but twice as energetic. The night was a flurry of bits and pieces of everyone's stories, which I couldn't keep straight. My brain was unfocused and I had low momentum, as always right before my period. I worried about keeping extra tampons dry and not bleeding through my shorts on the river. Pads are worthless if they get wet. And would I have enough energy to perform well?

I brushed my teeth in the parking lot restroom and slid my mattress onto the open tailgate so I could look up and see the hazy half moon. Nights were still in the thirties or forties, but no rain expected. This night, I was glad for the forecast since I'd thrown my river gear on the roof to make room to sleep. I hooked Allie's leash to the truck bed and we curled together under the moon's wink. *Home is where you park your dog,* I thought as I drifted off.

That first day on the river, I guided through everything but the first and last rapids, which are the Nanny's biggest at Class III. The water is always cold, drawing from the bottom of the reservoir on the ridge. Dam controlled, the river is turned on each morning and off each evening in an unnatural cycle. The lines were clearer on this smaller river, making it easier to learn there, though it was twisty and hard to see far ahead. On the left bank were the railroad tracks and on the right was Route 28. On both sides the tangled green of the kudzu-covered gorge leaped to the sky. In contrast, the French Broad was, well, broad, and it seemed as if there were always several options you could take. We worked on the commands and shouting them effectively to our crews over the water's roar. *All forward. Right back. Left back. All forward hard!* We learned the names of rapids and tried to memorize the order and where to be on the river for what was around the bend.

The next day I awoke at 6:00 a.m. in pitch black and watched the sun gradually squeeze into the southeast *V* of the gorge. The pale light grew into a periwinkle blue, revealing clouds like combed wool. The staff housing parking lot was quiet and chilly. I'd been offered a room for the night, but that would've meant hauling stuff to and from the truck. Why bother? Allie didn't care where we slept.

That day and the next were filled with more information. Watching Joy was instructive purely for her ease as a leader. I listened to her humor and how both she and Angus treated everyone. Gender didn't seem to be a factor. Strength was, sure, but Barbara and Joy were buffer than some of the guys, and clearly Angus lived a life in which both genders literally pulled their own weight. It was as refreshing as a cold Nanny splash. Joy showed me what to do to build up the muscles I'd rely on most—chin-ups, sit-ups, back extensions. I already knew the right stretches. But one of their main lessons was to not try to muscle your way through everything. Learn to work with the river rather than try to beat it into submission. A common bumper sticker said: *Whitewater—women do it with finesse!*

As an analytical learner, I wished that Angus, the instructor in my raft, would give me more specific feedback. I felt solid gauging the water's momentum and reading the lines, but weakest at using my crew effectively. I hadn't gotten up the nerve to talk to Angus because we always seemed to have too much to do, and I didn't want to seem less than confident. Same old story.

The third day, after dinner, Betty Ann came over to introduce herself. She'd been on taxi squad the year before, coming in when they needed extra guides for large trips, and had already worked a week or more on the Nanny, which was the busiest river. She'd joined us because she needed rescue techniques and other advanced training.

"Where did you guide before?" she asked me and was surprised when I told her this was my first time. "I was watching you. You had the strongest moves and knew the river best."

Whaaaaaat? Lordy, did I need to hear that.

"You're such a strong paddler. You could guide at the Chattooga," she went on, laughing at my stunned reaction.

That's the high-testosterone river, the one where *Deliverance* had been filmed. I was flattered but not tempted. We made plans to grab our kayaks after dinner and go to the lake.

That night I crashed hard and woke up achy. I thought about how much I'd enjoyed hanging out with Betty Ann and working on our offside rolls. She seemed around my age. I was grateful for her positive feedback and for showing me a better way to tie my kayak to the roof. Companionship made it easier to get my sore body moving.

The last day of training was bittersweet since I liked my pod members and didn't know when some would cycle through the French Broad outpost. Betty Ann would be stationed at the Ocoee, a long way from me, but we swore to get together on days off when possible. We spent our final day on the river doing drills, practicing back ferries, and running rapids with only one other person or by ourselves.

Then we did multiple runs of the Nantahala Falls, the last and biggest rapid, walking boats back up as we took turns. We had full rafts, but everyone paddled with their T-grip ends in the water, except for the guide and one other. This gave us heavy rafts and mimicked a weak crew. We practiced choosing where to put the strongest paddler. It was hilarious.

We all unintentionally took turns falling out, finding balance harder without a paddle blade for bracing. On my turn as guide, I was too far left at first; I hadn't fully broken free of the eddy line, so I did two 360-degree spins in the long eddy to get into a better position as we approached the falls. I was still a tad left but used my momentum to break free of the eddy current and made a clean run with some impromptu surfing in the hole, while my crew hooted with glee.

At the bottom, Angus grinned. "Way to go to Plan B."

"More like Plan F," I said. But we'd had fun and I'd shown myself I could adapt. It was a good day on the river.

Back at the French Broad, I talked to my parents on the phone. Mom asked whether I thought I'd made the right decision coming to NOC. I said, "Yes!" without hesitation. After dinner, Ciro showed slides from his summer travels. I'd given Scott money for beer and was looking forward to an evening catching up with my French Broad crew. The place felt more like home than when I'd left.

Windy was on the front steps of his posh plywood abode when I was heading to the slide show, and I told him about the ups and downs of training. He laughed and nodded and then got serious—like professor serious.

"You need to realize how much skill and potential you have," he said as he pinned me with his kind eyes.

"There are moments I do," I said. "More and more of them."

Settling into My New Frontier

Now I needed additional training as a guide on the French Broad. As I grew more competent, my sense of belonging increased. I started appreciating how much more I was learning because the French Broad's wildness was not made predictable with a dam. At first I didn't like how it kept me more on edge, but then I settled into checking the stair gauge each day, the same way I'd assess my raft crew's strengths and weaknesses when first sizing them up. Familiarity allowed me to make decisions based on new combinations of variables and built up my confidence in more than paddling and guiding. It also built a connection to the river that went beyond what I'd expected.

"One of the great losses of working rivers like the Nanny, Ocoee, or Pigeon is that you see that same world every day," Windy told me. "Wild places demand that we truly see them because if we don't really look we won't know, we won't understand."

As with close friends whose mood you can tell by the angle of their head when they think no one is watching, I learned to look at rocks and sections of stream bank to know how pushy the river was going to be, what the best ways to approach it were.

My schedule was split between photography and guiding, and as a photographer I had to learn where to station myself depending on water level and get my timing down. Those days of film and no picture previews seem long ago. But customers ordered photos before you even knew whether they came out, and refunds were a hassle. Scott, who was in his mid to late twenties like me, was not a boss to praise anyone but was quick to tell others about the shots missed or other mistakes. One day off, I hiked to the bottom of Frank Bell's rapid—the biggest there at Class IV—and practiced throwing the rescue rope. The bright yellow ropes were stiff nylon, and if you were assigned to be safety it was crucial that you could get the rope out far enough to be useful. I'd never thrown anything other than a Frisbee.

Scott paddled down ahead of the group, pulling his kayak up on the rocks where I stood. He looked up, surprised to see me, noted the rope in my hand, and said, "Huh." Then he got into position as the bow of a raft peeked over the top of the upper ledge, which made a horizon line from where we were. Immediately, a woman popped out of the raft, and while grabbing for her, the guide fell out too. At the bottom was a hole notorious for taking people deep. When I didn't see them, I worried they were recirculating without air. Then thirty feet downstream they popped up soaked and smiling. Scott already had his camera pointed at the spot. Carnage makes good photos, and he was grinning more than usual. I tossed the rope and pulled the happy women over to us.

At dinner he told the story, including how I'd been there practicing with the rope.

"She has a good throw," he said.

I tried to play it cool and not grin like a goofball. For once Scott wasn't teasing and he didn't undercut his praise with an innuendo.

At the Nantahala where there were lots of people—staff, guests, and paddlers out on their own—"Good throw!" was a common pick-up line. Betty Ann and I had compared notes and agreed it tied with "You know, I give great back massages." Talking with Betty Ann, I'd found she was also aware of the talk that added a layer of sexual tension to ordinary moments. Not all guys did this; like mist, such talk could be thick in some places on the river and nonexistent in others. I also noticed it'd become easier to talk to guys I didn't know when paddling or walking around. I'd started to give males the benefit of the doubt more and trust my instincts, no longer so tense about safety or worried that friendliness would be seen as an invitation. If it was misconstrued, I could sort it out. And I had backup. Instead of being alone in a new place, I was one of the tribe.

Someone would eventually notice if I didn't return to my room or truck, would hear if I yelled or was hassled anywhere around the outpost. I had a society of sorts, so I could risk more, stray a little further out of my comfort zone. It was a great chance to relax and enjoy new opportunities, and I did. But being more relaxed and less defensive also made it easier to analyze the ways many guys reacted to and talked about women. I could more easily forgive the guests who stared at my abs (*Oh my God, how did you get those?*) because this was an unfamiliar world to them. When a guy in my raft said, "I've never seen shoulders like that on a girl," I replied that I'd seen plenty. And hey, at least it wasn't my boobs they were ogling. But when the male guides waiting for dinner sat at the picture window watching and commenting as Jen mowed the front yard, it was annoying. Nothing she wore or did was asking for attention, but she was nineteen and pretty and blonde and hey, that's open season, I guess. It seemed as if they assumed she desired this kind of attention, that it was the reason she was here doing this instead of another summer job.

Even though the men I worked with (at least the ones who'd been at NOC for years) were accustomed to working alongside strong, competent women doing every job necessary, they were still products of culture as much as I was. American culture—in stories and images—constantly tells the story of men withdrawing from civilization to retreat to nature: the Boones, Crocketts, Thoreaus, Muirs, and almost every character John Wayne ever played (Hondo is my favorite). I loved these role models. When I was a girl visiting national parks with my family, I read all the exhibits about how men settled the West, saving a woman or two along the way. Now I lived among raft guides who often referred to themselves as whitewater cowboys. Why not? We had our version of bunkhouses and rodeos. But it was the romantic notion of the cowboy as a tough, solitary figure who chooses a hard life of few comforts over soft, city ways that was at the heart of the comparison.

We weren't the first to make ourselves over in this iconic male image. Take Theodore Roosevelt, a sickly boy from a wealthy family in New York City, who'd made himself into a robust big game hunter and cowboy by the time he became president of the United States, in 1901. He demonstrated this ideal masculinity when he said the hunter "must possess energy, manliness, self-reliance, and a capacity for self-help." Women, like nature, were considered passive and voiceless, existing as a resource for men, much like wild game. If a woman was self-reliant, she wouldn't need a man. She might not measure her value in how she served men. Egads, civilization might crumble.

Roosevelt was concerned by the 1890 census, which showed the frontier disappearing. He, along with others like Frederick Jackson Turner, feared that losing the frontier as the crucible for rugged independent spirit would result in American men becoming overcivilized. (And by overcivilized, they meant feminized and Europeanized.) Roosevelt advocated raising children under the superior moral guidance of their mothers but argued that taking older boys from their mothers to test themselves against the wilderness was the only way to make them real men. This view spurred his monumental conservation efforts, such as establishing the US Forest Service, five national parks, and many bird and game preserves. He protected a total of 230 million acres of public land. I wonder whether he'd be surprised by how many women enjoy these places.

Our national pride built up around being rugged individualists able to hack a life out of whatever natural resources were available, fancy clothes and manners be damned. I wasn't aware of how women's absence from such stories affected the way we'd be reacted to in outdoor professions, even in the late twentieth century. And it wasn't the sort of thing we raft guides were talking about while sitting under the stars, smoking cigars, and watching moonlight skip on the dark river.

I could relate to Teddy Roosevelt. I'd been motivated to test myself by enduring a difficult, physical lifestyle without all the familiar comforts of civilization (including money in the bank). What I hadn't realized was that this time-honored trial was not just about proving my toughness and self-reliance; it was specifically constructed to prove my manhood. Roosevelt himself touted the remaining wilderness as a way to promote "the vigorous manliness for the lack of which in a nation, as in an individual, the possession of no other qualities can possibly atone." He wasn't alone. "Society everywhere is in conspiracy against the manhood of every one of its members," wrote Ralph Waldo Emerson.

There I was, cluelessly enacting my version of the national pastoral plot in which the young suburban woman sets out to become a man. No wonder the men I worked with on the river, and most of the people on trips, tried to fit me into the category of either a mannish woman/lesbian or a wild (loose) woman in need of capture. After all, the *Oxford English Dictionary* lists the seventh definition of "wild (adj.)" as "a. Not submitting to moral control, . . . wayward, self-willed," and "b. Giving way to sexual passion, . . . licentious, . . . loose." Our national mythology indicates that like wilderness and the animals within it, a wild woman needs to be conquered. A proper, virtuous woman entering wild spaces was worse, like one of the guys bringing his wife on a buffalo hunt. Being a feminist straight out of grad school, I probably seemed at times like the unwanted leaking of a civilized female morality into the wild zone where savage instincts were encouraged to run free in men. How dare I suggest they watch what they said when ogling Jen out the window? The natural world was their locker room.

Girls Gone Wild

If women aren't supposed to be active characters on their own adventures in wilderness stories, no wonder Betty Ann and I met with resistance from many of the guys we guided and paddled with. I remember a Polish woman my age, Bianca, who would guide on the French Broad occasionally. In her beautiful accent that flowed around words like river current smoothing and rounding stones, she would express as best she could her bafflement over the way men spoke to and about her. It must have seemed especially confusing to someone outside American culture.

Literary critic Annette Kolodny argues that many American women have preferred domesticated nature, such as gardens and parks, to the wilderness, choosing society over a full-on retreat. Stacy Alaimo complicates this, pointing out that though rarely depicted, there are a variety of reasons women choose to play or work outdoors, and some of those activities or professions require more remote spaces. What's unfortunate is that women's motives for inhabiting wild spaces are often under such scrutiny and cause such suspicion. And that women can experience greater fear or danger because of this.

Back in the summer of 1994, as I was adjusting to life as a raft guide, I was lucky. There were women who led in the NOC offices and on the rivers. Many men in the company didn't feel threatened by strong, skilled women, and there were plenty of young males who were learning not to feel that way because of the examples around them. That year I was considering a career of raft guiding in the spring and summer and leading adventure travel trips in warmer climates in the fall and winter. Though I didn't pursue this path, many women do choose careers outdoors, partly because they are not routine. It can be risky. That's the point. Those risks are often greater for women, but not because they are weaker or less skilled. No, these threats arise from culture, not nature. The sense of community I felt at NOC was a tremendous gift, one I appreciated even more in 2016 when I read about the sexual harassment plaguing women in our public land agencies.

Imagine you are a female scientist studying a tiny endangered songbird that nests in a remote location and you finally get a seasonal position with the National Park Service (NPS) to do your research. You will get to spend nine days on the Colorado River going through the Grand Canyon, with an NPS boatman to take you where you need to go. You quit another job to take this one, excited for the adventure. But the first day out, the man, this professional, comments on your ass, asks frank questions about your sex life, and calls you a "hot sexy biologist." When talking about meeting up downstream with a female NPS staff member, he comments that he's hoping you'll have a "three-way." Here you are, dependent on this man for food, privacy when bathing or going to the bathroom, safety precautions in the rapids and weather conditions, and the satellite phone. He also controls whether or not you will get to the work sites that your research and probably future NPS employment depend on.

This was the situation in which Cheyenne Szydlo found herself in June 2006. Before that summer, she said, "there was never any place that felt safer or happier to me than the outdoors." A couple of days into the trip, she found herself responding to his comments by laughing uncomfortably and referring often to her boyfriend and their plans to marry. Her reaction is a familiar one to most women: she identified herself with a man so that the boatman would respect her boyfriend's claim, even though he wouldn't respect her lack of interest. After all, good men don't poach. But her status as unavailable was negated by her choice to enter this most sacred and macho of male spaces—the wilderness. The descriptions of this boatman and other NPS and US Forest Service employees that Kathryn Joyce recounts in "Out Here, No One Can Hear You Scream" demonstrate how much some twenty-first-century men still want to party like it's 1899.

In a few days Szydlo went from feeling uncomfortable to terrified. "This person was in complete control of everything I needed to survive," she told Joyce. One day he stopped the motor in the middle of the river, "came up behind her, grabbed her shoulders and asked her to describe her sexual fantasies so he could act them out." She immediately started crying, told him to "get off!" and to quit harassing her. The word "harassment" triggered a reaction, and he stopped. For the last five days they barely spoke. Later, when she tried to file a complaint, the NPS human resources employee told her she'd need dates, times, and *witnesses*.

On the river, deep in the canyon, Szydlo had no community to back her up. She felt alone. A number of women have been in similar situations, whether as Forest Service firefighters, rangers, or wildlife biologists, and some men have sided with them, like boatman Dan Hall, who was disgusted with how women were treated. There are many stories, including ones about male employees asked to narrow down female intern candidates by their Facebook photos. When employees lodged complaints, they were steered away from anything formal.

One NPS boatman covered his boat hatch with pictures of topless women and boasted to coworkers that he made money on the side recruiting college-age women for Girls Gone Wild–style pornographic videos. Boatmen like Hall who objected to the culture in the boat shop were blacklisted. Women who objected were labeled complainers and targeted with more harassment. And if they pushed it or word leaked out, they were retaliated against with bad evaluations and poor assignments. One woman described the work environment as trying to "walk the fine line between not being hated and not being desired." The same pattern occurred in the Forest Service with firefighters, especially in California. Elisa Lopez-Crowder, a Navy veteran, joined the Forest Service in 2010, and during her first month working fires in Eldorado National Forest an assistant captain asked her "whether she'd been a 'bitch' or a 'slut' in the Navy, and whether her skin was really that color or just dirty." It got worse from there. Joyce quotes her as saying, "In the years I served in the military, I never encountered such discrimination and harassment as I have working for the US Forest Service."

It broke my heart to read about these problems in the agencies I idealized. My brother works for the US Forest Service, and he's one of the best men I know. As often as I meet macho mountain men outdoors, I meet open-minded, thoughtful men who treat nature and women with respect. I had to face how deep my own romanticism of our American public lands goes. As a feminist scholar, I should've known better than to think any institution can avoid the cultural paradigm shifts brought about by women entering traditionally male jobs like the military.

But while the problem with sexual assault in our military hit the front pages in 1991, the similar culture of the Park Service remained unnoticed—outside the NPS, that is. An employee survey in 2000 revealed that more than 50 percent of female rangers and 75 percent of female park police had experienced sexual harassment on the job. Though park management would usually refer to these as misunderstandings, this time a task force was created to set up a hotline and help with training. But it never happened. The task force was eliminated in 2002. So what occurred a decade later shouldn't have been the shock many claimed it was.

In 2011 all Forest Service sexual harassment claims were turned over to the secretary of agriculture in DC to deal with because they'd been handled so poorly. (The national forests fall under the Department of Agriculture, and the national parks under the Department of the Interior.) In 2014, after having their complaints virtually ignored by park managers in the Grand Canyon, twelve women and Hall wrote to Secretary of the Interior Sally Jewell, requesting a formal investigation into the "pervasive culture of discrimination, retaliation, and a sexually hostile work environment" in the Grand Canyon. Jewell responded quickly, and soon the Office of Inspector General (OIG) interviewed more than eighty people and identified more than twenty additional people affected, one of whom was Szydlo. Greg Gransback of the OIG, who was familiar with sexual harassment cases from having investigated the Tailhook military scandal, told Joyce that he "teared up" when he read the stories of these Park Service women.

As of early 2017, there were some transfers, some retirements, but few if any firings. There are new regulations concerning allowable behavior on river expeditions, including "standard uniforms" and the need for an "outside supervisor." Uniforms! Why is it, when women complain of sexual harassment, the response is to look at clothing? Usually, as with high school dress codes, the focus is on regulating women's clothing instead of requiring men to regulate their behavior. Even if this new NPS rule includes requiring male river guides to wear standard uniforms, does anyone really think this will address the problem?

Sexual harassment has nothing to do with women's clothes. Men are capable of controlling themselves around scantily clad women, as raft guides and life guards prove. Nor did the harassment have to do with a lack of skill on the women's part. The women in these stories were highly competent when hired for these coveted positions. Their attempts to make a living outdoors and feel as if they belonged in that work environment were frustrated by common workplace sexism compounded by how much of their work took place in remote areas. The additional cultural baggage concerning women in wild places was like adding lighter fluid to a campfire. Joyce emphasizes the long-term impact the sexual harassment had on those involved:

In my conversations with the women, they expressed great pride in their strength. For years, they had performed dangerous, physically demanding jobs. Many of them had faced life-threatening situations. All of them had operated within environments in which women had very little room for error. The harassment they described had not only brought about personal humiliation or the loss of a job or even a career. It had shaken their entire perception of themselves—as tough and resilient, able to handle anything that man or nature could throw at them.

The sexual harassment and assault accusations were also investigated in depth by *High Country News* reporter Lyndsey Gilpin. It's important to read articles like Joyce's and Gilpin's because they bring what's hidden out into the open, and we can't confront what we can't see. But I'm concerned about emphasizing such stories, because they increase the perception of how risky outdoor spaces and professions are for women. They can influence women to restrict their mobility and are used by those who love them and are worried about their safety to keep them from exploring and adventuring.

In the 1950s, wildlife biologist and outdoor writer Anne LaBastille had a hard time finding any schools that would let her do field research. No one wanted the liability of what could happen to a female alone or with a group of men in an outdoor environment. She was the second female in Cornell University's Natural Resources program and the first to concentrate on wildlife ecology. They wanted her senior project to be based on library research, but she was interested in field research and refused, graduating in 1955. When LaBastille chose to go to Colorado State University for her master's, she turned down a scholarship contingent on her doing library research, footing the bill for her studies so she could do the work she wanted to do. While working on her thesis observing mule deer in the Rockies, LaBastille became the first woman to do research at a federal Cooperative Wildlife Research Unit in the United States.

Later, she went back to Cornell University for her doctorate. In 1969, after earning her PhD in wildlife ecology, she became Cornell's first female professor in the Natural Resources Department. After a couple of years, she moved to her cabin in the woods, working as a self-employed ecological consultant, writer, and New York State licensed guide, gaining regional and international recognition. The World Wildlife Fund gave her its gold medal in 1974. None of this would have happened if she hadn't been willing to break through those barriers to do her research and conservation work. Clearly, discrimination affects more than the opportunities lost to women or any other marginalized group. It limits the contributions people make to society.

I remember finding LaBastille's book *Woodswoman* (just now autocorrect changed that to "Woodsman") that summer as a raft ide. I lay on my sleeping bag in my yellow cinder-block room d read about how she bought thirty acres in the Adirondacks and built a tiny cabin on a lake. She could reach it only by boat, and during the warm months when she lived there she had the solitude and connection to the natural world she craved. This was the first time I'd ever read of a woman pursuing this kind of life. Published in 1976 when both the women's movement and environmental movement were on the rise in the United States, the book describes building the cabin, living without electricity or running water, and exploring the Adirondacks. Like many, she was profoundly influenced by Thoreau. She wrote about her adventures in more than twelve books and continued to inspire women to get outdoors and bulldoze through restricting cultural conventions until her death at age seventy-seven in 2011. More than twenty years after I read *Woodswoman*, her legacy touched me again when I spent two weeks on her lake in October 2016, working on this book as one of six writers chosen for the LaBastille Memorial Writers Residency. Yet one more thing for which I am in her debt.

"Too Much Safety Seems to Yield Only Danger in the Long Run"

LaBastille would have agreed with this line in Aldo Leopold's short essay "Thinking like a Mountain." She would have agreed with the sense in which he meant it—he was responding to the way we manage wildlife as we strive for "safety, prosperity, comfort, long life [ours], and dullness" rather than ecological health. But she would have also agreed with the sentiment as applied to women nowadays. If girls and women are discouraged from taking risks of their own choosing, they will be unprepared to face real dangers. They will also not learn the benefits of taking risks.

Women need to be able to read and hear stories of other women pursuing outdoor adventures—however they define them—so they have a quiver of examples of women having fun, learning lessons without getting hurt or assaulted, overcoming their fears, and finding their own way. Thoreau is fine and all, and I love Edward Abbey, but it's not the same. According to Paul Slovic, an expert on risk perception, danger is real but risk is perceived. Two people doing the same activity can experience different risk. This means risk is not objective but is influenced by many things. Turns out, his research shows, our sense of risk is affected more by stories, images, and experiences than it is by facts and statistics. This is true regardless of gender. If we all had more examples of adventuresome outdoor women who didn't end up being murdered on the Appalachian Trail or mauled by grizzly bears in Yellowstone—both the exception rather than the rule—we wouldn't be so quick to suggest it's too dangerous for women to travel or live or work in the wild.

According to Slovic, the biggest indicator of how someone will perceive the risk of something is how high or low they rate the dread. Dread is what he labels the spectrum gauging fear, which starts at that niggling unease and goes all the way to panic. A high fear rating almost always results in a higher perception of risk. And his research has shown that risk and benefit tend to have an inverse relationship. For instance, most people feel that the risk of riding in cars is lower than flying and the benefit higher, when statistically plane travel is less dangerous. But most of us benefit far more on a daily basis from driving than from flying, so it's more familiar and *feels* less risky. The stories we hear of women outdoors are disproportionately about women getting raped or disappearing when they are out jogging. These get stored in an associative pool, increasing our fear of doing similar activities. And that will increase how we perceive the risk.

However, in an online survey I developed in the early 2000s that had over a thousand responses, I found that a group of women who rated the risk of certain outdoor activities at moderate or high levels also consistently rated the benefit of such activities as extremely high, contradicting Slovic's findings. To understand this, I looked to his research suggesting that the biggest influence on one's perceptions of dread is worldview. So I analyzed perceptions of risk and benefit by how women identified themselves. Women who held traditional views about women and nature did not rate the benefit of such activities high. But those who identified as feminists, ecofeminists, or environmentalists did. Perhaps their strong appreciation of empowerment, equal choice, and the importance of nature enabled them to separate these particular risks as worth taking.

I spoke with Slovic about this, and he thought my findings and conclusions were intriguing. Personally, I felt relieved to know I wasn't alone. So often, I'd been unable to sleep well the night before a paddling trip because as much as I loved whitewater kayaking it often scared the piss out of me. The fretful nights of camping alone, wondering what those noises were (human or squirrel in dry leaves?), didn't keep me from backpacking again and again. I'd always known there were women who didn't feel such dread doing these things, but now I knew there were women who did and yet kept doing them. Why hadn't I read any stories of or by these women? Where were they?

In 1994, an anthology of new women's outdoor writing called *Another Wilderness*, edited by Susan Fox Rogers, was published. I didn't discover it until a few years later, but when I did I thought, *finally*! A variety of activities and geographies are covered, and there is a diverse representation of women's experiences in terms of ethnicity, physical ability, and sexual orientation. Many of the essays include the inner journey of the writers, much in the way that Cheryl Strayed's 2012 bestseller *Wild: From Lost to Found on the Pacific Crest Trail* does. I liked reading all the reasons these women tested themselves in the wild—to grieve for a loved one, to strengthen a bond or to reconnect, to engage in scientific exploration, to obtain spiritual growth, or to gain confidence after a breakup. Their experience and skill levels were different, but in most of their stories, fear is mentioned. This was what I'd long been looking for.

In "River of Fear, River of Grace," Geneen Marie Haugen recalls becoming one of the first female whitewater guides on the Snake River in Wyoming. Around 1980, she became one of three "lady boatmen" on that river and was almost cocky with pride. Although she was paid less than the men doing the same job, she admits that did not dampen her enthusiasm. Like me and the women I guided with, Haugen did not feel she could discuss her fears out loud with more-experienced coworkers. She writes, "In those days on that river, it seemed unthinkable to acknowledge uncertainty or fear—especially for the anomalous lady boatman, who was scrutinized for any trace of weakness by dozens of territorial river men. . . . I learned well to hide my wariness, even from myself."

But her fears came rushing to the surface when a commercial raft capsized and lives were lost because the guide panicked. She realized how much she'd been ignoring her unease over people trusting her with their lives. She hadn't been trained in CPR or first aid and was never taught rescue techniques. This was not unusual back then, and more than a decade later NOC guides were often mocked by other guides for being safety Nazis. (Not by guests. They seemed to appreciate it.)

And then there are the risks never mentioned on any waiver. While risk perception often focuses on the sense of physical danger, there is another aspect that concerns social or emotional risk. Women often assess the risk of seeming weak, scared, or stereotypically feminine as too great to take the chance of discussing their concerns, especially around guys. I'm sure many males recognize the emotional risk of being labeled sissies, pansies, or pussies if expressing concern or caution.

I'm hearing young boys now say, "Don't go all female on me" or "You're such a girl." This type of pressure is even greater in professional outdoor situations than in recreational ones; there's more on the line, and you usually don't get to choose those you work with. Lack of control or familiarity also increases one's sense of dread. When women choose the people they go backpacking or paddling with, this lowers their perceived risk, increasing their sense of both physical and emotional safety. But in a job where a woman is assigned a boatman or male coleader she doesn't know, or already knows she doesn't work well or feel comfortable with, her dread may rise like a creek after hard rain.

Haugen describes life on the river as constantly existing on "the edge between excitement and fear," though she "feigned boredom" like everyone else. A few years after pursuing work elsewhere, she joined some friends on a float trip through the canyon, eager to introduce her urban boyfriend to an activity she loved. She was one of only two who had any experience guiding (though her guiding had been on a different river), and that summer the Colorado River rose to extreme levels because of flooding upstream, which caused dam managers to release large volumes to reduce the swelling of Lake Powell. Haugen and her friends were notified of this by a plastic-wrapped message dropped from a helicopter. Already on the river several days, the relaxed float trip turned high adrenaline.

Though the French Broad is a smaller, less forceful river, I could relate. The summer of my raft guiding had been one of heavy rains and floods. Water levels rose above what most of us were trained for. One time, trips had to be canceled, but staff went out that day in rafts guided by the most experienced, who showed us how to navigate a river we couldn't have imagined. The water moved so fast there was barely time to look around and memorize the new context. This was wildness that swallowed my familiar landmarks and spit standing waves up where eddy lines had been. My dread rose to record heights, but I trusted my training and trainers. The next morning I hid my fear when I met my crew of Boy Scouts.

The situation on the Grand Canyon forced Haugen to explore her reluctance to admit she wasn't invincible, not only because there was no one to rescue her, but because she was one of only two leaders that the group was counting on to get them out safely. "I descended the artificial strata of myself: eager naiveté, arrogant confidence, blind machismo," she writes. This admission from a woman that she was susceptible to macho posturing was eye opening to me, and I recognized that I'd also used it as a coping mechanism.

An exciting account of her outer journey bucking through huge waves, trying to read rapids that looked nothing like the map, accompanies Haugen's chronicle of dealing with her fear over a situation unfamiliar and out of her control. She describes running Crystal Rapid, rated one of the hardest even at normal water levels: "Sliding up that sparkling tongue [of water], I was transported beyond myself, rising into grace. I *became* the boat, the oars, the river. Then, again, myself: a human woman immersed in living wild. My fear shrank to a small blur, a tiny hum, in a vast spectrum of sensation." I know the feeling of intense focus she describes, an absolute peace and centeredness. Her words express why doing what scares us outdoors is worth it for many people.

We're starting to see more accounts of women's adventures outdoors (see my bibliography, in which narrative and creative works are identified). As we read and hear more of them, I believe our perceptions will shift. Instead of warning our daughters, wives, and friends who want to do outdoor activities, even walk alone, I hope we'll encourage them and discuss any fears or anxieties they have—without putting ours onto them. Encouraging females to take responsibility for the challenges they may face, preparing them to handle any difficulties, also helps male-female relations. Many men I've spoken with say that when they take women backpacking or camping in wild places they feel a lot of pressure to protect them and make everything go smoothly.

A few years after my season raft guiding, I was on a weekend backpack trip in Great Smoky Mountains National Park. This was my first time backpacking with only another woman. Spring was calling, and we had to go. The air was warm. Creek crossings were deep and fast. The moss looked extremely content. After most of the day and miles were behind us, we crested a ridge. A side trail led to a shelter. We decided to check it out even though we carried a tent and planned to go a bit farther. As we got close we saw someone had taped a picture above the threshold. A few steps more and we stopped. It was a centerfold, the model with legs splayed predictably. In black marker, our unwanted decorator had scrawled "BABES IN THE WOODS." We turned and left so fast, I can't remember whether we tore it down. I don't think we could bring ourselves to touch it.

Zaron Burnett, who blogs at *Huffington Post*, writes in his piece "A Gentleman's Guide to Rape Culture" that he has a hard time imagining what it's like for people who have to constantly think about their safety in public places or how they can protect themselves. "As men we can enjoy this particular extreme luxury of movement and freedom of choice. In order to understand rape culture, remember this is a freedom that at least half the population doesn't enjoy." Exactly. I want that freedom to move around outdoors, to do so without always feeling watched, threatened, restricted, or accountable to someone. To not be a babe—innocent or lusty. To just be in the woods.

RISKING PLAY

What I Play At

Kayaking. Climbing. Skinny-dipping. Surfing.
Writing. Cycling. Knitting.

Learning to Risk

Lightnin' watched me, pretending he wasn't. He knew I was nervous, but neither one of us wanted to talk about it. I'd kayaked the chilly Nantahala River, a Class II–III run in Western North Carolina, twice before with Lightnin' and the other instructors acting like cowboys with water wings, herding us into eddies and away from hazards. But now I was paddling with more experienced boaters, Lightnin's buddies. So, in addition to not wanting to get hurt, I was anxious not to make a fool of myself.

Deep breath. "You're here because you want to be," I reminded myself.

Others were already in their boats, ferrying back and forth, limbering up. They looked so confident. One flipped upside down, his gold helmet disappearing, and a beat later, rolled back up. I'd recently learned the Eskimo roll myself, but in a pond where the water was warm and still. This was the real test.

Getting down the river while staying topside was my goal. If I did flip over, I wanted to roll rather than punch out and have to chase whatever gear I didn't hold on to. If I came out of my boat, there'd be a high probability of knocking shins and other delicate areas, of trapping a foot between rocks. I knew this from experience.

Helmet cinched, paddle in hand, I sealed my sprayskirt to the cockpit like high-quality Tupperware. I put on my nose clips. I pulled off my nose clips. I ferried across and stretched. I decided not to try a practice roll, telling them I didn't want to get cold. They were kind enough to let me get away with this fib.

Oh, to be able to turn off the fear the way they could the water released from the dam upriver.

We came to a moderate section where rocks stuck out with obvious eddies behind them. I eddy hopped to loosen up, sticking my bow into the reverse flow in back of the rocks, which then spun me upstream to a stop. I'd made four out of five, hitting them high. It wasn't control I was gaining, it was understanding. I'll never be able to stop anytime I want on a river, but I was beginning to learn the language, to listen when it said *you can stop here*. I'd entered the country of rivers, and nothing my culture taught me was of any help.

Ahead swayed and darted the brightly colored paddlers, who seemed some hybrid of fish and flower. Lightnin' looked over his purple shoulder, wide tawny mustache dripping above his grin.

And then I flipped. Fast. But . . . underwater time moved slowly, bobbed along rather than raced. Everything was muffled, even the fear. My paddle was already sweeping, presumably propelled by my hands. My body sprung like a stretched rubber band. Air. Noise. I saw Lightnin' downstream. He was roaring with laughter. And then he wasn't. Water claimed my ears. Silly. I'd raised my head too soon, throwing off my balance. But I'd gotten a good breath, so, more slowly, I tucked hard (my hands in the air above my butt, in another world of water-rim and sun), swept out (the end of my paddle scraping over a low rock) and hip snapped, keeping my head snug on my shoulder as the water changed to something that was on me, not around me. The air burst with laughter. Lightnin' again. And me too, I realized. My first combat roll! The splashes around me seemed like river laughter, the rocks just under the surface like . . .

And I flipped. Damn. Full of adrenaline, I'd rushed again, raised my head too soon and saw Lightnin' grinning as I tipped back over.

"Heads get us into too much trouble," I thought.

Decades later, I still think heads cause a lot of problems. But it's not their fault exactly. They're overworked. Our culture has pinned too much responsibility on them, treating heads like the older sibling that must always watch the younger child, the body. Someday, maybe, our culture will mature and our minds and bodies will relate without the condescension.

When I took up kayaking at twenty-one, for the first time I was learning something that required my body to take the lead, to fail or succeed in both public and painful ways. Nothing prepared me for this type of activity. I'd been a good student, but that taught me how to shape knowledge in private before making it public. I sang on stage in school and church, but again, I practiced and didn't risk physical pain. The most important difference was that I could assess the risk of failure and embarrassment in these situations, and from that came my confidence. By my early twenties, I had some pretty ingrained notions about how I learned. I learned headfirst.

So when I wanted to kayak, I had to learn how to risk with my body. I acquired good technique and skill, the fine points of style and power. I could read the river. All the things I could study and do, I did well. Still, my nerves froze me above all but the most familiar rapids. I wanted to be sure I wouldn't fail, the way I was when I showed up for a test at school. But you can't learn how to kayak without ever making a mistake that has you feeling like you'll never breathe again. I kept thinking I'd discover the key to what made me hold back when less experienced paddlers tried harder moves and bigger rivers. It didn't happen. For seven years I paddled the same rivers, having good days and bad days but never any big breakthroughs.

The river spoke to me in this way: it said, above is the conscious mind, sensory overload, anticipation, and fear.

Underneath is the subconscious, focus, reaction, and peace. The river is where air, earth, and water meet. Sometimes these elements flow side by side, and sometimes they collide. Kayaking has taught me that planning ahead is possible only half the time. I must be able to react when swept up in the momentum and collision of forces surrounding me. At these times, instincts emotional and physical help more than logic. Logic says the quickest way from point A to point B is a straight line. The river tells me that progress is not always forward. I give up my desire for control in order to dance with the unknown. Each day I get better at following the river's lead.

What I Don't Want to Risk Death or Injury For

Winning. Doing something first. Saving face. Proving I don't have limits, or shouldn't. Keeping up with others, even my husband.

On Not Being an Adrenaline Junkie

Paddlers call a roll in whitewater a *combat* roll. Mountaineers call the part of the mountain that will let you ascend a *weakness*. There's a lot of jargon I'm not fond of that implies humans are in competition with the natural world, a view inherently self-defeating and not a whole lot of fun.

Once I was dismayed to read in *American Whitewater* a short piece by a man whom I'd paddled with once. The tone was lighthearted. The account was of paddling a bigger river than he should have been on, getting the shit kicked out of him rapid after rapid (each time blaming his troubles on equipment or bad luck), and taking out early only when he'd lost his paddle. Though in the introduction he describes the day as a lesson in humility, his conclusion is a jocular "It was a good day on the river." Somehow, I didn't get the feeling he took the risk or river seriously. Bravado stories like this perpetuate the Hollywood image of outdoor recreation in which the land is a toy or an enemy.

In our culture, all risk is lumped together, and therefore so are all risk takers. A *Time* magazine article titled "Life on the Edge" posits that athletes in extreme sports (another term I dislike) are fueled by the same impulses that make people play fast and loose with sex, gamble high stakes in casinos, and invest wildly in the stock market. But there is a difference between responsible and irresponsible risk, between feeding the ego and feeding the soul.

Case in point: at the time I was learning to kayak, I was dating a guy who called me "Mother" when I was the cautious voice in the crowd. One February day when we were with friends at Folly Beach, South Carolina, I got sick of being on constant risk-assessment duty and cast my better judgment to the gulls. I really wanted to go sailing in the waves. No matter that this was our friend's first time sailing on the ocean, or that there was a full-blown tornado watch in the middle of winter—I was tired of denying myself adventure. My boyfriend, who hadn't planned on going, climbed aboard to add weight so righting ourselves would be easier if we capsized. There were only two wet suits, so he wore a raincoat and swim trunks. We flew a hull for three miles out, our side of the boat lifted entirely out of the water. The three of us leaned back over the rollicking water to weigh it down. My cheeks were raw from the salt as waves slapped flat against my face before slamming into the guys. A glorious ride—until we tried to tack and went over. We got into position to pull the sail back upright, but instead the pontoons always turned at the last moment and dumped us back in the water. Not knowing why it wasn't working, we repeated this again and again. We finally had to stop trying because my boyfriend was turning blue. We huddled to keep him warm for an hour until the Coast Guard finally arrived. He was borderline hypothermic.

What did I learn that day? That if I didn't take risks incrementally, if I played life too safe, the urge would build up and I'd be a candidate for the Darwin Awards. These awards celebrate Darwin's theory of evolution by recognizing "individuals who contribute to the improvement of our gene pool by removing themselves from it in a sublimely stupid manner." Today, I enjoy many outdoor activities that involve risk. But on the spectrum of possible risks, mine are mostly modest, and they progress sometimes by baby steps.

One way of approaching outdoor recreation is combative and egotistical, but that's not the approach I aspire to. I choose teachers and companions outdoors who have humility and inner goals, who seek challenges as opportunities for growth. Bigger is not always better, and more dangerous is not necessarily more impressive. Sure, I like how a climb that turns epic tests my ability to adapt and endure. But even when backpacking alone in moderate conditions, I still confront, as eco-philosopher Paul Shepard says, "the full weight of the cosmos on [my] head without the shield of society." I don't set out to have an epic; epics are inevitable if I regularly forgo the manufactured safety of civilization for something wilder. The fear of paddling fast-moving water reconnects me to the wonder of life, the sacredness of the earthly, physical creation.

This spiritual aspect to outdoor recreation is what keeps me coming back for more after a wet, cold day and sore body parts. But so often in the media, spiritual gratification is ignored and ego gratification is played on by big-city marketing teams with high-dollar accounts. "Somewhere out there is a mountain calling you a wuss," claims Toyota. So, if I drive my 4Runner to the top of a mountain, that makes me brave? Subaru Outback ads read, "Coming soon to a wilderness near you." That sounds like a threat to me. And then there are the ones that commercialize the spiritual aspect, like Oakley eyewear: "If you believe the man upstairs is watching you and looking after you, you'd better pray he's wearing optically correct goggles, too." Now this might be funny except that outdoor recreation is becoming more and more about gear and less about any basic connection to self and earth and whatever invisible power you believe in. Nature is being pimped out.

"Play and worship," writes Shepard, "are the two human activities removed from commonplace life. One is necessary for the other." I agree with him but also see how, in media and the classroom, nature is relentlessly diminished and demystified even as play is commercialized. I've witnessed how the junkie mentality that craves the chemical rush, and the yuppie mentality that craves the rugged image, can eclipse the spiritual component. When Diane Ackerman details how "deep play" is the way we gain "altered states," she's referring to a kind of wholeness—not the rush that leaves you empty afterward, but the rush that leaves you filled. A merging of the physical and spiritual. I've often wondered whether it's a coincidence that "sacred" is a letter switch from "scared"; and when I tell a friend I was "awed," she hears I was "odd."

Most outdoor magazines give the impression that risk is the rage, that everyone's climbing impossible routes, paddling the most dangerous rapids, backpacking thirty miles a day uphill, and skiing off cliffs—or else they're couch potatoes. Those of us out doing these activities at less extreme levels know that's not true, but how do people who've never been initiated into such activities find out? Everywhere the message comes that you need more money and guts than the average person to get started. And for all the effort industry and our public land agencies have been putting into diversifying images of who plays outdoors, and appealing to people other than straight white males to buy their gear, in 2016 *Outside* magazine was still being shelved near *Men's Journal, GQ,* and *Maxim* in airport newsstands.

What I Think Is Worth Risking Death or Injury For
Connection. Stretching my limits. Warm granite on bare skin. Joy.
Accepting I have limits. Remembering I'm an animal. Wonder.
Cold river currents. Losing control. Teaching myself how to endure
struggles. Grace.

Our Woman, Afraid of Nothing

"Remember to breathe," my husband, Jimmy, reminded me as I started up the climb. The crack in the rock slanted right at an angle before shooting skyward. I shook my hands and arms out behind me, trying to get the blood flowing. Then I placed one in after the other, palms facing up and out, moving hand over hand in the smooth red rock. Where it steepened, I switched my weight left and started to layback, a technique that uses opposing forces to hold you to a sideways edge.

Walking my feet up the face of the rock, I moved one hand out right into a horizontal crack above me. I'd have to commit both hands before I could reach where the hold got better. No other options. My arms weren't strong enough to wait. After positioning my feet high, out of sight beneath the rock pressing into my belly, I pulled on fingertips, right hand first, left hand crossover, the edge finally deep enough to take my second knuckles as I moved my right hand higher. From there I could reach the bolt and safely clip myself to the rock.

"Way to go!" Jimmy hollered once I was crouched on a small ledge.

Gasping and grinning, I tipped my head back and looked at the rest of the climb. I had already passed the hardest section.

When I finished, Jimmy lowered me from the top,

simultaneously proud and bemused. He'd been climbing much harder routes for longer than I'd even been climbing. I asked him why he'd backed off that climb. "It messed with my head. I kept thinking what the fall would be like. Didn't you?" he asked.

I realized I hadn't. When I got close and saw it was within my capability I didn't stop to reflect. Still, there's a difference between knowing you can do something and knowing you will. I no longer needed to be certain I'd succeed, a guarantee no one is given. I'd come a long way since first learning to kayak or climb and felt more confident matching my abilities to situations. Still, I'm bound to get hurt sometimes. Accepting that I'm going to make mistakes has been the first step toward accepting I'm going to die.

Just as taking risks keeps me from becoming complacent about the gift of life, a healthy awareness of mortality makes me choose my risks more wisely. In 1997 my parents died in the same month, and the following year of emotional struggle was filled with physical breakthroughs. No longer did I think I was risking death when I kayaked. I knew death was inevitable, and not kayaking wasn't going to change that. And since I enjoyed kayaking and wasn't doing it to prove something, I stopped holding back. I finally paddled a harder river I'd been eyeing from a safe distance, rolling when I went over, but mostly staying up. Since grief is life at flood stage, rivers had a strong pull for me then and tutored me in the complexities of their currents and my own.

A friend in Alaska told me that the Bella Coola, a Pacific Northwest tribe, call one of their most important spirits Our Woman, Afraid of Nothing. She said, "That's what I thought of when I read your essays about your parents' deaths." I asked for a picture of her, this spirit. Today it's pinned above my desk, a simple pen and ink of a woman with one arm draped around a snow-capped mountain. Fish swim in her hair. I love this image, its femininity and simplicity, its caring, its strength. Do I dare be like her? Yes. It's worth the risk.

After climbing Cathedral Peak with Jimmy, Yosemite National Park (photo credit: Michael Cohen)

Rock-Climbing Thirties

TOY EQUITY

"You don't understand. I need it more than you," he tells her, this man she means to marry. Not sex. The outdoors. Beyond the window's blur and across the slick road, the creek rages from days of rain. It pounds against the glass. Leaning against the wall, he is morose as a basset. And she feels nothing. At least not pity.

Of course she responds. She always responds, but she can tell he's still locked in his precious desperation. Turning to the sink, she mixes dish soap with running water, the white suds rising around her hands. It's not as if she didn't have years of shedding her shirt under the sun, trading malls for trees and highways for trails. That's what he likes about her. And in Alaska that first summer, when they'd realized her backpack was larger, that she carried more, hadn't they both laughed? Even her guilty memory of shoving his kayak off a wave she'd been surfing—he'd been a beginner after all, hadn't meant to squeeze her out—adds to her disbelief at his words. He knows nothing about needs, she decides. Or is it that he knows nothing about not getting them met—something she feels, if not expert in, then advanced.

She hands him the last dish, moves to the table to watch him finish drying. His careful hands are marked with gashes, his calves chiseled, leading her eyes up his legs to his shorts, like a favorite climbing route. At that moment, she gets a glimpse of what she's afraid of, more than the divvying up of dishes, cooking, mowing, scrubbing, vacuuming, and reproducing— some of which can be negotiated, some not. Wives and mothers are not expected to want to play. Not on their own, unless play means shopping or getting their hair done. She likes getting her hair done but also likes feeling the wind mess it up and going for days without looking at it or thinking about it. And if she had to pick one or the other . . . but why should she?

She leaves the room to think. How can she make this man, this good man who loves her for the best reasons, understand what society doesn't? It starts when toys are pink and blue and kept on separate aisles, and never really stops. But he doesn't buy into that. She guesses this is the work of relationships (close ones, real ones)—exposing the unseen parts of us. The parts that don't match the off-the-shelf narrative.

Her dog jumps on the couch, noses under the afghan, and knocks the book—ignored in her lap—to the floor. Rain hammers the trailer roof. True, it's easier for her to put her mind to tasks indoors, to enjoy the quiet, curled-up moments even if she'd rather be climbing. Her fondness for rearranging furniture and painting rooms annoys him at times. As if nothing inside the walls lures him. Except his books. He loves his books, so orderly with their colorful spines, now mixed together with hers. Across the room, leaning against the shelves are both kayak paddles, kept there to remind them who they really are, while their boats, bikes, backpacks, climbing gear, and his surfboard from college days huddle in the shed.

It's more than fitness he misses when stuck behind the window like this. Yes, he complains about the lack of endorphins, though it's only for a few days. But there's a sheen that dulls and changes his reflection. Not the way she sees him, but how he sees himself. A man in a certain place, using his body, feeling entirely awake and involved in the messy, sweaty web of life. People notice him riding his bike everywhere. They stare from their cars or wave. They comment on it in meetings and classes. "You're that guy," they say with the same respect and awe they have for the purple mountain majesties or the redwood forest. He verges on becoming an American icon, likes being "that guy."

She gets it. She's been "that girl" when it brought a good feeling. Said by her writing students who wanted her to teach them an Eskimo roll, or by friends who see she's dressed to hit the crags after class. But more often, "that girl" has been said in the same amazed voice one uses for the largest Komodo dragon in a zoo, or the puzzled voice used to point out a juggling unicyclist—both oddities to stare at for a bit. Worse is when it's the voice used to comment on someone else's children who're too young to be doing what they're doing, where they're doing it. It's not wise. This behavior will come to no good. Someone should watch over her better.

It seems as if he belongs wherever he is. Has probably never changed a space just by entering it, unless he's walked into the ladies' restroom by mistake.

Her eyes trace the retro wallpaper up and down. She scratches the dog's scruff. When she thinks about what she loves about this man, she thinks in verbs: climbing, paddling, hiking, backpacking, mountain biking (less so), kissing (more so), road tripping, talking. Next, she thinks of places: Rumbling Bald, Kruzof Island, Pisgah Forest, Green River, Auke Bay, Looking Glass Rock. Things they've done, places they've been together. Their love active and 3-D. Tangible and like nothing else she's experienced. She doesn't think she needs him more than he needs her, or the other way around. Maybe it's the word "need" she hates.

She would willingly give up the unessential. Haven't they agreed that a simple, rural life in a university town with low cost of living is their goal? That way she'd be free to pursue her art and keep whatever type of house she wished. Teach if she wanted. He understands her need to create but feels no such impulse. Perhaps this is the crux. Her desires are more numerous. Can she feel each as strongly as he feels the singular pull to flex his freedom outdoors?

She growls, making her dog look up. She doesn't have to

think about her answer. Desire was not rationed at creation, she's sure of this. So maybe it is essential, her yearning to be outdoors, since, like her art, it makes her who she is. Both are how she seeks and finds herself. To write a poem, even a line or image, as long as it's fully felt, brings energy to the atmosphere that makes each object she focuses on, leaf or limb, cup or comb, recharge. And when she climbs, the rock holds her captive in mind more than body, making a mockery of the responsibilities that wait on the ground, giving her back to herself. And if he can understand her art as essential, she has faith she can show him the play they love is essential to her too.

It will require a vow to go along with the others. An agreement to share joys as much as dishes and, someday, diapers. She's not interested in comparing hours spent outdoors. But equal access, equal emphasis. And equal toys. Her eyes slide from the wallpaper to the paddles. He hadn't even been kayaking a year and they'd gotten him a used boat. And when he'd suggested better suspension would make her mountain biking more enjoyable, he'd been right. She knew they were lucky. Getting cheap, used gear was easy in an area with outdoor resorts that constantly upgraded. Still, they chose toys over stereos, new trucks, or fancy trips.

Throwing off the afghan, her smile is a crack in the clouds. She calls his name. A rainy day is a good day to go shopping for their wedding gifts. He hates stores unless they sell craft beer or outdoor gear. Today he can pick out the backpack she'll give him. In his truck she'll explain her theory of toy equity and how, in case his doctorate takes them somewhere salty and sea-breeze blown, she wants him to give her a promise, a tease, a surfboard of her own.

OUTSIDE EXPECTATIONS

But theory precedes exploration . . . we are, actually,
pioneers trying to find a new path through the maze of
tradition, convention and dogma.

—Anne Morrow Lindbergh, *Gift from the Sea*

I'd known Jimmy about three weeks before we went climbing
at Looking Glass Rock in Western North Carolina. What I
knew of him was from conversations on the phone about our
common interests in education, literature, and the environment, and from looking into his oceanic eyes, broad face
framed by brown surfer-length hair, trying to keep my head
above water as his laughter and sincere care for others drew me
like the tide. We'd shared stories about outdoor excursions,
usually moderate adventures that turned epic. But this was our
first day sharing one of those activities.

We were with his friends, preparing to ascend Sun Dial and
The Nose, classic 5.8 friction routes. Jimmy started uncoiling
the rope, and one of his buddies got ready to lead the first
pitch. "Want to belay?" Jimmy asked me. I buckled my harness
and clipped to the coral-and-blue lifeline. My job was to monitor the amount of slack the lead climber had and catch him if
he fell. Jimmy watched as I got in position. As Sean moved up
the rock, placing gear to catch him if he fell, Jimmy talked with
his friends below while watching my technique and yelling
support to the leader.

"Nice belay," he said when Sean was on top, setting up for
us to follow. "Want to go next?"

What the hell. Tying in, I felt on the spot, as a high school
boy does when he picks up his date and the girl's father is
waiting to give him the once-over. No way around it. All those
stereotypical female concerns—like whether my butt looked
big with the harness hugging my black Lycra shorts—competed

with concerns about getting up the rock face. But fresh air and dirt grounded me. As much as I liked Jimmy, if he was the type who judged me by my butt size or my climbing ability, then he could go jump off a cliff. There were plenty handy.

Rock climbing focuses me like nothing else. Even that day. I flattened my palms against rough granite in greeting. It was just us now, the rock and me. Up a few steps, I searched under what climbers call eyebrows, looking for enough space to hook my fingers, palm up. These underclings are a Looking Glass trademark. Limber and strong from yoga, I steadily rose above the male eyes below me. I felt my back muscles absorb the warm sun. Once safely on the belay ledge beside Sean, I turned to face the autumn-spangled hills and valley. And to wait for Jimmy.

After that great day of climbing, you could say we both fell—in a good way.

Most of our getting-to-know-each-other phase occurred outside. Climbing provided opportunities to learn how we each handled competition and dependence. To my delight, I found Jimmy could offer suggestions about my climbing without being condescending. When he led routes with me belaying him, we grew experienced in interdependence—he needed me to make sure he didn't hit the deck if he fell, and I needed him—with his experience and skill—to climb the rock first. Active time spent together outdoors taught us about each other faster and more concretely than hanging out talking. Of course we talked too—on quartzite ledges far above the everyday world, on hand-holding hikes through spring wildflowers, and on campouts on windy Appalachian balds.

Our first night together under the stars came the weekend after our first climb. I was in a nervous frenzy over what to do about sleeping arrangements. Privacy was the issue, not sex. We lived over an hour apart and had decided he'd drive my way and stay the weekend. But I had a one-room apartment below the schoolroom where I taught tenth graders. Life in the close community of an alternative residential school was great except when it came to dating. My bed was my living room, and my neighbors were mostly fifteen-year-olds who knew my daily habits. In a flash of brilliance, I decided we'd camp on Black Balsam nearby on the Blue Ridge Parkway. After dinner, we hefted our small packs—filled with only sleeping bags, pads, and a tarp—and followed my dog up a steep trail to the rocky bald. We used flashlights at first through pine and spruce but, once in the open, walked slowly in the dark. No moon. Stars flecked the sky like serviceberry blossoms awakening the ridges in early spring, their promise somehow the same.

That night, in sleeping bags zipped together, my dog between us, I talked more candidly, less fearfully, than I ever had with a man. Maybe it was Jimmy, maybe the example of starlight's faith as overhead it careened through space at an unknown future. But both of us, in that place, starting the second month of our lives together, cleared so much air I expected to wake and see all the smog blown in from Ohio Valley factories gone, and wave upon blue wave cresting before us.

Besides the future, we discussed why I enjoyed backpacking and car camping alone. In a curious, not challenging way, Jimmy asked about trips I'd taken, whether I'd ever gotten scared. Earlier in the night there'd been a couple of drunk fellas walking around, probably unaware of us flattened against the dark bald. Or were they? At some point, after it'd grown quiet, Jimmy called my attention to a couple of silhouettes a hundred yards away. "Is that those guys?" he whispered.

I squinted but couldn't tell. "I reckon."

Throughout the night, we checked periodically and they were still there, though quiet. "Would you sleep out here alone?" Jimmy asked.

"Probably. And I might worry all night too."

"Take me." He said this in a tone pleading rather than commanding. "I might not be able to do anything, but I'd like to be there."

I rolled on my side to look at him. He actually seemed vulnerable. "I like to go by myself," I said gently. "But not always, and not everywhere."

I wonder how long it would've been before we discussed my need for solitude if we hadn't mistaken a couple of young spruce trees for drunks. As it was, that conversation freed me from fretting about my actions and habits as we spent more time together. I knew that no matter how much I grew to love him, I'd always want stretches of time alone.

One particularly memorable evening, Jimmy burst through the door of his one-room apartment after a late class discussing Milton's portrayal of Adam and Eve. "I figured out what it is I love about you so much, about *us*." The words were flung as the door slammed closed. After striding to where I sat curled up reading, he stressed each word: "Neither of us dominates the other." As if released, he rocked back on his heels. "I've never had that happen before," he added before kissing me with eyes open wide.

There followed a stretch of growth in our relationship when we routinely experienced being insecure in each other's company. During this phase, every time I tried an activity that scared me, or chose not to do something, I wondered whether I was risking our relationship. Would he think I was a sissy for being frightened? Would he get tired of climbing with me if I didn't always want to do the routes he did? These were important fears to settle, and I'm sure through outdoor recreation we built our trust more quickly. Some activities provided more challenges for our relationship than others.

Jimmy had mountain biked for years, even raced some. He was a mud machine. I liked mud fine, but steering around rocks and roots, hopping logs, and catching air were not skills

I possessed. What's more, I wasn't sure I wanted to acquire them. Much as we tried to be clear about what type of ride we were going on, each turned out more full of obstacles than I was ready for, more scary than he realized. Insidious trees (remember *The Wizard of Oz*?) would hook my handlebars with their branches, dry leaves cackling hysterically. I did have the pleasure of giving Jimmy a heart attack when I launched over my front wheel into the mud. And so it went, with me gritting my teeth on grit because he loved this sport and I was afraid to disappoint him. To make matters worse, we were usually with his buddies, and I couldn't shake my anxiety about holding everyone up. In the aftermath of that hell, I can calmly state that a man new at mountain biking often rides more slowly too, but as the only woman I felt pressured to represent my gender well. And wouldn't you know, these rides happened at the same time every month, that time when I'm more emotional and my body channels its energy inward. I don't have as much to spare for physical activities and judge myself more harshly. Who wants to explain that to your boyfriend's buddies the first time you meet? "Hi, I'm Lilace. I'm on the rag."

Meanwhile, as I was trying my bipeds at biking, Jimmy began whitewater kayaking, something I'd done for years. As he learned more and we began going down easy rivers together, our roles reversed. I confess, I reveled in his terrified expression as he entered small rapids. The way he held his breath, cheeks bulging Louis Armstrong style, afraid he'd flip. And when he did and cut his brow slightly, I washed and Band-aided it. Reading the river, surfing a wave, paddling straight on flat water all came relatively easily to me, while the thrill and fright of being in the water's grip made the rapids seem many times faster and bigger to Jimmy at first. Then one day, I checked the knots after Jimmy had loaded the boats. There was more slack than I liked, so I retied them. I must have made some snippy comment because he retorted, "Don't talk to me as if I'm one of your tenth graders!" I got my first taste of his anger and a real lesson in leadership. As much as I hated condescension, I had done exactly that to Jimmy.

Over a six-month period of climbing, mountain biking, and kayaking, we consciously broke down our cultural conditioning and built up our partnership. We took turns being the leader. Jimmy learned when he was pushing me without meaning to and got comfortable letting me often call the shots when paddling. I learned to quiet the critical voices in my head that nibbled at my confidence, and to handle being the most knowledgeable one without going on a power trip. We grew into new roles in unfamiliar realms. We adapted to shifting roles, reading the currents of our relationship better and trusting that direct communication would help us navigate any rough water ahead.

During this period my parents died. Dad first, then three weeks later Mom. If I hadn't known Jimmy was "on belay" for me, I would've felt even more untethered. Still, asking him to fly up to Mom's service with me was hard. We'd known each other barely three months. But if we were going to spend our lives together—and we'd begun talking that way—then he needed to be there. Not because I couldn't handle it alone, but because this would be one of the most significant events in my life and I wanted him to share it.

Asking for help, asking for *anything*, makes me choke. If we hadn't already established a pattern of asking for more rope, less slack, help dumping a boat, or a rest break, I might not have gotten up the nerve. A hole would've been created that we couldn't have gone back and filled.

In most of my previous relationships, all the getting-to-know-you part consisted of us telling the other who we were. Going to the movies, dinner, hanging out with friends are all great, but there's a trap. After a few months something would happen, something bizarre or seedy, which made it clear to me that the guy was not the person he'd pretended to be. Sometimes, sadly, it was news to him as well. After perfecting the get-lost speech, I still wondered how to troubleshoot for self-deluders who talked like enlightened Romeos. Actions *do* speak louder than words. Hell, they holler. After a couple of months with Jimmy, I didn't worry about any grand surprises. We'd spent too much time together in intense situations, reacting under pressure. We each knew the other didn't become verbally abusive, cast blame, or turn into a useless, sniveling blob. I learned he would actually forgive me for tossing his front bike tire onto the pavement when unloading the truck; and once I realized it wasn't *my* tire, he saw I was so horrified and distraught, I forgot to reattach my brakes when we started riding. I loved how Jimmy used humor to lighten the mood when we were hungry or hurting and farther from the car than we wished. And he appreciated that I didn't have hang-ups over how much either of us carried or how we looked. Now, you don't have to bike or kayak or climb. But I highly recommend going camping with anyone you want to really get to know— how a person acts when facing a little discomfort and a lot of dirt is extremely revealing.

So, after many long trails hiked and biked, many cliffs scaled and rapids run, Jimmy and I decided to get married. But what now? The only other long-term relationship I'd had, other than ones I was born into, was with the mountains and rivers of North Carolina. Everything I knew about appreciating the familiar, about how deepening contact means deepening understanding and greater love, about stay-put-ed-ness, I tried to transfer to my relationship with Jimmy. But climbing one 5.9 route or paddling one Class IV river doesn't prepare you for the intricacies of all others. As a blunt, outspoken woman who didn't wait around hoping for a boyfriend, I lacked experience with all but the first and last stages of intimate relationships—as if I'd known bookends without the books. I knew what people on talk shows and in self-help books said about the difficulty of keeping the thrill alive as you wake up to that same face every day in the same room with water stains on the ceiling. Nothing like wet plaster and responsibilities to dampen romance.

Suddenly we'd moved to Reno, bought a house, and were thinking about kids in the next few years. Finances needed planning, small repairs needed making, and when the puppy joined us, a lot more chores needed doing, like holes dug in the backyard ready to trip us. But the snowy peaks of the eastern-most range of the Sierras lurked too. In forty minutes we could be up there with dogs and snowshoes, laughing at our clumsy pratfalls, at the dogs disappearing in drifts, at the icicles on our nose hairs. In North Carolina, Jimmy and I knew the terrain, access trails, and what to expect from the weather. But we learned more about each other in an unfamiliar landscape— Nevada's desert climate, the Sierras' deep snow and fast rivers— where we had to cooperate and maintain flexibility.

"Lilace, John wants to know if we'll paddle the American with him Saturday." Jimmy had been itching to get on a river since we moved here.

"That's in California, right? How far a drive is it? What level?" Always extremely cautious about jumping on new rivers, I liked a lot of information.

"Class II–III mostly. There's one Class IV but you can walk around it if you want. And it's less than two hours away."

I didn't respond. He knew the nervous me was arguing with the eager me. I'd barely met John and wondered what kind of boater he was. Still, the longer we waited, the more effort it'd take to get back in paddling shape.

Hoping to tip the odds toward going, Jimmy said, "A friend of his is boating too. Dave, a doctor at the medical school."

"Fine. At least there'll be someone to pick up our pieces who knows how to put them back together."

We beached our kayaks and hiked down for a view of Troublemaker, the Class IV. A huge jumble of rocks on river left offered a challenge. It forced the current to narrow, speed up, and turn hard right. After the turn, a large rock in the middle, called Gunsight, demanded you commit to one side or the other. We watched John run it. Doctor Dave looked at Jimmy and me.

"I'm going to walk it," Jimmy said.

"I'll run it," I said at nearly the same time. We exchanged looks, each surprised by the other's answer.

Back at our boats, Dave and I waited so Jimmy could get in position to watch. I breathed deep. It was a wonderful sensation to be sure of my ability, when I'd so often underestimated it in the past. Jimmy was a quick learner, and I often got annoyed with him for not being more cautious, and with myself for resenting his ease at taking physical risks. Yet here I was. That morning the current had seemed pushy, and I hadn't been making my moves with the precision needed in big rapids. By midday, though, I'd been hitting all my moves, working with the river instead of against it, feeling the thrill of courting a force of nature. And I knew this rapid was within my ability.

From the calm spot where we sat, I looked downriver. The big drop meant only a horizon line was visible, the rapid hidden below. "You go first," I told Dave, "and I'll watch where you enter."

With a big smile, he dug his paddle deep and nosed into the current. Bloop, he was gone. I memorized the little rooster-tail wave his boat disappeared left of. My paddle whirled almost of its own accord, and my eyes never left that wave. Then I was close enough to see turbulence beyond. Dave's line was good. Waves shouted in my ears. A sweep with the left blade, lifting that knee and hip to carve right, I aimed down the chute left of

Gunsight and eddied into the calm below. Jimmy and the others stood grinning. "Way to go, Honey." He slapped my padded PFD. "I'm proud of you."

I don't know about most people, but what scares me or thrills me can change from day to day. Jimmy and I have to be in constant communication about what we're doing, what we're planning on doing, and how we're feeling. We're always revising what we know of the other person, and this happened even more once we moved to Nevada and built our skill in new activities. When I started climbing harder, Jimmy didn't have a problem with me finishing routes he'd backed off of—in fact he bragged about it to friends: "That's my wife!" But he *was* concerned over my apparent lack of fear. I, of course, reminded him that when he'd first kayaked I'd watched and seethed over his gutsy approach. It helped that we'd each experienced both sides. It was like mystic marriage counseling. Our culture expects every relationship to have a stronger and weaker partner, one who loves more and one less. But nature has no such expectations.

In the same way the sun moves closer and farther from the earth, varying its heat and light, Jimmy and I began our marriage moving through a shifting balance of self-reliant solitude and interdependence. We thought about how all life is interconnected, how no one is truly independent. Getting up early and hiking as the sun rose, or climbing a few hours before fulfilling worldly responsibilities, kept our friendship fresh.

As we recreated, we re-created our love over and over.

EN CORDÉE FÉMININE

Moving from North Carolina to Nevada with my husband a couple of months after our wedding meant we spent the early years of our marriage exploring lots of new territory together—emotional, academic, and geographic. Some was sublime and some was rocky, but being climbers we made it through fine.

High stepping in Owens River Gorge, California

He was in the PhD program in literature and environment at the University of Nevada, Reno. Soon I signed on in the same program for a second master's degree, so our days revolved around shared study and shared play. The eastern Sierras were less than an hour away, but our schedules didn't allow us to get up there as much as we would've liked. When the leaves were off the trees in our backyard, we could stare at the snow-laden peaks while we studied. One way we stayed sane and got in better shape than ever was by joining the local climbing gym, Rocksport.

Until this time I'd had female mentors in paddling but not climbing. Melanie, the woman who had introduced Jimmy and me, would often go climbing with us, her husband, and other guys in North Carolina. She'd been climbing longer than I had and was good but didn't love it. I *loved* it. It felt more natural to me than paddling. I never worried about falling the way I worried about being trapped underwater. I felt in control of the pace more, like I wasn't always in reaction mode.

Of course I was older now—early thirties—and the self-esteem gained from backpacking and paddling transferred over. The additional benefit of having found love and companionship meant less energy spent on sexual politics and mate hunting when outdoors. After a couple of years of climbing regularly, I'd relaxed into trusting my body and was confident in the basic mechanics of the equipment. But I hadn't really challenged myself. I followed Jimmy up rock faces and cross-country, happy to have joined my life to a man who shared my love of climbing and would make me a part of this outdoor lifestyle.

Now at Rocksport I met women who loved climbing. It wasn't uncommon to find that the Russian woman who had given me beta (information) about the bouldering problem I was working on was in the latest issue of *Climbing* magazine, or that the teenage girl working the hardest route in the room would be competing in Europe next month. More common were the women who worked as counselors, lawyers, booksellers, and stay-at-home moms who came for the climbing and the camaraderie. It was here I met Jackie Hueftle.

Jackie, nineteen, had been on the local team competing in the Junior Competitive Climbing Association (JCCA) and now worked at the gym. Her curly blonde hair framed a serious and unadorned face. At first I didn't pay much attention to her because she seemed so young and went about her tasks quietly in an otherwise raucous place. But she was friends with Bill, another worker there whose tips were helping me become a better climber. He said I could learn a lot from Jackie. I started seeking her out. Indoors, I was learning to read routes—much like reading a river. Unlike in the outdoors, here I could climb a route without seeing someone, usually Jimmy, do it first.

In a gym, someone sets the routes at a wide range of difficulties, identifying the holds on the route with colored tape. They assign a rating and then it's up to the climber to ascend using just the taped holds, or any "natural" features, which indoors most often means smearing your foot against the blank wall. Reading a route in a gym meant seeing the climb from the eyes of its creator, as opposed to outdoors where the Creator didn't have climbers in mind at all. I'd ask myself, what moves were they expecting or hoping to make me do? The better climbers get at reading routes, the less energy they waste trying to figure out what to do when on the wall, and the longer before their forearms pump out. Jackie saw the routes through the eyes of an experienced climber, but she was also a female about my size, certainly closer to my size than any of the guys I'd ever climbed with. She even set routes, sometimes asking me to try them and give her feedback.

We'd been there over a year when Jackie and I had the best idea ever: let's go on a girls' climbing trip, just the two of us. (Jackie, who was technically still a girl, called it that and at thirty-three I was happy to be included.) Jackie had often told me how frustrating competing had become before she'd aged out, how hard they pushed her when she was on the local juniors team, how she'd get frustrated with them and with herself, and how her coach would push harder. The pressure had started to take the fun out of climbing. Listening, I felt a deep connection. Even though I'd been in my late twenties when I started climbing regularly, I often got so frustrated I'd cuss at myself and the rock and cry in the car on the way home. I'd hated myself for it, had judged myself harshly for not reacting as the guys around me did.

What's more, as a late bloomer, Jackie was at the rope end of puberty, hormones pinging around inside her like buckshot in a box canyon. A self-proclaimed tomboy, she didn't worry about not dressing femininely. But like many girls, she was uncomfortable being looked at and singled out. Her role models were into modesty and humility, qualities long expected of women, which created tension inside her when competing for the title or spotlight. Many female athletes have struggled with this conflict.

It's easy to understand that a male coach who saw her climbing ability as on par with that of the guys on the team might not realize all the ways she was unlike them. As Karen Warren explains in "Women's Outdoor Adventures: Myth and Reality," American males tend to be raised with a greater familiarity with mechanical things, lots of outdoor adventure role models, and an internalized assumption of success. Jackie's coaches' expectations of her were high. But, while justified, their opinion of her might have also been influenced by a culture that says a woman with the same ability as a skilled man in activities like climbing is exceptional—a superwoman or freak. Such a view suggests her abilities are simply natural rather than also learned through training and struggle. There were fewer girls than boys competing in the JCCA, and the coaches may have seen Jackie as one of the team members with the best chance of competing professionally. I'm sure it was disappointing if she didn't pull as hard as they expected. "You can do better than that" is not a helpful comment when the person agrees—she *can* climb harder than that—and wonders what was wrong with her that she didn't. Okay, so I'm projecting. I hadn't been around when Jackie was going through this, but I could easily imagine the whole scenario. From our conversations, I sensed she'd tried to deny some of her love of competing so she didn't have to deal with that pressure. Also, I overheard comments from some of her former coaches who climbed at the gym (one dated Jackie's mother) about her never having lived up to her potential. That she could have really been something.

"You need to climb without these guys around," I told her. Even if they weren't judging her now, it would be hard to escape the sense that they were.

"I've always wanted to do a girls' climbing trip, but I've never had anyone to go with," she said. "Let's head out to Wild Iris. We can take my truck."

I had no idea what or where Wild Iris was, but I did know two things: (1) Jackie could lead much harder routes, so I would learn a lot, and (2) I knew about road tripping and camping without guys, so she could learn from me. It already had a different feel from any other climbing trip I'd helped plan with my husband. Suddenly I thought, *I wonder if I'll climb differently without guys around?*

Jimmy enthusiastically supported the idea. It's not as if my going off alone outdoors was new. Our first year in Nevada I volunteered with an environmental group, mapping wilderness study areas far out in the Great Basin Desert. I didn't know a thing about the land when I left (though I asked questions to prepare myself), but when I came back I felt I was making a home in a deeper sense than learning the best grocery stores and bars. I'd taken my husband's V8 GMC Sierra and got that truck in and out of situations that are our little secrets.

Jimmy's stories of his climbing trips out West with buddies before we met had always sounded like fun. "Wild Iris is in Wyoming. Supposed to be awesome limestone. You'll have a blast," he told me wistfully. Jackie and I got a guidebook for the area, she arranged time off, I turned in my final papers, and off we went. But first I had to learn to shoot a gun.

I'd always had a dog instead of a gun. It was deliberate. Even if Allie "went off" accidentally, she'd never be aimed at me. But she was staying home this trip. The only thing I knew about guns was that if I was going to be around one I needed to know how to use it. Jackie owned a handgun, given to her by family, and I couldn't dissuade her from bringing it. Maybe it wasn't my place to. Everyone has a right to self-defense, which means they have a right to choose their method, within legal and reasonable limits. So one afternoon she took me into the desert, where we met her grandfather. Under his tutelage I learned to load, unload, and shoot a regular and semiautomatic revolver. How to tell whether the safety was on or off. I was no Annie Oakley, but that didn't break my heart.

We drove eleven hours northeast, up and over the Continental Divide. Whoever wasn't driving read to the other. I read from the Wild Iris guide about routes, making note of climbs that sounded good to us. Jackie read from the novel *Invisible Monsters*, with a plot so grotesque and bizarre we couldn't stop laughing. We pulled in late to Lander City Park, which the guide said had free camping. In the dark we didn't see any sites so we pitched our tents on the grass right behind her truck. The next morning we awoke to a lawnmower's drone. I peeked out the tent flap. Hmmmm, maybe this wasn't where we were supposed to camp. I crawled into the sunshine. There were already kids riding bikes and people walking dogs. As the mower circled closer, we threw our tents in the truck and headed to Limestone Mountain, where bolted climbs abounded.

Both of us preferred sport climbing where, instead of the heavy gear a traditional lead climber carries, we had to carry only quickdraws—short slings with a carabiner on each end— that clip into the bolt and rope in case a climber falls. At nine thousand feet, the ridge crowned the bright green meadows dotted yellow and purple with wildflowers. Polished almost white by the morning sun, it rose above the aspen and pine trees that shaded belayers at the base. Most were single-pitch climbs, which meant that the lead climber lowered down to the ground rather than setting an anchor and belaying the next climber up to that spot.

Years later, when Jackie was head routesetter at the Spot Bouldering Gym in Boulder, Colorado, she'd write, "The truth is that rock climbing is a misunderstood activity—an activity that is often lifestyle-defining to those who participate in it and an activity that is, contrary to popular belief, much less dangerous than more common pastimes like skiing, jumping on a trampoline, or driving a car." I enjoyed how she didn't love climbing because it seemed cool or extreme; she loved it despite that.

Climbing Manless

Though I didn't know it then, women's mountaineering has a long history. Miriam O'Brien, 1898–1976, was the first woman climber and mountaineer to encourage women to climb manless, though she was not the first to do it. Women, predominantly European, had been mountaineering in the Alps throughout the 1800s, and some had gone with only hired guides, and a few without men at all. Though by the late 1800s American women climbers hadn't reached the same standards of boldness and technical skill as their British sisters, social acceptance seemed to advance faster in the United States than in Europe. Maybe because being an American meant you prided yourself on being less proper than those Brits. At the end of the nineteenth century, when the American suffrage movement was in full swing and European mountain clubs were still for men only, the Appalachian Mountain Club and Sierra Club accepted members of both genders and even fostered women's climbing. While in Reno, I met and climbed with Americanist David Mazel, whose book *Mountaineering Women: Stories by Early Climbers* was the first to introduce me to the inspiring, frustrating, and amusing history of women's climbing. Learning of their experiences and sauciness so long ago was revelatory and showed me how some women climbers had used their achievements to promote women's equality, while others had doubled down on their modest behavior and attire when off the mountain to compensate.

O'Brien reaped the benefits of following pre–World War I climbers like Annie Smith Peck and Fanny Bullock Workman. Born and raised in New England, she began climbing in 1920 in the Alps and then went on to ascend Mount Rainier, Longs Peak, and several mountains in the Canadian Rockies. These climbs without "the assistance of overly solicitous Alpine guides" shaped her confidence—along with one winter evening on Mount Washington where, after a full and exhausting day of climbing, she went alone through the snow to look for her brother. He turned out to be fine, just late, but in her autobiography, *Give Me the Hills*, she writes about an invaluable lesson that rescue attempt taught her: "I learned that the sensation of fatigue may be very misleading; that one has enormous unsuspected reserves of strength and endurance. . . . I have been too tired to eat, too tired to sleep. But I don't remember any occasion when I couldn't have walked another mile if my life had depended upon it." It was 1925. Five years earlier, American women had gotten the vote after a seventy-year test of their endurance.

In 1929 O'Brien made her first manless ascent with Winifred Marples. (I adore that name and like to think that I was Jackie's Winifred Marples.) O'Brien had learned how to "lead the rope" so she'd have the necessary skill to attempt ascents *en cordée féminine*—with only women on the rope. Once she'd learned to lead, which was easier than men made it sound, she set out to do climbs like the one with Marples that would prepare her for harder, more noteworthy manless ascents. The evening before the climb, the two women went outside to scout the path they'd take the next morning when they left before sunup. Being a trip leader, she knew, is about more than climbing; it's about the planning and preparing of all aspects. "It would be entirely possible, and embarrassing," O'Brien wrote, "to get lost leaving the hut."

At Wild Iris, after claiming one of the primitive campsites, Jackie and I loaded packs with a rope, gear, snacks, water, and rain jackets. We brought the guide book to read the descriptions of areas, looking up at the wide strip of rock from afar before it was obscured by the trees, trying to decide which trail to take. There were no signs there or at the base of the crag. Which trail would take us to the Main Wall or OK Corral? Once at the Main Wall, we looked back and forth between the book and rock, doing our best to confirm we were at the Five Ten area of the wall. This was our first challenge of going manless. We were willing to ask other climbers, but there was the chance they'd be new and winging it, or there wouldn't be anyone else where we were going. I requested to see the guide book more and more when Jimmy and I went climbing, but I deferred to his judgment because he'd been doing this longer, and I figured it'd be quicker. Yet there were times when my instinct or interpretation of the maps was the correct one. Now, Jackie and I were prepared to figure it out ourselves. Even the sharp edges of the limestone pockets lost much of their sting as we made all the decisions, choosing the routes we would lead. I laughed at the names inspired by cowboys and country music as I tied in at the base of "You Picked a Fine Climb to Leave Me Lucille." An ode to manless climbing!

O'Brien became a loud proponent of women climbing without any men because that allowed women to share equally in the joy of accomplishment as well as the responsibility. How else were they to gain competence and good judgment, if not in the same way men had? Even though a few women had already led climbs, including Lily Bristow, who'd scandalized the world by sharing tents with men, many were still insisting to O'Brien that women weren't capable, partly because "they just come walking along behind, looking at the scenery." While she didn't agree, she saw that if women were going to be prepared to lead, they needed to go completely manless—meaning not even a guide or porter. "In any emergency, particularly in an outdoor sport like mountaineering," she writes, "what man wouldn't spring to the front and take over?" Women, she knew, were just as prone to revert to their conditioning in such situations.

Even for me at the dawn of the twenty-first century, taking on a leadership role among men was not an easy step despite how much skill and judgment I'd cultivated or how outspoken I was. On this trip, the good routes we climbed were even better because we chose them. The ones that we misjudged or that disappointed us were clearer lessons in making assessments. When the clouds grew thick and dark over the Wind River Range as Jackie and I sat atop the OK Corral ridge, it was up to us to decide whether to head back to the campsite. Summer storms blew in fast. We agreed to choose caution and retreated to our tents to read while listening to the rain and eating chocolate O's, the small chocolate-covered doughnuts we bought in gas stations that'd become our signature snack. We thought that in order to climb hard, having O's—which stood for ovaries—was as important (or as unimportant) as having balls.

Three days after the successful climb with Marples, O'Brien set her sights on ascending the Grépon manless. At the time, it was considered one of the finest climbs in the French Alps, and not all the licensed guides in the area could do it. O'Brien had climbed it before on lead, but with a porter. The assumption was that if a man was around, the woman did not do it all on her own. To choose the Grépon was also to make a spectacle of herself and her partner Alice Damesme; they could be assured of other climbing parties being in the area. They had a true alpine start at 2:35 a.m., hiking in the dark for hours until stopping at a breakfast spot. Several groups set on different goals were there as well, and their reactions to the two women's project were disbelieving though polite. After breakfast, the other parties held back, allowing the women to go first across the glacier and bergschrund—the crevasse at the top where the glacier pulled away from the rock. "The bergschrund really did give us quite a lot of trouble," O'Brien remembers, "but we couldn't waste much time on it with that large and rapidly-growing audience below."

They negotiated many challenges, such as route finding in mist and well-meaning help. "We declined with thanks [a] superfluous rescue," she writes, when a porter offered to throw down a rope. In fact, the only male assistance they accepted on the ascent occurred when Damesme was leading the Mummery Crack (having changed from nailed boots into lighter shoes for technical climbing) and O'Brien wished to take a picture. A male climber, who'd gallantly allowed their team to go first, though he and his partner had been ahead and he was known as a speed demon, handed her the camera. He was enjoying watching their momentous ascent of a sixty-foot crack that was deadly should a leader fall near the top. After a "brief but severe blizzard of snow," they climbed the many pitches left before reaching the summit. Here, having lunch with the pair of men who'd passed them on the traverse above the crack, they were all visible through a telescope to O'Brien's mother and others who spread the news back in town. Successfully completing the ascent and feeling sure their point had been made, the two women accepted the men's offer to use their rappel rope, already in place, to descend. "As Alice was roping down and I was belaying her, I saw Armand's hand shoot out a time or two to grasp her rope. He thought in time and did not touch it, but his desire to do so was almost irresistible," writes O'Brien.

Sadly, but not surprisingly, not all men adjusted well to the women's accomplishment. That evening in Chamonix, Etienne Bruhl lamented that "the Grépon has disappeared. . . . As a climb it no longer exists. Now that it has been done by two women alone, no self-respecting man can undertake it. A pity, too, because it used to be a very good climb." O'Brien and Damesme had broken into the clubhouse, ignoring the "No Girls Allowed" sign, and made themselves at home. The fact that one was American might have especially galled Bruhl. His comment underscores how experience—our own and others'—creates a sense of place that transforms a blank space. For Bruhl, this layer of experience by two women erased his previous sense of the Grépon. British poet Helen Mort responds to him in a poem called "An Easy Day for a Lady":

> When we climb alone
> *en cordée féminine,*
> we are magicians of the Alps—
> we make the routes we follow
> disappear.

In the third stanza she confronts the entire history of male mountaineering by taking Bruhl's comment seriously: "Where you made ways, / we will unmake." Here I imagine the paths laid out by patriarchy being unraveled, as one might rip out several poorly knitted rows of a sweater (or jumper, since Mort is British). Women's accounts of outdoor adventures repeatedly show how men and women can be in the same place while still in different worlds.

I don't know whether these worlds can ever be fully merged, but they can be changed for the better. Leisure time spent outdoors, especially in wilder, more removed areas, helps women take leadership roles back at home and work. It's no surprise that so many women breaking trail outdoors are also making an effort to change society. In *Women on High*, Rebecca Brown chronicles how many pioneering mountaineers, especially Fanny Bullock Workman and Annie Smith Peck, used their mountaineering accomplishments as they competed against each other to promote women's equality. There's a photo of Workman atop a Himalayan glacier in 1912, holding a newspaper with the headline "Votes for Women." It sent a clear message that women were moving into all sorts of places they hadn't been before. Peck had been a pioneering professor in archaeology before she gave up teaching for a life of mountaineering and public lectures (necessary to raise funds). In 1911 she stated:

> A woman who has done good work in the scholastic world doesn't like to be called a good woman scholar. Call her a good scholar and let it go at that. I have climbed 1,500 feet higher than any man in the United States. Don't call me a woman climber.

Following in their knee-deep, snowy footsteps, Arlene Blum has been breaking down barriers for women in environmental science fields as well as mountaineering. She led the first all-women expedition to Annapurna in 1978, when only three women had ever successfully summited above 8,000 meters (26,000 feet), the oxygen-thin death zone. Also in the late 1970s, her research and advocacy were instrumental in developing regulations for carcinogenic chemicals being used as flame retardants in children's pajamas. She's currently an executive director of the Green Science Policy Institute, which she cofounded, working to bring scientific research into policy considerations about toxic chemicals that affect public and environmental health worldwide. She also holds workshops and lectures on women in leadership. To me, Blum is the peak example of using the skills honed through outdoor adventure to improve the world.

On our women-only trip, Jackie and I weren't terribly aware of being female. We didn't give a damn what we looked like. Oh, I did advise her, when we first claimed one of the primitive campsites near the climbing area, to park with the truck facing the dirt road. That way if we were ever bothered, especially in the night, we could make a fast escape. And she showed me a new pee stance that was really good for slopes (squatting on one leg, while the other stretches out like a brace—this also aims the pee away instead of straight down). But other than that, we weren't women in a man's world; we were just two climbers— happy, physically exhausted, sore, and mentally relaxed. So much so that I didn't mind my pillow of coiled rope with only a sweatshirt laid over it.

We did what we wanted without feeling pressured and communicated easily about everything from dinner prep to how much we'd climb each day. There were other people around, but it wasn't crowded. We didn't avoid people, but we barely talked to anyone.

A few days into the trip, Jackie found a route she wanted to try in a new area. There were trees close to the rock, but she could see at least five bolts and it looked good. This wasn't a route of limestone pockets, as most of our climbs had been. We couldn't decide what route it was, partly because we weren't exactly sure where we were. We didn't know how difficult it was rated. Ratings are often unreliable anyway and can either falsely boost your confidence or psyche you out. *So what?* we thought. She could see the anchors and knew it was definitely a single pitch, and she would have plenty of rope to lower off if she couldn't finish it.

I spotted her as she bouldered to the first bolt and clipped, and then put her on belay. The crux came where she thought it would, just below the third bolt. But her plan for how to move through the hardest section wasn't working. Being maxed out below an unclipped bolt is the worst feeling. On lead, if you fall you will fall the length of the rope to the last bolt clipped, and then that distance again as you pass by on your way down. The rope will catch you, but that can be a long way to fall. And if you fall when you've just pulled up some rope to make the next clip, then you fall even farther. Even though we do it more than most people, climbers despise falling.

Jackie kept backing down to where she could hang and rest. I could tell she was getting frustrated because she kept attempting the same moves. Then the swearing started. Her legs started to shake. Her fingers must have been screaming. She didn't want to lower off, but this was not going to get any better until she could calm down and rest. On the ground (rope left hanging, waiting for her next attempt), she fumed. As she berated herself about not figuring it out—saying she knew she could do this, why couldn't she do this?—I sat quietly. I wasn't in a hurry and there was no one around. Then she started to cry. We sat there, hanging out, until she stopped. In my experience, crying is like a reset button. Jackie lost the tension in her shoulders. She started talking about what she'd been doing that hadn't worked and running through new possibilities.

When she stopped talking I said, "You ready to give it another go?"

She nodded.

At the second bolt she paused, took another close look at the rock below the next clip, and put her best plan into action. It wasn't effortless, but she did it. Hearing the click of that quickdraw clipping the bolt, and then seeing the rope slide through the lower biner as I took in the slack, was a moment of pure grace. As a preacher's kid I know that grace isn't earned, it's given. Still, Jackie earned this all the way.

Crying is often seen as showing weakness or manipulation in our culture and is associated with females. But it's also a physiological response that has many benefits and many causes. In Jackie's case she was frustrated and physically spent. Crying was an involuntary way of purging the tension. Crying can often be a sign of low blood sugar or hypothermia. A woman I bike and climb with tells people, "If you see me sitting down crying, don't ask me what's wrong. Offer me a candy bar or cola. If I shake my head, just leave me alone. I'm working something out." She doesn't care what people think if they see her cry; it's part of her process.

For me, being able to get frustrated, cry, regroup, and problem solve is one of the skills I learned from outdoor adventures, especially solo and women-only ones. Now I rarely get to the point of crying when frustrated in group settings. I've learned to let go of whatever isn't working, or take a break, before I reach such an emotional state. I get some more calories and water, take some deep breaths, cleanse my aura (just kidding), and start working it out.

I've gained from all my outdoor experiences, but I almost missed out on the benefits that come from women-only trips. When I was a raft guide, there were a few skills clinics for women, but they were always full. Staff could take a leftover spot only at the last minute, and I couldn't afford to pay for a course or any other guided trip. Besides, I'd heard stories about how those tours or wild women outings were a way for lesbians to hook up. I'd spent enough of my twenties around folks who assumed I was gay—maybe because I bought my jeans in the men's department, sometimes had really short hair, and always had a really loud mouth, especially about gender equality. I had lots of gay friends and had no issues with people loving whom they loved. But it was irritating as a young woman looking for a male soul mate to not be taken at my word about whom I was attracted to. Taking up knitting helped, though I'm not sure why my coworkers thought lesbians didn't knit.

There are lots of different reasons women enjoy women-only excursions. I prefer them when they're with friends I want to spend more time with and we don't have to accommodate the schedules and whims of spouses and kids. As a way to learn a new skill, I like the idea of a women's surf camp, especially Las Olas with the slogan "we make girls out of women." Yes, lesbians do these activities (and some knit!) and also have outdoor groups only for them (because let's face it, sometimes they don't want to be around straight women).

When I get asked why I would want to do something in a women-only group—climbing, biking, backpacking, community theater—my answer is simple. For the same reasons men have been doing things in men-only groups for all of civilized time. *Calm down*, I think, *it's not a conspiracy.*

Maybe because I was married, or maybe because I had matured, I wasn't worried that going off with Jackie would make people think I was a lesbian. What they thought was their deal. But there has been a long history of athletic, physical women facing homophobia. When the Title IX Act was passed in 1972 and women's participation in professional sports started increasing, women of all sexual orientations often adopted extrafeminine dress and behavior off the court or field. Sports are meant to be played in front of an audience, unlike most outdoor recreation, and are more of a public spectacle. People are going to talk, especially if you're as good as Serena Williams. Even in 2016 I found this exchange in a gay news and gossip site when someone asked whether Serena was gay or straight and was told she was straight.

Then why does she go around looking like a femmed-up bull dyke?

I was thankful that someone replied, *What are you talking about? She's a professional athlete; she's a strong woman with muscles. Nothing wrong with that.*

And there's an additional layer of race-related abuse she gets.

She's violating the spaces of many privileged groups by using her God-given talent and hard-earned skill to compete physically. We have a lot of issues in our country about who deserves to play and what types of leisure they're allowed to pursue. When will we accept that women like to play with more than dolls and Easy-Bake ovens?

Girls Like to Play Dirty

For the week Jackie and I were camping, we didn't bathe. We had only the water we brought (and could refill in town). No biggie. We were both used to this, and it was part of what we *liked* about camping. I'm sure you've noticed that plenty of little girls like rolling in grass, climbing trees, and stomping in mud puddles. Around puberty, when all sorts of rules change and kids who were treated the same get divided into "boys" and "girls," females get told they shouldn't get dirty. (Even if a girl's parents support her tomboy inclinations, our culture lets her know it isn't normal.) Think of what the word "dirty" means when it describes a female over the age of twelve. A *dirty girl* is a slut and will no doubt grow up to be a *wild woman*.

On the surface we've come a long way, with outdoor clothing lines for women, ads, and catalogs that show active moms and girlfriends. But just including women isn't enough. It's great to now have smaller sizes, but do we have to divide gear and outdoor clothing into men's and women's? Most people have recognized there are more than two genders, and among women and men there are more than the stereotypical body shapes. I don't need a curvy-cut jacket, but I'm glad it exists for those who do. And men with short or narrow torsos, or who can't carry as much weight, shouldn't have to buy a "women's" backpack. Women snark online about how easy it is to keep pastel outdoor clothing clean and share ways to cover up the ubiquitous flower appliqué or design. In 2015 Target

announced it would start removing distinctions between girls'
toys and boys' toys, so maybe the outdoor gear industry could
remove them from adult toys too.

How women are depicted and marketed to by the outdoor
industry reveals how deep our cultural assumption is that women
need—or want—to be pretty at all times. Pretty, that is, by
cultural standards of what is feminine. As Cheryll Glotfelty's
rhetorical analysis illustrates, this has been a recurring theme
since the first backpacking guides in the 1970s aimed specifically at women. In addition to discussions of women-specific
hygiene and personal details, they had a more motivational tone,
dialed back the discussion of gadgets, and went into great detail
about how to keep feeling feminine and looking attractive while
camping. I'm uneasy with this emphasis. Though women share
beauty secrets with their girlfriends in bonding rituals, they also
use beauty standards as a way to judge and bully—doing the
patriarchy's work for it. As someone who in her twenties kept one
eye out for male mate material when I was climbing or camping,
I'm not saying I didn't want to feel attractive. What I enjoyed as
much as anything else at those times was how my idea of what
was attractive changed outdoors. I felt no expectation to be particularly clean or well coifed. A big smile (even in pouring rain or
when lost), gung ho spirit, and sense of humor were what made
me feel dynamic. The guys I was interested in were attracted to
low-maintenance women who liked these activities.

The emphasis on femininity also shows up in recent guides
to glamping (glamour + camping), which are mostly about
creating less rustic campsites but are sometimes about women
being more glamorous and feminine outdoors. I agree with
MaryJane Butters that now "girl campers have ditched the
notion that camping equipment is the domain of men," but I
shake my head over the idea that "we hang our prom dresses
right by our lanterns." Why would anyone waste space bringing

a prom dress unless the tulle skirt could double as bug netting? Seems to me it would attract annoying males as surely as a bug zapper's blue light pulls in pests. Take *Backcountry Betty: Roughing It in Style*, which markets itself this way: "Discover your inner 'Betty' with this fierce and fresh approach to camping and wilderness. Tongue-in-cheek wilderness manual for women who appreciate nature but prefer to maintain their coiffure while interacting with it." The slang term "Betty" does not mean just female; according to *Urban Dictionary* it means "hot chick." I know the book is supposed to be funny as well as helpful, but to me it's sliding back to almost where we started. I prefer *A Woman's Guide to the Wild: Your Complete Outdoor Handbook* by Ruby McConnell.

Guides like *Backcountry Betty* reinforce the assumption that women don't want to physically exert themselves or sweat; that "women relax, men mountaineer," as Adrianne Wadewitz puts it. She points out that "much of the gear that is produced for women assumes less of a desire to do activities that are as physically demanding as men—the gear is often less hardy and more decorative." These designs perpetuate the notion that women are "physically weak, . . . fascinated by fashion, . . . [and] 'soft.'" In her 2013 research, she compared climbing harnesses from a well-known brand and found that the names and colors of the women's line were sexy, passive, and decorative. Women could choose from "Primrose," "Lotus," and "Siren," while the men's line offered bold colors with powerful, active names like "Chaos," "Focus," and "Momentum."

Outdoor clothing is a huge industry currently being marketed to everyone, no walks in the woods required. But for those who *are* active outdoors, clothing is also equipment. It affects temperature, ease of movement, safety, and general comfort. It should fit and it should work. When Jackie and I were climbing, that's all we cared about. Back when Miriam O'Brien was climbing, there were no harnesses—you just tied the rope around your waist. She either made or had made her own nailed boots for the sections of snow and ice. But at least she could wear pants.

When I was a little girl, it seemed obvious to me that dresses were an attempt to keep me from climbing trees. I wore them to church but made it a point to do a headstand each week in Sunday school. I was so sure dresses were tools of oppression (no, I did not use those words) that I threw down my copy of *Little House on the Prairie* in disgust when I read that girls wore dresses on the frontier, sure it was more propaganda.

But, my apologies to Laura Ingalls Wilder, I grew to learn the historical truth: women spent centuries in skirts and still did amazing things. When women were scaling the Alps in the mid-1800s, they generally wore two skirts over bloomers, which might weigh ten to fifteen pounds when dry. Even more impressive when you consider that wool and flannel soaked through with snow would weigh twice that. Skirts became entangled and threw women off balance or got them so stuck they had to be cut loose. A safety hazard for all in the climbing party, skirts regularly knocked off loose rocks onto those below. They might not have climbed men's routes backward and in high heels, but, like Ginger Rogers, early women climbers did not merely do what men did. They had to be tougher and more determined.

And sneaky. Meta Brevoort and other climbers in the late 1800s started wearing knickers under their top skirt. When they left the village and reached the base of the crags, they took to "slipping on and off." This rather racy term referred to the act of stashing their skirts in knapsacks or behind rocks. All was fine and good unless you forgot which rock it was or, as happened to Elizabeth Le Blond, an avalanche whisked it away while you were climbing. With her guide, she stealthily made her way back toward the village in drag. She hid behind a tree while he went in search of appropriate attire and returned with an evening gown. I hope she was still wearing her boots when she walked into the lodge.

"Our dress has done all the mischief," wrote Mrs. W. G. Nowell in the Appalachian Mountain Club's journal in 1877. "For years it had kept us away from the glory of the woods and the mountain heights." Indeed, in pursuits such as mountaineering and cycling this was true. At the same time that these women were entangled in skirts, they were still being stifled by corsets. Women had to choose how much of convention they would throw off, literally. Those who weren't willing to throw off their corsets completely could wear them more loosely when hiking, or at least leave the whalebone stays at home. One of the things I enjoy about outdoor recreation is how it brings me into contact with people who don't judge my clothing in terms of fashion or acceptability. (Okay, there are a few of those, but I avoid them.) It's about functionality and comfort. It seems to me that guys who are around women in these situations drop a lot of the cultural expectations of how women should dress, even when they are back in the village. As one man jovially called out to Henriette d'Angeville in 1838 after she became the second woman to summit Mont Blanc, "Here's to courage, in whatever dress!"

Once mountaineering clothing became less gendered and women's skirts were no longer knocking rocks on men's heads, there was still a sense among many established male mountaineers that even qualified women were a disruptive force on expeditions. Experienced climbers such as Arlene Blum repeatedly met resistance when applying for spots on teams. In 1969, with great recommendations and an impressive list of high-altitude accomplishments, she was denied a place because "one woman and nine men would seem to me to be unpleasant high on the open ice, not only in excretory situations, but in the easy masculine companionship which is so vital a part of the joy of an expedition," according to the leader. No wonder Blum went on to organize all-women teams to climb Denali and Annapurna and write about her adventures with mountains and sexism. Sometimes women climb with other women because it's easier to shed the sexism that often creeps into climbing. But sometimes women climb with other women for the easy female companionship, which lends a different quality to the experience. Not that it was automatically easy to communicate on all-women expeditions. Blum's books (unlike most male mountaineering literature) detail the group dynamics and leadership struggles and solutions.

I've never done a large all-women trip of any kind. Going on a climbing trip with Jackie, I knew pretty well whom I was going with. It wasn't just that she was female, it was that she was Jackie. There's nothing magical about having another pair of ovaries around. But there is a lot to be said for finding a friend who has shared certain experiences because she too grew up with the same kind of body, and who wants to sleep in a tent, sport climb, and sing 1970s rock ballads while making dinner. And who wants to share decision making.

It's not that the climbing world is more sexist than our culture at large. I find it less so. In 2017, Jackie shared with me several blog posts on women's climbing that debated whether the familiar forms of sexism (assumptions about women's abilities, anxiety over women encroaching on male territory, and unwarranted worry over women's safety) still exist out on the crags and in the climbing gym, or whether oversensitive women are interpreting comments and actions in ways that give rise to "complaint feminism." From what I can tell, the women writing these blogs are younger than I am and are more active climbers, so maybe it's my age and out-of-touchness speaking here. (Hush, you make up words too.) However, I see their differing interpretations of the same scenarios as more revealing than opposing. Is the guy who won't leave you alone in the rock gym clueless, or creepy? Was he really following you out to your car in the public parking lot? What did that man mean when he said you had "nice moves" or said you needed to "sack up" and do the climb? There is no way for someone not in that specific moment to answer that. And I might have a different experience of it than another woman in the same moment. Actually, I would have a different reaction than the twenty- or twenty-five-year-old me. It took lots of outdoor experience and reflection to become confident in reading those scenes, avoiding guys who set my radar off, and speaking up when nonthreatening guys could use some gentle enlightening as to how their actions or comments could come across.

For instance, mansplaining is as common outdoors as indoors. I've read about "Bob," the man some women climbers conjure when strange guys hover near enough to hear what they are discussing. Hoping to head off unwanted advice, the women recount the tips "Bob" gave them and how they are doing what "Bob" suggested. In this way they are showing that they are under the guidance of a male, and that Bob will no doubt be back soon to check on them. Though Jackie and I didn't evoke Bob, we'd experienced our share of unwanted advice and attention at times.

Instead of the fictional Bob, I had a very real Jimmy. After my climbing trip with Jackie I participated more in the planning of Jimmy's and my climbing trips, sometimes struggling (with myself and with him) to speak up about what I wanted to climb and how. About a decade later, we were reminiscing. He listened to how difficult it'd been for me to start trusting myself back then when he'd say "that's too hard" or "do you really think you can . . ." and fill me full of doubts. Whatever it was had seemed within my capabilities, but, you know, he'd been climbing longer and maybe I'd missed something.

"I'm sorry I did that," he said at the dining room table on one of those blissful early days of parenting when both kids were in bed by 7:00 p.m. and we had quiet time to share a drink and stories of the glory days. "I was an ass."

He wasn't, I assured him. At least, not for that. If I could have articulated back then what I was able to that night, I think he would have understood. I was acting out of habit as much as he was, and habits are hard to break.

Unfortunately, one habit many women have is the internalized fear and lack of self-esteem a culture of sexism ingrains in us. Individual women get this in different amounts, even if, as in my case, we have not been the victim of violent acts by individual males. It can be hard to undo internalized sexism, but climbing and other outdoor recreation are great subcultures for women to experience interactions with men who are comfortable having physically and emotionally strong women around. But we can't expect women or girls to enter the subculture without some general baggage. Likewise, many good men in the climbing subculture may be unaware of the internalized sexism they've accrued without realizing it.

Despite our gains, in 2010 the American Mountain Guides Association (AMGA) listed 294 people they'd certified as rock, alpine, and ski mountaineering guides, and only 26 were women. The AMGA executive director at the time, Betsy Novak, said only 7 of the 60 guides certified in all three areas were female, but that was more than in many other countries. Jackie is one of only two female Level 4 Certified National Routesetters in the United States. The goal is not to get even numbers. But the numbers and anecdotal evidence show that there are additional access issues facing women climbers—ones men don't encounter. James Edward Mills, journalist and climber, coined the term "adventure gap" to refer to the fact that so few people of color participate in outdoor recreation. There is also an adventure gap when it comes to gender, though not nearly as severe. Women of color have a double hurdle, yet they have made great achievements outdoors. Did you know that the first African American to summit Everest was a woman? Sophia Danenberg summited in 2006, unguided, accompanied by one Sherpa.

After my trip with Jackie, I applied the lessons I'd learned, and the spark of new habits, to climbing with women but also with my husband and other male friends. My own thoughts were clearer and communication improved, though a one-week girls' climbing trip can do only so much. I wasn't like Miriam O'Brien, who laid out a series of objectives she wanted to do manless. After she and Alice Damesme traversed the Grépon, they easily summited the Matterhorn in 1932. Their friends threw them a party back in Chamonix, but Miriam didn't show. She headed off to the eastern Alps, this time with her former climbing partner Robert Underhill. They married later that year and climbed together for nineteen years. She writes, "Manless climbing is fun for awhile, but this other arrangement is better!"

Even though adjusting to my new confidence in climbing wasn't automatic, Jimmy enjoyed climbing with me more because I wasn't always asking him what he thought I should do, or what the best route or moves were. We learned each other's strengths. I took a weekend clinic on trad (traditional) climbing to increase my knowledge, skill, and judgment in that area, but I still relied on his experience in placing gear for protection. And my greater gymnastic skill at climbing steep and overhung routes meant that I could often suggest techniques he could try. Now he could relax more, no longer feeling that the burden of us having a good day climbing was completely on his shoulders.

Like Fanny Bullock Workman, I had a husband with whom I could share the responsibility and enjoyment of our expeditions. In 1897, she and her husband bicycled four thousand miles from the southern tip of India to the Himalayas. They then became besotted with alpine mountaineering. Over the next fourteen years, they planned eight Himalayan expeditions, alternating the responsibilities of planning logistics and running scientific projects. When they had trouble with labor such as porters demanding more money or rebelling, they dealt with the challenges together.

Poor Annie Smith Peck, Fanny's main rival for altitude records. Not only did Annie not have a husband or male relative who climbed with her, it appears she never knew what it was like to climb with only women. Of course, it might not have given her a better experience, but she certainly regretted being dependent on hired men to staff her expeditions to South America. Either she was a bad judge of character or there just weren't enough open-minded males available then. In 1904, she headed for Peru again, having been thwarted from making a first ascent by bad weather. There she hired Victor Sintich, an Austrian she'd met the year before who had some experience snow climbing. She also hired Indian porters. She was single, she wasn't from a wealthy family (unlike Fanny), and all her funds were raised from sponsors and lectures she gave back in the States.

Who knows what Peck said to Victor Sintich about his role and responsibilities? We do know that according to her, he "dearly loved his own way." Not any more than she, no doubt, but she was the one with the most experience and, ahem, the one who was paying his fee. The Indian men took their direction from him, and at one point Sintich declared that they would turn around, just when they'd gotten within range of the summit. It was cold and dangerous, but what, Annie must've wondered, had they expected? She insisted on at least climbing the ridge to get a view of the summit, and, roped to the head Indian (next in command after Sintich), she used her ice ax and crampons to navigate between crevasses. The terrain had steepened and become a difficult ice climb when Peck turned to look below and saw the rope trailing behind, having been untied. When she carefully backtracked and reached the two men, Sintich said if she didn't listen to him he wouldn't follow her. "Oh how I longed for a man with the pluck and determination to stand by me to the finish!" she wrote.

People often assume the woman in a partnership is holding the man back from adventure. Clearly Peck would disagree. In my experience, Jimmy and I have equal pluck and determination, but we sometimes prefer different styles and challenges. I'm more eager to sleep on the ground and go backpacking, but I'd never been interested in ice or alpine climbing, which Jimmy had always wanted to do. There we were out West, with the snowy Sierras constantly looking over our shoulders, and with the shadow of kids visible on the horizon, getting closer and closer. When I told him to make a list of things he wanted to do before becoming a father, alpine climbing was at the top. I sighed and went out with him to buy crampons, plastic boots, and an ice ax. His and hers. Our goal was Mount Shasta in the Cascade Range, the first major peak Annie Smith Peck scaled in 1888. And though more than a century later our gear and clothing were better, the dormant volcano stood little changed at 14,179 feet.

I didn't have to go, but sharing a new adventure with Jimmy before the extreme adventure of having kids together felt right to me. Several friends from the university jumped at the idea. Kirk was older and had a lot of Nevada experience, and I'd enjoyed exploring the Black Rock Desert with him. Ceridwen was in my master's program, and her husband, Bruce, liked to climb and mountaineer. I didn't have much of a hand in the planning, though I listened and asked questions of those with alpine experience. Jimmy didn't have alpine experience per se but had read a lot about snow and ice mountaineering. For

Kirk it would be the biggest alpine peak he'd attempted, and for the rest of us it would be our first.

Jimmy trained in his way and I trained in mine. His class load was heavier, so he ran on Peavine Mountain behind our house to build cardio endurance. I wasn't a runner, had more time, and wanted to be really familiar with my new gear. I asked Kirk to help me train. We carried packs, did long hikes in snow that winter, and went up shorter peaks. I got to see whether it was worth wearing other shoes to hike in to the base, or whether I could stand hiking in my plastic boots to save weight. I found out that on a flatter approach, plastic boots irritated my Achilles tendon. Good to know! I tested my lungs at altitude. We practiced glissading—sliding down steep snow or ice slopes on our feet or butt—which I loved but my dog was infinitely better at. Glissading also gave me a chance to practice, with Kirk's guidance, how to use my ice ax to self-arrest. Knowing how to stop myself if I got blown off a narrow edge was reassuring, even if the thought of getting blown around on high, slippery surfaces (and having to scramble and hack my way back up) was not.

Though Shasta is a common choice for a first alpine experience, it packs plenty of risks in its snow, scree, rock, and ice. There are steep slopes, avalanches, glaciers, rockfall, altitude, and extreme weather to consider. Winter-like temperatures can occur any time of year, and Shasta can turn into a fourteen-thousand-foot lightning rod. My main concern was wind. With no other peaks within a hundred miles in all directions, gusts can accelerate without interference. I read that speeds could reach one hundred miles per hour at tree line—only eight thousand feet. We all discussed the risks and what precautions to take and agreed on a cautious approach to changing weather. We would camp at the closest trailhead and get a 3:00 a.m. alpine start. This would ensure the best snow conditions for the longest time. We'd try an up-and-back in one day, not carrying the heavy loads camping on the slope would require, and be okay with turning around if the going got too tough. No heroics or summit fever allowed.

As Kirk and I trained, I felt that even if we never climbed Shasta, the views from Freel Peak were worth it. At 10,886 feet, it was the tallest peak ringing Lake Tahoe. Still, it didn't prepare me for my first view of Shasta rising like a god straight out of the valley floor and looming above us.

In the driver's seat, Kirk turned to Jimmy and me and said, only half in jest, "We're gonna die."

It was intimidating, but also enticing. How could you be around such a marvel for long and not want to set foot on its slopes, if not its summit? Jagged rocks poked through icy ridges, flanked by gulches that were sometimes white, sometimes dark gray. All this thrust up from a swath of green conifers and, if you were standing 140 miles away on a clear day, the golden plains of the Central Valley. The first ascent, after many attempts, was made in 1854 by Captain Elias Pearce. Soon he led five women up to successfully summit in 1856. It amazes me how easily I find such accounts of women doing what we've been conditioned to believe they rarely did.

At Bunny Flat Trailhead, about seven thousand feet, I knew I shouldn't complain about my gear, which was a darn sight better than those ladies' split skirts for riding pack mules, but my boots were heavy and the layers seemed endless. I had two sets of mittens because losing any would almost certainly mean frostbite. And there were shell pants, shell jacket, gators to keep snow out of the boots, and even shells for my mittens. Ski goggles, wool hat, fleece neck gaiter. And packs full of the essentials including lip balm, sunblock, headlamp, bivy sack, first aid kit, plenty of fluids and easy-to-digest calories, and the free poop pack-out bag we got with our passes and permits. (Nothing biodegrades

above tree line.) Cramming it all in at 3:00 a.m., while trying
to eat oatmeal and warm up after five hours on a foam pad in a
sleeping bag on the parking lot, had me groaning inwardly. Then
I packed my helmet, crampons, ice ax, and red plastic boots
because we'd wear running shoes for the approach through the
trees. I don't know how eager I was, but I was ready.

Lucky for us the snow was hard, and we moved as fast as our
loads and lungs allowed. Not particularly speedy or talkative, I
kept my gaze on the glow of my light weaving through the red
firs and sugar pines. We stopped briefly to sip. To chew. Then our
five lights would bob off again, mine next to last, with Jimmy
behind. After we broke from the tree cover, the slope steepened,
and we traded our running shoes for boots. My hands in their
thin liner gloves were cold by the time I'd tied my boots and
attached my gaiters. Kirk was the only one with older leather
boots. He joked that if we got stranded in a blizzard he'd be the
only one to survive because he could eat his footwear.

After we'd plodded for hours in the dark, the sun came
like the miracle it is. From where we were, low on a southwest
ridge, the peak donned a thin halo and grew more angelic by
the minute, until it was framed by a golden mane. Sipping and
chewing, we turned around. The valley below was cleaved by
a huge dark triangle, the shadow of the peak. I felt the magic
and sacredness of the place that had earned it the reputation as
a power center and drew three to five thousand people to gather
there in August 1987 for the Harmonic Convergence. Of
course, I feel this energy in lots of wild places, but the effort it
had taken to be in that spot at that time added to what nature
threw in for free.

We were moving slowly. I sensed that at least Kirk could go
faster. We were warming up in the sun, which felt great to me
because I'm always cold. Jimmy was overheating and stripping
off layers, like a dance of the seven polypro veils. He was also

complaining about his stomach. Our approach, called Broadway, joined Green Butte Ridge at 9,200 feet. One small yellow dot sat ahead on a rare dip wide enough to pitch a tent near some exposed rock. The book said that camping was possible at about 10,200 feet, so these landmarks were how we judged our distance. Unlike during most hiking or even climbing I'd done, we weren't passing anything. The head game was as different as the view and pace. The rest step (placing the forward foot, rocking back on the rear leg with knee locked while taking a breath, and then leaning forward and kicking the back leg up and ahead into the snow) helped me keep my breathing steady, but our speed never picked up.

Not long after we passed the tent, Jimmy stopped.

"I'm gut-bombed. I wish I'd brought some water, not just Gatorade. Y'all go on and I'll head back to the car."

Kirk got his keys out of his pack.

"Not alone," I said. "I'll go with you."

"But you're doing great. You should keep going. It's a straight shot down and nowhere to get lost. I'll be fine."

It's true, I was finally warmed up and feeling confident in my crampons. And though there didn't seem to be much chance of anyone making the summit at our pace, I was interested to see what lay ahead. But not so interested I'd risk Jimmy cramping up or worse on the descent. We were at 10,500 feet, not even close to as high up as we'd been other times in our life, me on Mount Whitney and Jimmy on Longs Peak. But we'd gotten a taste of mountaineering in snow and ice. I didn't know whether it'd satisfied Jimmy, but I'd enjoyed the experience more than I'd expected to. Going down now didn't mean never coming back up. We took Kirk's keys, wished the others well, and turned around.

Hiking down, we had a great time just the two of us. Not that Jimmy didn't still feel nauseated or disappointed, but we were safe and the view was grand. Midday now, hikers were out ant-dotting the mountain's base. There were also backcountry skiers, and to our left just outside the wilderness boundary, snowmobiles buzzed. It felt so different from the isolation of the dark and early morning. And both were good. I thought about how automatic my choice to come down had been. It wasn't because I was tired, scared, or bored. It was because there are certain expectations when climbing—that as a belayer you will never let go of the rope with your brake hand, and that you don't leave your partner to descend alone unless one of you is injured and can't go on. These habits had become ingrained.

While the snow got softer under our boots and I could start to pick out Kirk's red Trooper way below us in the lot, I thought about how I'd developed my independence, confidence, and judgment, but how in many ways it was even harder and more important to be a good partner. The trip with Jackie had taught me that too. Climbing required communicating frequently and clearly, being comfortable checking another's equipment and preparation (and having mine checked), sharing decision making and risk taking, and trading off on whose goals were pursued when they weren't the same. Good habits to have developed with any partner, but, looking over at Jimmy's scruffy, tanned face, I thought how fortunate I was to have this foundation for our marriage and family. Then I had another thought.

"Uh, Honey," I said. "I have to go."

"Go where?"

"Right here. I can't wait till we get to the trees." They were hundreds of feet away. People, however, were heading toward us from below and above. "What do I do?"

Jimmy pointed to the side of the ridge where there was a little dip. "Once you squat down, they won't see you until they're closer."

I dropped my pack, grabbed my resealable poop bag with odor-absorbing kitty litter I'd gotten at the trailhead, and opened it wide. The man I loved stood with his back to me, keeping watch so I wouldn't be surprised by anyone. For a second I was embarrassed. Then I simply felt lucky to have a good partner.

BECOMING ALL ANIMAL

But she didn't entirely forget. We are always in both worlds, because they aren't really two.
—Gary Snyder, from *The Woman Who Married a Bear*

You study the sky, hesitant to have left shelter. Wind pushes clouds over the granite ridgelines like predator and prey, the white ones seemingly chased by darker ones. But for now the sun is warm on your hair. You have time and needs to meet. Something in your bones surges and you feel your feet make the decision to proceed. Your load is winter ponderous, not the light lift of warm weather, but your back revels in being useful, capable. As you move, your breasts, fuller at this time in your cycle, amplify the sway of your body over land. Your haunches rally as you step up rocks; shoulders, hips, and ankles balance-dance as beneath your feet the granite shifts color, clouds still dashing across blue plains above.

This is not just another solo backpack trip. I am on a mission, sent by that inner voice that, when I hear it, I cannot disobey. Though the forecasters call for the first winter storm of the season, and though I'm used to the milder climate and terrain of the southern Appalachians, I doggedly stuffed one more warm shirt under the top pouch of my pack this morning and drove an hour and a half to South Lake Tahoe to get my permit. There is irony in having to gain society's permission to escape it. The ranger wrote out the parking pass and hunted down change. That's what I'm hunting too, in another fashion, and I was glad the ranger was female when she asked, "How many?"

"One."

"Any dogs?"

"No."

Locking my car, I pause before hefting the pack, always unreasonably heavy when I go alone. If I were a werewolf, or the bear husband of the old stories, this is when the hair would quickly sprout across my cheeks and shoulders, the claws emerge and back hunch. People watching would know then. But here in this parking lot, a family walks by and looks only at my pack and ponytail. They have no idea the changes going on inside me as I attempt my first shape-shift. As I deliberately become all animal.

You are away at college and have gotten up the nerve to kayak. Bobbing with what comes, hips starting to react on their own, you follow the experienced paddlers. At the end of the drop the back wave catches your edge and you're underwater. So slow and dark and cold. And then you're up, shaking your head like a spaniel. Such a different world beyond the familiar surface—now you know. This is what you came for. To belong somewhere like a frog or heron. Like the people cheering you who belong on the river—so beautiful and strong and free— so unlike the suburbs you grew up in. Laughing, you peel off wet clothes by the side of the road, not caring who sees. Later, in front of your mirror, you stare at your back, neck twisted, flexing both arms at once. There, between your shoulders, new ridges. The beginning of wings.

Of course, I know and you know that we *are* animals. But like the phrase "boys will be boys," the fact that we're animals is treated as something we can't help rather than something to cultivate. I don't remember when it first occurred to me that by inhabiting my animal nature more I might find a way around my fears, which had grown rather than shrunk over the years of traveling, hiking, and backpacking alone. Fears of meeting human males in the wild; of being told, if I made it out of a bad situation, that I should have known better; of believing all the voices out there that say it's a woman's fault for going anywhere—but especially into the wilderness—alone. Maybe it was when I read about grizzly sows having to avoid and ward off attacks from the large males. They can't hide away all the time and they don't look for an even larger male to protect them. They adapt. They use their senses to discover whether a male is around. If so, the sow tries not to feed in the prime areas when the male is likely to feed. But if she or her cub is charged and the sow must fight, she fights tremendously. And who of us would suggest that if she fails and is killed, or her cub is killed, that she asked for it?

At the trailhead I check the map for distances. A man with a toddler is ahead of me.

"How far you going in?" he asks.

"Don't know yet." I evade the question. Though my instincts say he is harmless, I won't give my destination. Smiling, I leave them behind. My goal this trip is not to act as a female grizzly would, though I often think about what I know of animal behavior. I want to become my own animal. To do this I must shut off the cultural white noise and remember what it is to think with my body. My cerebral cortex has been thoroughly colonized, but my haunches are still pretty precultural. My hands and feet are quick to solve problems when I trust them to.

I approach two middle-aged women at the top of a long stair-like climb. They've been resting and watching my small steps and deliberate foot placements.

"How much does that pack weigh?" one asks in fatigued awe.

"I have no idea," I say with a breathless laugh. "Never weigh your pack. You want to believe it's lighter than it is when you start out, and to brag it was heavier than it was when you get home."

This attitude is more self-preservation than suicidal tendency or ego. If the pack is too heavy, my back will tell me (I try it on at home). But put a number to it and my brain will convince my body it's too heavy regardless. Or worse, if I'm having a bad day, I don't want to know the pack is plenty light and should be no problem. Animals don't weigh loads, and I know that when I'm out on my own, my body amazes me. What seems heavy in the driveway seems infinitely doable on the leaf-strewn trail.

You are thirteen, swinging down from the cherry tree by your window. It is quiet except for the sounds of cars nearby and your mother's voice in your ear: not after dark . . . never alone . . . don't you read the papers? No one understands your restlessness. The suburbs suck. Your brothers get to go where they want, even at night. You get to go to your room. Because there's nothing else to do you walk the black edge of the road, with each step daydreaming of woods, dogs that come every time you call, and strong, kind boys. A half moon winks through the trees. Then someone whistles. "Hey baby, you don't have to walk." You remember where you are. Stuck. The car doesn't stop. What if I want to walk? you think. What then?

Like many female adventurers, I've had to learn the hard way, and I break society's rules. I've struggled free from some of the traps Western culture has set out to extirpate my instincts, and I feel lucky not to have lost a limb so far. Although I was a mouthy child, *always be polite* was firmly ingrained by the time I became an adult. Attached to that was *don't make a scene.* Following these rules makes it almost impossible for the civilized female to prevent a threatening encounter with a male, so caught up is she in giving him the benefit of the doubt until he has his hands on her, is forcing her into the car or onto the ground.

I laugh at the centuries-old message that civilization is created for and maintained by women. Civilization—that place with walls where humans deceive themselves about the extent of their control and buy into the myth of security. The only place, we're told, where women can be safe. I am not less safe in the wild. Statistics show I'm at greater risk of attack in my house or on a city street than I am miles away from a trailhead or parking lot. I don't trust what civilization and culture tell me anymore. I trust my gut. Out alone, I look everyone in the eye once and then avert my gaze (but never, ever look down). I turn to face anyone coming up the trail from behind. I can look ornery and unapproachable in seconds. I don't wear the shroud of fear and vulnerability I'm told is attractive, is feminine. I bare my aggression, like teeth. If a man does not understand how to respect my privacy—a kind of territory—then he deserves whatever growls he's given.

Two young women are day hiking ahead. One steps aside and as I pass, whispers *courageous*.

It breaks my heart.

Someone rounds the turn below you. Something about his size, or that he's alone, or the way he cocks his head sends a tremor up your back. There is a large boulder and you slip behind it. What about this person makes your ruff go up, makes you not even want to sniff out his intentions? It doesn't matter. There are no walls here and disappearing is not hard. As he reaches the boulder and moves past, you're crouched, ready to pretend you were peeing if he looks. He doesn't look. Why would he? No one expects you to be here. A little amazed, you watch him march uphill, oblivious. A

wren perched without moving in the bushes nearby meets
your gaze.

Men are animals. This is what I've been told countless times
before driving cross-country or going camping by myself.
Most often it's male friends who have drummed this into my
skull. I understand them to mean that men are driven by their
dicks, which pulse with instinct, not reason. They mean that
men can act badly. Well, women are animals too—treated like
pets, many feel. And animals are animals. I leave civilization
to be with animals and to be an animal, and surely I can allow
men inside this definition in the same, less derogatory way
I'm including myself. Most animals, especially the best killers,
the bloodthirstiest, have ingrained inhibitions—both social
and genetic—that keep deadly conflicts among members of a
species to a minimum. Especially prevalent are the inhibitions
of males of these species (most birds and mammals) that keep
them from physically attacking a female. It seems our culture
evolved too fast; our hereditary inhibitions couldn't keep up.

Or maybe the messages given to females are social inhibitions devised by patriarchal culture rather than biological evolution. Messages such as "You're putting yourself in danger!"—
as if women should never take risks or don't want to; "You're
asking for it!"—the "it" presumably the same as in "doing it";
and "Don't go alone, take a guy with you!"—an especially
problematic message for single women since more than 80
percent of sexual crimes are committed by someone they know.

Women are domesticated through fear. We're taught that
we need—no, *deserve*—protection. A privilege that we enjoy
like poodles who're primped, dressed in bows, and carried
around. I don't want to be a decoration or a pet who waits
for her husband to come home. My husband and I do things
together—climb, hike, kayak, bike, read, debate. But we also

do things separately. And when I go into the wilderness alone, he has to defend both my decision and his to others (not to stay but presumably to have *let me go*).

Even in other primates, possibly the most social of animals, members take time by themselves. For some people, being alone in a crowded city street or bar is enough, or having the whole house to themselves. I need the woods, mountains, and rivers, which remind me that dirt and sweat aren't undesirable, that I have muscles for a purpose. I need places without mirrors. In all their good intentions, people who've tried to keep me safe have helped keep me from discovering myself and exploring my creativity, my body, and the land. A room of one's own? Sounds great, but an isolated canyon, peak, or valley occasionally is just as necessary. Let me go, I begged my mother. Let me go, I begged the voices in my head. I never would've married a man I had to beg this way.

When you reach the lake it's still sunny. You hurry, hoping to get in a quick dip while the sun is full force. After scouting out a place in the steep granite walls that will let you camp above, unseen from the banks, you reclaim your pack and huff it up manzanita and scree to the flat. The wind, as if it'd been waiting, surges as you pitch the tent. You check from below to make sure it's hidden. Once it's weighted down with rocks in each corner and over the stakes, you explore the shoreline. All the hikers have left. Each time the sun's consumed by a cloud you wonder, is this it? Kingfishers rattle. You strain to hear the sounds of conversation carried a long way, relax when you determine it's the wind-thrown water hitting logs and rocks. As a Steller's jay cries and heads for the lone Jeffrey pine, you settle in to listen to the voices.

Even with everyone gone, I have to concentrate on the sounds
around me, make them familiar, before I can completely relax.
The animals that live here know these sounds, but I'm new
to this habitat. I'm used to rustling leaves and eastern rivers,
not the irregular slapping of lake water on a rugged shore.
Sun heats my face and I strip, hoping it will hang around
long enough for me to run into the cold, clear water. Then a
cloud shoulders the warmth aside, and reluctantly I pull my
shirts back on. Am I being wise or wimpy? Skinny-dipping is
an obsession of mine, even when it's too cold to really swim.
Immersing myself in natural waters is a conscious reminder
that I don't have control over things like temperature, depth, or
what's on the bottom. It's a reverse baptism, one that celebrates
my body and mortality by baring myself to this beautiful,
relentless creation. Two mallards come right up to where I'm
filtering water, and I enviously lose myself in their antics and
the iridescent blue, green, and purple feathers up close. As they
paddle away I screw the lid on my bottle.

"Is that water potable?" I spin. The man has stopped a
respectful distance away.

"No, that's why I have a filter," I fumble. I didn't hear him. *I
hadn't heard him.*

At first this is all I can think, but as a woman catches up
with him I realize this time it's okay. Maybe animals stalked
from downwind feel this way when they finally get a sniff of a
too-close stranger.

"Sorry if I startled you. I didn't expect to see anyone out
here," he's saying. "You know there's a winter storm watch."

I nod. I've categorized him as one of my kind—pleasant
outdoor enthusiast who appreciates solitude. "The weather
report called for snow down to seven thousand feet. That's why
I didn't go any further in."

"Fifty-five hundred is what I heard."

We all look toward the lake, imagine snow covering the shore, pines, and granite ledges. The hush of the next morning.

After they leave I feel truly alone. It's wonderful. The wind has picked up and I've started the stove even though I ate my sandwich only two hours ago. Like the other animals, I must scurry for food before the storm hits. In my case, hot food. The temperature is dropping fast. As creamy garlic pasta burps in the pot, I squat on a boulder to get a better view. Like an animal, I stayed when people fled to their cars. Like an animal, I'm not uneasy that a storm is coming. Perhaps, as it is for the other animals, this can be a kind of home. At least I feel at home, the way when the curtains are pulled you can walk around in your underwear, not caring whether your hair's combed or teeth brushed. Here on this ridge, I've escaped society's gaze.

The steep scree and aspen slopes rise above on three sides. Could the black bears around here scramble up them? It's hard to imagine. I stare at the nooks in the rock walls as I eat way more than I need, trying to hoard all the fat against a cold night. I compare each gust with the last, and each one's stronger. No bears pass through. The barometric lows before a major storm make animals lethargic, I recall. That and my full belly have me thinking it's time to den.

A few drops of rain convince you to take a last pee in the half light. Something moves, a dark head bobs in and out of the tall manzanita. Your heart stops. They've come for you. More follow the first, but they're in baseball caps. You look back and the bear becomes a guy whose navy hoodie is pulled tight around his head. You're disappointed.

And nervous. They come from another direction, off trail, and head toward the high point of nearby rocks. They don't see me but can't help but notice the tent from where they're going. My brain says to zip up tight, avoid contact, but my body wants to stand its ground. They know where I am; I want to see where they are, where they go, and when they leave. Can they tell I'm female? Probably not in my rain shell and hat. But if they come closer . . . ?

They're not dressed for the weather that's coming. They don't even carry daypacks. What brings them out here? To *my* place? Ethologists say an animal will be the most aggressive toward others of its species in familiar territory. The fact that I've settled in may be why I'm not interested in retreating. It doesn't take long for them to wander out back the way they came, and I consider how I'd feel if I were holed up in the tent now. I wouldn't know they were gone. Even if I peeked out and didn't see them, I'd wonder whether they were hidden. I'd worry all night. My body made the right decision.

It's started raining and I consider keeping the food bag in my tent. What animal will be out in this? Or I could stash it in the crook of a small tree. I mean, there aren't many tall enough, and all the lower branches on the pines are broken off so that . . . but my body is not listening.

My hands grab the cord and double-bagged food, while my feet and eyes hunt for a suitable spot. There is really only one option. The pine is on a steep, scrubby slope, which makes it difficult to get into good position for an underhand throw. I tie the cord around a fist-sized rock. I didn't often have to hang food where I'm from, but after a couple of tries I lob the rock over the branch and the tied rope follows. Now I stand amid juniper and granite. It's only me, with no reinforcements, and I'm enough.

Finally in the tent, wet gear off to the side, I think about how I came to doubt myself. Was it that I was born with a suburban spoon in my mouth that fed me all those white middle-class fairy tales about how great it is to have men do everything for you? Was it that in the 1970s and 1980s women were working hard to prove their competence in the indoor male world of commerce, emphasizing their minds and masking their bodies? Was it that no women I knew sought solitude outdoors? In the metropolitan area of my youth, the wild was something only men were supposed to crave, and then only a few weekends a year when they valued their brawn more than their pin-striped brains.

> *You are five, racing around the front lawn behind your older brothers on the first really warm spring day. Your mother calls you aside and hands you a shirt. You start to cry and point at your brothers. "Little girls are different," she says. "Little girls wear shirts." But you cry harder and beg for one day more, one day, and she relents. No longer sure what the game is, you roll down the hill again and again. Grass sticks to your back and belly. Climbing the magnolia, you pay special attention to how smooth the bark is as you hold the trunk. Your brothers go inside. It's getting cool. Looking out through the large waxy leaves, you tuck your knees to your bare chest for warmth, afraid to go indoors. Afraid of never being let out.*

A girl with short hair and a penchant for dirt, I was always mistaken for a boy. I prided myself on being a tomboy and wore my brothers' hand-me-downs until puberty dropped me into a vat of glitter lip gloss. Luckily, once I was at college, the hippies got me comfortable with a clean face again, and the rednecks showed me that flannel could be flattering.

Now I'm still caught off guard by the people—both males and females—who describe me as butch. When single, I learned it was easier to move around in social circles if I grew my hair long. A man I'd been working with for over a year and whom I admired asked whether I knew how much taking up knitting had changed my image. This man and I took high schoolers on hikes and longer trips. In the woods I felt no qualms about spitting if I had to, competed in belching contests, and—like the male leaders—didn't suppress any gastric emissions caused by the rice and bean diet. Not my behavior in a restaurant, but they didn't necessarily know that. It now occurs to me that those actions construed as manly are really me at my most animal.

How did it happen that men get the freedom to act like animals? Do we really think they can't help it, or rather, that we can help it more than they can? Maybe it's feared that women who let themselves be a little wild will, like the woman who married a bear in Pacific Northwest Indian tales, choose not to turn back. I don't know whether that's still a possibility anywhere in the world, but it's not one I'd choose. Still, I'll claw and kick for the chance to temporarily drop as far out of human society as possible. And to spit when I need to.

The wind is crazy now, pushing your tent's dome from all sides, bending the poles concave at times. You hear each gust gather in another valley and grow to the great growl of Ursa that charges over the ridge and shakes your den. Maybe you are trespassing. Your full bladder whines insistently, so you slip out of your bag and into rain gear. Outside it's dark, as if the earth had rolled into a cave. The cold rain stings your butt with its quills. Shadows everywhere shift and settle. Remember what the elders say: if you meet a bear, open your coat and show that you're a woman.

Back in my sleeping bag trying to warm up, I wallow in memories of sun on my skin: hiking the Cumberland Island beaches on my first backpack trip, all of us naked except for what we carried; stripping my shirt off every lunch stop during desert day hikes; standing nude, shin deep in the Colorado River, admiring the rich colors of the Grand Canyon while a breeze slips between my legs; celebrating Independence Day by skinny-dipping solo in the Rio Grande, stroking back and forth from America to Mexico.

I've always wanted to get rid of barriers between me and the earth, but it wasn't until my freshman year in college that I finally returned to the outdoors as the little girl I was before impending breasts and periods separated me from boys and nature. I remember nervously approaching the reservoir's edge with others for a dip to wash off all the grease and stress of the restaurant's late shift. I said I'd go but wouldn't strip. No one cared. When I'd almost reached the water, others were just starting to splash into the shallows. The dark swallowed the details and suddenly I felt more self-conscious in underwear. The next instant I was wading to where the black water could slide over my naked chest.

What do we lose when we become afraid to ever bare ourselves, emotionally or physically? When we're uncomfortable being naked except to make love or wash? Our distrust of our bodies is crippling. As girls, we're told they beguile ceaselessly and cruelly, so we wear clothes designed to hide or accent them. We're told they're weak and can't protect us, so we cower. Then, sometime when we're older, we hear from women who've found their voices, who have begun to expose these lies. They tell us that together we can fight to make the world safe someday. I know their work has made it easier for me to shape my life, and I'm grateful. But I don't believe the world will ever be completely safe for anyone. And I'm glad, because a safe world has no room for wildness.

At midnight the rain slaps the nylon even harder, unlikely to ever gentle into snow. Can this cheap tent hold up for six or seven more hours of this? I feel certain a pole will snap or nylon tear. As it is, I'm riding on the raft of my Therm-a-Rest, the decomposed granite outside unable to absorb this much water. It's pooled underneath my ground cloth, and the tent floats between where the corners are staked. The fly doesn't even cover the back of the tent, where the full force of the storm has soaked the wall. I imagine trying to hike the steepness in these gusts with a full pack in the dark. I don't think I could get down the manzanita slope, let alone keep from getting blown off the narrow cliff-edged trail. For a few minutes I stare anxiously at the nylon sides pressing in on me. Then I remember why I'm here. No animal would stay awake worrying about what might happen. It'd just react if something did. Abruptly I release the tension in my body. The reality is I don't want to have to deal with a busted tent or stashing my pack so I can get to the car in the dark, but I know I could. Now I concentrate on the noise and let it drown out the cultural messages my brain tries to send. The storm distracts me from pointless human worry, and I welcome it.

You're on the borderline between awake and asleep, afloat in a deep pool of belonging. Your heart reaches out to other creatures burrowed in this place, enduring the same forces. To creatures nested in places you'll never know, living lives you can't imagine. In their world the expectations are simple. You sense that their world is your world but without the lies. You release those lies, which turn into ravens calling and winging above the dark valley. You have not taken back the night.

Better, you are sharing it.

Storm coming, North Carolina (photo credit: Melanie Derry)

Bicycles, Motherhood, and Midlife

BLIGHTED

The Reno rock gym's noise faded as soon as I left the mat and my belayer, a fortyish woman I'd never seen there before. She'd been volunteering at that rope for hours as folks climbed, trying to earn as many points as they could. Her smile encouraged me. I'd never signed up for a competition before and almost didn't this time. The plastic holds felt familiar against my hands. Heck, they should—this was my third time that day trying this climb. It was rated 5.12, and I'd normally consider it out of my range. But Pootey, my friend and climbing coach for the day, was right. The moves were the kind I excelled at. Each time, I'd gotten close to the top but hadn't kept my balance enough to control the big reach that'd set me up to grab the last hold. Stopping at the highest secure stance, I took a breath and focused on the new sequence I hoped would make the difference. My last chance. I'd rested an hour without climbing anything in order to give it one more best shot. It was a calculated risk, and Pootey approved. The comp was almost over.

Stepping up, I back flagged my leg to help keep my body close to the wall, moved my left hand to the small intermediate hold, and paused. My body wanted to bring my feet closer, but I knew from experience that without the leg flagged my weight would pull me off before I could reach the good hold. We had a new plan. I wasted moments and energy second-guessing and then heard Jimmy yell from across the gym, *You've got it, Lilace!*

And I did. I rode the sound of my husband's voice to the hold, stepped left, and grabbed the final jug above, hanging by my right arm as I made eye contact with my belayer, who'd confirm my climb. The crowd below erupted. Pootey clapped and shouted, her short blonde hair bouncing as she jumped. I let go. Once lowered down, I thanked my belayer. "Glad to," she said. "It's a pleasure to watch you climb."

I'm back and better than ever, I thought. No one but Jimmy, Pootey, and a few other close friends had any idea what my body had been through recently.

🌲🌲🌲

Three weeks earlier, Jimmy and I had eagerly stared at the lima-bean shape on the screen in the OB-GYN office. The doctor, whom we'd known for fifteen minutes, zoomed the image in and out. "I'm sorry," she said. "I don't see a baby." I stared harder at the screen, not comprehending. She explained, "Sometimes a placenta develops without an embryo. We'll do tests of course, to be sure."

But I'd had tests, at home and at the clinic. I'd thought we were sure.

Jimmy watched me closely. He was sad for this nonbaby. Mostly he was sad for me. He had no doubt I would get pregnant again. At home I went online and looked up blighted ovum to be reassured. "Common occurrence." "Most find it easier to get pregnant afterwards because the body's been prepped to nurture a baby."

Jimmy stroked my cheek. Held my hand. "I love you." he said. "All that matters is you're healthy," he said.

The doctor was kind and made my appointment to get blood drawn for fifteen minutes before the lab opened. She didn't want me to have to sit in a room full of pregnant women. Even though I waited for the results before I had the dark beer I craved, I knew it was true.

Jimmy said he had a new appreciation for technology. "It would scare me to death if you just started bleeding."

I was glad to be spared that shock, but the weird limbo was

hard. I was still tired. The hormones still flowed through me.
I pictured the black-and-white swirl in my abdomen. The dark
lima bean inside. The beanless bean. The nonbean, nonbeing. I
was still pregnant. I was never pregnant.

All those books I read, and none mentioned this possibility? Rather than wait for nature, we scheduled a D&C when
the doctor found out I had a trip in a week. Spring break we
were heading to Bishop, California, to camp and climb, and
I wouldn't stay home. I needed the eastern Sierras more than
ever. She said there was a risk of hemorrhaging if I miscarried
out in the middle of nowhere.

Why do they call it a miscarriage if I never carried a baby?

Blighted, adj.: spoiled, ruined, destroyed. Anything that
prevents growth or prosperity.

The bar was packed with regulars and some of our friends from
the university who showed up to hear poetry. Jimmy, Pootey,
Ross, Valerie, and Michael came specifically to hear me. At
the break before my turn, I went to the toilet. Inside the small
room painted purple I started bleeding. At least this would save
me the bother and cost of a D&C.

Only five people in the audience knew I was pregnant and
was not pregnant anymore. Only I knew I was bleeding. I read
my poems, the little worlds I could make.

It took three days of cramping to expel a two-month-old
placenta. Don't believe anyone who tells you it feels like a
heavy period. On the outside I was thriving. My spring break
climbing went fine. I threw myself at the routes in Owens River

Gorge, and then a couple of days at Happy Boulders and the Buttermilks. I drank in the desert heat. Soaked up the view of pink-tinted Mount Tom on the horizon. Dogs ran free and so did the beer back at camp. At least I could drink now.

Jimmy, Pootey, they knew I was not myself. I knew I was only myself. *I won't compete in the comp*, I told her. *I hate competing. I feel like a failure. It's a horrible idea.*

♣♣♣

Blight, verb: Subject to neglect.

♣♣♣

As usual, Pootey had been right—climbing in the comp was a big rush. It felt like giving the finger to fate. *See that? You didn't shatter my world.* So why has everything been shit this trip? Hiding from the midday summer sun in Idaho's City of Rocks, I'm seething. I thought because I was climbing fine that I was fine, but over the last couple of months my climbing has stagnated. Tucked in a narrow slot of granite, I've found shade and solitude enough to let down my defenses. Somewhere closer to the campsite, Jimmy and Bill are resting and chatting, still having fun. Still clueless. I want someone to see what's going on with me, and then I want someone to explain it. It doesn't help that the guys are having such a good time. The three of us usually make a great team, and I love where we are, had begged to come back rather than explore a new area. This trip I've slingshotted between worrying I'm ruining their trip and seething that they're so unbothered.

I'd been plenty involved in the planning, but ever since we arrived I've had no opinions. All I've been sure of is that their goals haven't been mine. I get on the climbs they choose and shake, freeze up, or get so frustrated I pump out. Even when I do finish a climb, I'm aware of how choppy and graceless my movements are. It feels all wrong. We have to go home in a few days. I've been wasting my time here, reading in the tent more than climbing, fuming over how left out I feel. But today I realize I dread going back too. Nothing makes me happy. If I could have or do anything I want, I can think of only one thing. And that, apparently, I can't have. At least I can't make it happen.

Jimmy's head appears in the air between the granite slabs shielding me. He and Bill want to head over to the Flaming Rock area and poke around. I don't want to hang out while they window-shop, and besides I feel as if I might finally be ready to face my demons.

"I'll come in an hour. Where should I find you?"

"Not sure. We'll be checking out the climbs, but we'll watch for you," Jimmy promises.

We go over again the area they'll be in before they set off.

Out here where there are no distractions like classes or work, where it's simply the earth, these good men, and climbing, what I've been hiding from myself sits on the ledge in full view: I don't trust my body anymore. I thought I'd be pregnant again by now. I'd looked forward to only following on this trip, never tying into the sharp end, taking breaks to read or lie in the shade because I'd be doing the hard work of making a human. That's the project on my mind. I have no others, can't think of any routes I want to work on, especially since my performance has been so unfocused.

Suddenly I need to lead a route. I don't know what route, but I want a challenge, to take a risk I have more control over than trying to have a baby. This I can make happen today. I fill water bottles, grab my pack, and head to Flaming Rock.

On the third time through the area, shouting for Bill and Jimmy, I start looking off trail and find them behind some trees in a niche, Jimmy tied in belaying Bill.

"There you are," Jimmy says, lowering Bill down.

"I've been walking around calling for you for twenty minutes, goddamn it."

"What? There's no way we could've missed you."

The ridiculousness of that statement only irritates me more. "I want to lead something," I say.

"Great," Bill says. "What?"

I take the guidebook he hands me and flip through it. I'm looking for something that's not crimpy or vertical crack climbing. Something balancey, with overhangs or roofs to pull. Away from the more popular areas, farther back where we haven't explored much, there are two bolted 5.10a climbs on a feature called the Slabbage Patch. We hike over and uphill, crossing a creek and stream, to check them out. The boulder, when it comes into view, is beautiful in a rougher, less symmetrical way than the classic, smooth granite around us. It has a warm copper patina, and the pale pocked surface, interrupted with jutting features, seems slightly out of place. I feel an immediate connection.

The line I like is the center feature on the face, one that's been dubbed "I Can't Believe It." The name is either a mind game or a bad omen.

"You sure?" Jimmy asks. "The start looks hard."

It's tricky; even the guidebook says so. I'll have to get to the horizontal crack under a thrust of rock that will make it hard to see the first bolt above. This is not Jimmy's kind of climbing, but with my smaller size and comfort hanging on my arms, it calls to me.

"Yeah. I'm sure, if you'll spot me."

So with Bill belaying, and Jimmy ready, I breathe deeply and put my hands against the rock. I follow the wide crack right as it ramps down low enough for me to get both hands on and paste my climbing shoes against the granite. With a grunt I mantle up, like boosting onto a counter, and swing my right foot up, then my knee into the gap. Unfortunately, it's not tall enough for me to crouch onto and not deep enough to pull most of my body in lying down. I'd planned to scooch back left. I try inching that direction, but my rear end and left leg dangle, pulling me out. The crack isn't wide enough to stuff an arm or fist in to counterbalance, and I see that in my rush for stability I've sacrificed it. The only reassuring thing is I have the Jimmy Rope. He'd gotten that nickname when bouldering—climbing short routes without ropes. Being spotted by my tall, strong husband puts me at ease. Him I trust.

I roll out of my awkward position and am back hanging on my arms. The lip of the crack is slopey and polished. I work my way six feet over as Jimmy shadows my slow progress. I'm only five feet off the ground. I know I'll survive the drop if I slip. But could I deal with knowing I'd failed again?

I hold on, and when Bill says I'm below the bolt I lever up again, reach for what I hope is a good hold above the thrusted rock, pull up, and clip into the first bolt.

"Good job, Honey," Jimmy says.

"Right on," Bill says.

"Somebody else could climb that a hell of a lot better," I say.

Immediately I want to strike the words from the air. I'm doing it again, blaming myself, blaming my body for not being perfect. Yet my body is what got me here. And it's my body that refuses to let me off the hook, refuses to let me pretend I'm over the miscarriage. On this climbing trip, on the rocks, my body put its foot down, saying *deal with this*. And I will, starting now.

I look up at the next bolt. There's a pretty big span of face climbing until I reach it. Above that one is another bolt right below the roof, and then barely the glimmer of another. Finally, somewhere I can't see, the anchors are waiting. I don't want to focus on them—like the baby I want so much, which seems as if it were here once, so clearly did I imagine our future.

Just bolt to bolt, for now.

The rock is warm and pleasantly gritty against my palms.

No matter what happens I will not say nasty things to my body for doing what it has to do to get my attention. *I'm listening*, I tell it. *What next?*

SELF AS HABITAT

"I just want it to happen naturally," Jimmy said to me from across the table of our romantic Valentine's Day dinner in a crowded restaurant. I was bringing up new information on conception, asking him to give up caffeine and alcohol and start taking a supplement until we got pregnant. The way I looked at it, if he went all in right away, he might soon be back to beer and coffee, while I'd have nine more months of abstaining.

"Well, it's not happening naturally. You're thirty-five. Your sperm might need a little help. In any case, the zinc won't hurt. Unless you'd rather get your sperm tested? You know what you'd have to do, right?" I had him there. He was a bit of a prude.

It'd been almost a year since my first miscarriage. I'd had another in the meantime, which I might have thought was a late period if I hadn't been charting every bit of my body's intake and output. Really sexy stuff. I'd approached this like a farmer improving her soil before planting. I was only one year younger than Jimmy. Though extremely healthy and in the best shape of my life, I worried now that there was something off. I'd never had regular periods. Maybe it wasn't age, but something that'd been wrong all along. I was working hard to trust my body and let go, but with each month it was getting harder.

What is natural, anyway? It's natural for women to have babies. Unless they can't. Does that mean it's unnatural for women to not want to have babies? I don't believe that for a second. Am I natural? The primary definition is "existing in or caused by nature; not made or caused by humankind." I'm a biological creature created by two humans who raised me in society. How can I make any sense of this?

Those days my head was a mess. So much of my life had been lived on high alert because I had female parts. Partially because having them made me a target for rape, but it wasn't only that threat. For over a decade I'd been determined to avoid pregnancy. Especially in college, biology seemed so unfair. Unlike guys' bodies, my body could turn sex for pleasure into a result that lasted longer than, well, you know. I didn't believe the slut-shaming messages of society, but I was keenly aware that if I didn't protect myself (with birth control and good choices), only I would suffer the consequences of pregnancy. The cultural message has been that for a married couple a baby is a gift from God, and out of wedlock a baby is a punishment cast upon the woman by the same God.

Luckily, this was not the God I'd been raised with. I was brought up Christian by a Presbyterian pastor, and my sense of God was foremost as the Creator of the natural world that I adored. When I connected with nature, I felt the full force of God's love—a love of me as an individual, no more important than the rest of creation. The Bible sounded best the rare summer Sunday mornings Dad led an outdoor service at Greenbelt National Park campground. We'd sit on the grass with a few strangers and sing our favorite hymns, Dad's voice leading us in the suburban wilderness.

Nature's plan? God's will? Even trying for a baby, I didn't see any point in those questions. But I was preoccupied with deciding what steps I would and wouldn't take to increase our fertility. That night at dinner, I started out talking about a pre-conception plan and we ended up deciding on a mutual training program. There'd been many times Jimmy had regulated his food and alcohol to get in shape for some physical challenge like a bike race, so this framing was familiar. And language matters. By dessert, I felt excited about doing this together. No longer was I on a solitary journey. Some things I still did alone, like seeing an MD who specialized in women's health and Chinese medicine. But we both dropped caffeine and alcohol from our diet. The crocuses were only starting to come up, so we were mostly climbing and cycling indoors, but as often as we could we went bouldering outside in a new desert area nearby called Purgatory. We'd decided our guideline would be that anything I did in hopes of helping us have a baby had to be good for me by itself and in its own right. Even nonfarmers should take care of their land, right?

At this time, I was climbing at my personal best. That winter we'd taken a couple of trips to Bishop, California, where I'd sent my first V4 problem at Happy Boulders. And another had followed. It felt strange to be pulled between wanting to push myself to break into V5 and wishing to be pregnant, which would end my bouldering until the baby was born. I knew I didn't need to completely stop climbing when pregnant (much to my in-laws' dismay), but I wouldn't climb without a rope and I wouldn't lead routes. I'd miss the thrill and challenge of bouldering with no harness or rope to constrain me.

One of my favorite things to do at the Happys and Purgatory was climb on top of a sun-warmed boulder in winter and lie against it, the heat transferring directly to bare skin around my sports bra. I'd close my eyes, let everything seep away: the Reno cold, graduate school stress, questions about fertility. I thought of lines by Chase Twichell, a favorite poet: "I lie again on a warm rock / and feel the hand of God on my back." In another part of the poem, she describes being overcome "with love for the world outside myself."

Yeah, that was it exactly. But how to channel that love?

For instance, did trying so hard to become a parent undermine my love for the world the way it was? For my body and marriage the way they were? Could I love everything just as much if I couldn't have a baby? I wanted to say yes, but I wasn't

sure. I believed adoption was a fine alternative. But I had no
way of knowing whether I could really let go of my desire to
experience the changes pregnancy would put me through. I've
known plenty of women who endured the physical contortions
of having a baby only because they sought the result. But I
really wanted to undergo this process, was curious about this
ability of the female body. I felt weird admitting this because
I hated it when women were reduced to their reproductive
capacities, as if that were their primary purpose on this earth.
It wasn't that being pregnant would confirm my womanhood
or femininity. I felt no social pressure to have a child and
knew there were plenty needing homes if biology didn't come
through for us. But in the same way Jimmy had always wanted
to alpine climb, I'd always wanted to give birth. To me, it
seemed as simple as that.

So I decided to do everything I could short of medical intervention. I took supplements, vitamin and herbal, and went for
weekly massage and acupuncture. After my massage therapist
had worked on my neck for almost an hour, I asked why it was
so tight. "You've been smiling a lot when you didn't want to,"
she said. Jimmy and I started private couples yoga too. Best
date nights ever! Dr. Christie Bonds did a full traditional medical workup to rule out anything hormonal. Then she studied
my tongue, had me fill out a long Chinese medicine questionnaire about what flavors I craved (sour), and asked other
unusual questions. Several times she emphasized that she made
no claims about helping fertility. However, the body networks
my questionnaire revealed to be unbalanced were the ones
that dealt with reproductive organs. She mentioned something
during the first consultation that stuck with me. She said that
unlike most who practiced Chinese medicine, she wouldn't do
acupuncture on women when they were menstruating or pregnant. Women's bodies were not out of balance at those times;

they were doing what needed to be done and she didn't want to interfere.

Who knows whether changing my attitude to my body helped? But a month and a half later I walked into her office beaming, and she knew I wouldn't be getting any more treatments. She hugged me and said to be sure to come back for postpartum help. It was understood that if something went wrong this time, she would be there for me too. But I didn't dwell on that. I had faith in my body, even though I'd taken the pregnancy test on April Fools' Day.

We had a busy spring, or it seemed that way because I was in a happy, sluggish daze. Mild nausea was the worst I got, but the first trimester I felt as if my energy had been sucked out. Or maybe pushed in, as if it were all directed at that tiny swirl of cells dividing, multiplying, and differentiating. I was lucky. I didn't work full time or have other kids at home. I had a husband willing to cook or run across town at all hours to Super Burrito. I could sit and read or go for slow walks on the gravelly lower slopes of Peavine Mountain at the northern edge of Reno. Arid and mostly devoid of trees, Peavine was beautiful in its solitude, especially when the clouds, purple and orange, blew in at sunset. This was not official wilderness but part of a large tract under the Bureau of Land Management (BLM), an agency created to handle the land homesteaders hadn't wanted. It wasn't uncommon to see where someone had driven in and dumped old appliances, as they do on the steep creek banks in Appalachia. On Peavine there was nothing like kudzu to cover it up. BLM land was said to be just rocks, sand, and ice, and I was grateful some of it was a few blocks from my door.

Yet I yearned to be among the Sierras. Everyone said my energy would come back in the second trimester, so we planned a summer trip to Tuolumne Meadows for some easy climbing. In the eastern section of Yosemite National Park, Tuolumne would

be less crowded than the iconic valley, and the granite domes
sprinkling the meadows held shorter and less difficult climbs.
We'd done Cathedral Peak there with friends a year and a half
earlier. After the three-mile hike, it had been an easy ascent to
the 10,911-foot summit, a small area that could fit only a few at
a time. John Muir first climbed it 132 years earlier. The day we
were there, the sky felt as silent and free of civilization as when
he'd made his ascent. Around us several different languages
floated through the otherwise quiet air. It was a few days after
the September 11 attacks, and everyone's flights back to Europe
had been canceled. It was a gift of peace at a tragic time.

This trip would be our first time camping there. I made
reservations and packed the food (it was all about food for
me then). Jimmy packed the gear, tent, and guidebooks. Five
months pregnant now, I was feeling better and not showing
so much as pooching. We left Reno's July heat early and drove
to the clear, cool air at 8,600 feet. The sun, intensified by the
altitude, reflected off exposed glaciated bedrock and alpine
lakes. After pitching the tent, we set off for Stately Pleasure
Dome and were on the rock by 11:00 a.m. We climbed the four
pitches of Great White Book, rated at 5.6 (well below my usual
climbing level), a long, wide crack big enough to wedge yourself into. It looked as if someone were starting to open a book
that'd been lying on its front cover.

Later I hung out by Tenaya Lake, soaking my ankles and
feet. Sleepy and satisfied, I leaned back against a stone near the
water's edge. I felt as if I were in a postcard or had walked into
an American wilderness calendar photo, as I long to do when in
my kitchen. I loved many landscapes, but something about the
exposed granite up against the brilliant blues of sky and water
and the green sedges lent drama to my lazy moment. Maybe
the life growing inside me prompted my heightened awareness—the way light and smells were now more intense—but I

couldn't look around and not think about the uncertain future
of places like this in our warming climate. Wilderness areas like
Yosemite were protected under a specific management approach
summed up by "leave it alone." We had Muir to thank for waking us up to the importance of preserving large areas in their
natural state. This has provided the best chance for wildlife
and plant species to thrive, and where I lay was in the northern
part of the largest continuous swath of roadless wilderness in
the United States outside of Alaska. While there were plenty
of people in the area we were staying in—at least July through
September—that was because we were near the highway. If
you wanted to explore the rest you went by foot, like any other
mammal. Scattered through the wilderness area to the south
were several groves of giant sequoias, trees my Grampa's uncle
Will Colby had worked to protect. Scientists had thought they
were pretty indestructible—and in comparison with most trees
they are. But there are new stressors for that species because
of the climate getting drier and warmer. I wondered what we
could do for them, and whether we *should* do anything.

I put my hand on my belly. My responsibilities as a parent
had barely begun. Ahead was an unending series of decisions
Jimmy and I would have to make about what was best for our
child. Foresters and rangers in our public lands had a lot of
unknowns and hard decisions ahead of them as well.

That night at camp we missed the breeze off the lake that
kept the bugs away. We cleaned up and bear-proofed the food
before turning in early. The mosquitoes were too thick to sit out
and enjoy the July evening.

The next day Jimmy gave in and led a 5.7 route I wanted to
do: Hermaphrodite Flake, called that because there are many
ways to go. You can climb around to the left or right, or go
up the middle under the flake for eighty feet of shade. My feet
had burned up in my black rubber shoes the day before, so the

central enclosed "chimney" called to me. Or maybe it was the womb-like associations. As a big guy, Jimmy tended to avoid tight areas like that, but when you're pregnant you get your way a lot. On the second pitch, in the cool darkness, my shoulders rubbed the rock as my feet pressed against both walls, inching me up. Since no one could hear me, I talked to the baby out loud, explaining where we were and what was pressing against the outside of my belly. *Do you like to be in snug spaces like this, or are you eager to get out?*

We ate a bug-free dinner at a lodge selling teddy bears that were way more like real bears than the usual flat-faced toy store variety. Jimmy looked at me as if I were a stranger when I insisted on buying one. The next day we explored around Puppy Dome, where I took photos of Jimmy bouldering shirt-less as well as making funny faces and poses. He knew these were going in the baby's journal along with photos he'd taken of me by the lake. I pulled Tuolumne Bear from my pack and put him in a pine tree for his picture.

"That'll confuse the kid," I said happily.

"Never too early to start messing with their minds," Jimmy agreed.

Back at camp the mosquitoes swarmed. I refused to come out of the car while Jimmy made dinner and felt no guilt claiming that as a perk of pregnancy. I watched him slap at the bugs in between stirring pasta and swigging beer. I ate in the car too.

By early August I was sporting a belly with a name—Gabriel. When Jimmy and I headed to Lover's Leap for the day, I had to borrow one of his harnesses because mine was too small. I looked forward to being on granite again. My midwife was fine if I followed Jimmy up climbs. Switching to a midwife in Nevada—where they couldn't have a working relationship with OBs or hospitals—was a big deal, but I'd felt better since. We lived only ten minutes from the hospital. Jimmy said it was the best check he'd ever written because my stress level dropped immediately.

That stress had spiked at our twenty-week ultrasound. The doctor had named all the parts she was viewing, stopping to record measurements. We were still basking in the news we were having a son, when she got to the kidneys, the last on the list. It seemed they were dilated more than they should be.

She turned to us and said, "This can be a sign of Down syndrome, but maybe not, because he's a boy."

What did that mean, we asked her? But she clammed up. Only said she'd make us an appointment for a 3-D ultrasound. We'd have to ask the specialist all our questions.

Lord, I was a wreck as we waited for that appointment. Our plan had been not to have anything beyond the basic blood and urine tests, and ultrasound. It'd been obnoxious how my normal pregnancy had suddenly become high risk when I'd turned thirty-five in the second trimester, and the pressure grew to have an amniocentesis. Jimmy and I had agreed that we didn't want anything to do with a test that had a slight risk of miscarriage and wasn't 100 percent accurate. And there was that long scary needle . . . Sure, not much in life is 100 percent certain, but the pressure to have a ton of tests rather than letting God and nature take care of it made hormonal-me a mess. At home I cried and howled that now we had to get a test that wouldn't tell us anything conclusive, and we needed to start reading up on Down syndrome.

"No we don't, Honey," Jimmy said, pulling me down next to him on the couch. "We just need to take it a day at a time."

Bolt to bolt, I thought, leaning into him, and decided to let his words comfort me.

Turns out a 3-D ultrasound can definitively rule out such conditions. When the specialist and technician cheered, all we saw on the screen was a fist. I assumed we were looking for his face, but the clear view of his pinky finger with two joints, long and curving perfectly alongside his others, told them all they needed to know. We should continue to monitor his kidneys, but they were often dilated in boys because of all their extra plumbing. It'd probably sort itself out.

As we hiked slowly through the trees at the base of the Lower Buttress, we passed climbers who all had something encouraging to say as I went by, my belly counterbalancing my pack. Jimmy carried the heavy stuff. We started with a 5.8 called The Groove and then headed to Surrealistic Pillar, a 5.7. Surrealistic was a good description of the photos from that first 3-D ultrasound. We'd left with a grotesque image of our son's face at twenty-one weeks. He had my nose, and I had a renewed appreciation for the role of medical technology. As Jimmy consulted the book about what nuts and cams to carry up this climb, clipping them onto his harness, I was also thankful for modern gear. Not only did these pieces of metal and nylon protect us from falls, they were better for the rock than the iron pitons hammered in and often left during the early days of climbing.

I'd climbed at Lover's Leap before, but never in this area. The wall waved in front of us in vertical undulations—one of which had been dubbed the pillar—but also in horizontal dikes that looked like ripples. These dikes formed unusual ridges spaced close enough to make face climbing doable for me in my current state. The first pitch was fun and had a variety of features, and it was easier than the high stepping that The Groove had demanded. When Jimmy was about twenty feet up the second pitch, it began raining. What was no problem dry turned into a sketchy slip-fest. There were no bolted anchors to rappel from, so we decided the best way off was up. He moved as fast as he could, and then it was my turn as thunder growled in the distance.

The wet rope dragged more than usual. My feet couldn't smear well on the wet rock, which normally had such good friction. Below me I saw all those we'd passed earlier heading down the trail to their cars. I concentrated on finding any little edge or crystal I could for my feet. The crux was a short blank section—no holds at all. I should have been able to smear my feet in front and brace my arms off the flake behind me, scooching up until I could grab a handhold. I tried and tried, as my feet slipped and thunder prowled closer. An old piton stuck out of a crack. I gave up and clipped a quickdraw into it. Unable to free climb that section and not able to lower, I hung on to that quickdraw and pulled my body up until I could grab the hold above. There's no such thing as "I can't do it" when you have to. It felt good to complete the pitch in good mental form, if not pure free-climbing form.

When I finally made it to Jimmy, we went over our options quickly and decided to break our rule of my not leading since this would get me off the rock sooner and lightning was now visible over the valley. The third pitch was the easiest and there were not many options to place gear anyway. I moved carefully but quickly. Jimmy kept me tied in, feeding rope as I climbed. If I fell there'd be consequences, but I was still attached to the mountain at the point where Jimmy stood.

"When you're done, just pull up the rope, untie, and get off the rock," he told me. "I'll deal with the rope when I get there."

I yelled down to let him know I'd reached the top, and he untied. After pulling up the rope, I counted the seconds between lightning and thunder. Gauging the distance, I took a couple of minutes to coil the rope, leaving it ready for Jimmy to grab and run. Then I rushed down the switchback trail. Our wet dog met me halfway and we hustled back to the truck. Everyone else had gotten off the rock, and the parking lot was otherwise empty. Jimmy blew into the truck cab minutes later, and we all grinned like wet puppies.

There are storms, literal and metaphorical, that you can see coming from a long way off, and some that give little warning. It was good to know that Jimmy and I were able to communicate and react in synch when a situation arose, and I hoped that would carry over into parenting. In his climbing journal, Jimmy wrote, "We kept our shit together well." He still loves telling about topping out and finding the rope already coiled for him.

Anyone who's had a baby tossing and turning in her belly, or has sat beside a woman whose stomach seems ready to hatch an angry alien, will comprehend what I was feeling in the final trimester. I was a vessel. Not the weaker vessel, obviously. What a ridiculous old term for women! Thanks for that one, Apostle Peter. I was stronger than ever carrying this creature and extra weight besides. Meanwhile Jimmy, that jerk, was getting thinner. Since we weren't climbing together as much, he'd started cycling with his buddies. He could get in a good workout in less time and so got home quicker. He figured he'd be doing more road riding than climbing right after Gabriel was born. Books for new dads often said they would gain weight right along with their wives. Not him, he vowed. It was annoying how he was drinking beer *and* getting skinny.

In September, Gabriel was really starting to squirm and contort. Now that he was bigger—and bigger than average, according to the midwife—I'd sit on the couch with my hands on my bare belly. It was best if I did this right after I ate. Digestion made him fidgety, so his elbow would jut out and then scroll across underneath my palms as he rolled over. Soon a foot would pop out lower. If I pressed gently on it he'd push back.

One afternoon while doing this, I looked up as a Steller's jay flew into the spruce by the picture window. The branches bobbed down right, then up left, but I couldn't see the jay. *I'm like that tree*, I thought. *I'm not a vessel—I'm habitat.* I told my friend Lorraine Anderson about this. I'd met her that year at a conference but had known of her anthology *Sisters of the Earth* for a long time. It had first been published in 1991, and a new edition was due out when Gabriel was. She'd been my companion on many long, leisurely hikes recently, and I enjoyed our conversations on my favorite subjects: gender, the outdoors, and food. I told her I wanted to go backpacking. No longer sleeping well in my bed, I might as well sleep poorly on the ground.

"I don't want to hike far, but I've got to get away from cars and houses and lie under the stars one more time before he's here," I said. "I need it to get me through those days I'll never leave the house. Like storing up food for winter."

"I know a perfect hike to a hidden lake. It's a mile from the car and only the first third is uphill."

We watched the weather and chose our time before the fall nights got too cold. I wasn't going to bring a tent but could share hers if necessary. I packed a foam pad, sleeping bag, water filter, food, and extra layers. Lorraine would carry the tent and stove. It was a lovely autumn day and we trudged slowly up, my breathing heavy but not gasping. I inhaled the vanilla scent of western pines. The white pine woods back East smelled so different, the way Atlantic and Pacific beaches smell different, the way people smell different. I was curious about the new baby smell I'd been reading so much about. Wouldn't every baby have its own smell?

Tuckasegee, our young Akita-shepherd mix, ran ahead. Allie, my companion indoors and out for thirteen years, had to stay home on hikes now. I missed her. Tuck was also a good trail dog. Her long brindle fur fluffed in the mountain air as she ran.

Our campsite was spectacular. The floor of pine needles lay soft beneath my sleeping pad. Sugar pines above pointed up forever, and Smith Lake sat only a short walk away, reflecting the dark greens and aspen yellows of fall in the Sierras. After dumping my pack, I scooted out on a log to pump water while Lorraine set up her tent and the camp kitchen.

As she heated water over her old stove, I teased Lorraine about her gear. The tent was old nylon, but at least not army surplus canvas. However, she wore flannel and jeans. "Cotton kills," I said.

"I've been backpacking in cotton since before you were born," she pointed out. "Stop worrying I'll get hypothermia. Rain isn't as much an issue here as it is out East."

That was true. I'd been taught to never buy a down sleeping bag because it couldn't keep me warm if it got wet. But they were lighter, and more common out West. However, her Sterno stove was not doing the job.

"I don't know what's wrong with it," she said. "I've never had trouble before."

"Have you been using it since before I was born?"

"Not quite," she laughed.

We decided it was warm enough to plop the sealed foil packets of Indian food into the pot. These were right off the grocery store shelf, easier and cheaper than dehydrated backcountry meals. After a few minutes, we opened and ate our chickpea curries out of the pouches. Lorraine stirred some hot chocolate mix into the water and poured it into two mugs.

"Sorry it's not hot," she grinned. "Maybe we should've brought your high-tech camp stove."

"Here's to technology," I said as we clinked aluminum mugs.

That night, I rolled from one side to the other, not really sleeping. Not really rolling either, since I had a pad only the width of my body. At least here I stared at the dark silhouettes of pines rather than a wall. Tuck was curled nearby, her leash hooked around my wrist in case she wanted to take off after something in the woods. But she was sleeping better than I was. Should I wake her? I had to pee and wondered whether it was okay to leave her. So far she hadn't been tempted to run off. I didn't want to get out of my cozy bag. Damn warm cocoa.

I sat straight up. Warm cocoa. *Shit.* I thought back hoping, but no, I was sure we'd heated dinner using water that Lorraine had scooped from the lake, saving what I'd pumped for drinking. We'd planned for it to come to a boil before stirring in the cocoa mix but then forgot it hadn't been treated when the stove gave out. Eight months pregnant, I'd put myself at risk for the giardia parasite. Always unpleasant, the diarrhea, nausea, and abdominal cramps resulting in possible dehydration and loss of nutrition could be serious in my condition. Had I just polluted myself?

Being land and woman wasn't easy.

Inside me, especially in my gut, lived lots of critters. True for all animals regardless of gender, this means everyone is habitat as well as inhabitant. But at least since Aristotle, Western civilization has promoted the idea that women are closer to nature because they give birth. Being associated with our bodies rather than our minds, women are considered overemotional, not rational like men. This justifies the domination of both women and animals, and the assumption that they and the land are resources for men's pleasure and projects. I didn't think of myself as land in that way, as a passive resource. I didn't think of the land as passive either. The last thing I wanted to do was flip the binary by arguing that women are better because they're more natural and nurturing than men. That'd be the same problems in different packaging.

Now that I carried something much larger than microorganisms in my belly, I was aware of both letting nature take its course and consciously making decisions based on the outcome I desired. It was possible to be both an individual and a part of the ecological whole. In fact, I now believed that was the only possible existence. I lived in a time when technology had a lot to offer but was also scary in the changes it could cause. I'd idealized pure nature for much of my life, but being pregnant had me thinking about how problematic the concepts of ideal wilderness and ideal motherhood were. Pregnancy was only the beginning of changes my body would face that I'd need to come to terms with. Some aspects of mothering are natural, instinctual, but I was not a spider mother who lets her babies devour her like locusts laying fields to waste. I had a say in how I navigated motherhood. And I really wished I hadn't drunk that cocoa. It wasn't even very tasty.

With Tuck trotting and squatting beside me, I peed and drank some filtered water. Not sure whether dilution was any solution in this case, I dropped off to sleep comforted by the fact we were staying out only one night. I'd be home if I developed any ill effects, and I'd have the help of science and technology.

According to loads of books and websites, pregnancy lasts an average of forty weeks from conception. We knew what week we'd conceived, and several ultrasounds had confirmed gestational age, but in week forty-three Gabriel showed no interest in separating from the mother ship. Or should that be leaving the den? We saw the midwife daily and kept her Doppler with us to check the heartbeat every hour. Gabriel was still growing, his vital signs were excellent, and he was head down. When the phone rang, we let the answering machine pick up. I'd stopped talking to family long ago. Back East and helpless, they wanted to know when I'd give up and head to the hospital.

Science still doesn't know exactly what triggers labor. Is it something in the baby? The placenta? The mother? All I knew was the signal hadn't happened yet. There are lots of stories of ten-month mamas if you look (and I had), so as long as this was the only reason to suspect the ignition system wasn't functioning properly, I'd continue to wait. Jimmy's mom had arrived two weeks after my due date, having made flight reservations months in advance. The tension in our house was tighter than my belly as Terri sat on the couch knitting another baby blanket.

My midwife, who'd put our plan to naturally induce labor on hold when another client went into early labor, called the second day of Terri's visit. I was to drink a tall glass of orange juice and castor oil with a bit of baking soda three times that day.

"Keep stirring it in between swallows or it will separate. The baking soda will make it fizz, easier to get down," she instructed. "And stay near a bathroom."

Jimmy and I had already tried other things said to help, like walking, having sex, and getting acupuncture. (Maybe I should've tried them all at once.) The castor oil stimulates the bowels, putting pressure on the uterus, sometimes indirectly inducing labor in women who are ready. The only person more ready than me was my mother-in-law across the room. When the midwife explained about the cramps, explosive gas, and frequent loud trips to the bathroom, I told Jimmy we needed to find his mom another place to stay. It didn't matter that she was the best mother-in-law in the world.

The castor oil did get the baby, and other things, moving. Jimmy's mom moved into our friends' house, empty since they were visiting family over winter break. While Terri stayed there and knitted, I was in back labor that got stronger every day, but not by much. Terri went home, leaving our friends a throw she'd knitted for their couch.

I really wanted to give birth, but not at the expense of Gabriel's well-being. He was doing fine other than being sunny side up, a not-uncommon situation that makes delivery harder and more painful. Having a midwife meant that I'd been able to eat and drink and walk as needed during labor. But I wasn't sleeping at all anymore and had no more desire to eat. From backpacking and climbing, I knew how to gauge my body's fuel. Almost all my reserves were used up.

"I've got one more night left in me," I told my midwife. "What would they do first if I went into the hospital?"

"They'd break your water. I can do that here, if you want."

We tried it, and I had the strongest contractions so far, but by morning I was still only five centimeters dilated and barely effaced. Jimmy and I headed to the emergency room. There I went from a natural approach to trying almost every intervention I'd heard of. Scalp monitor for the baby. Catheter for me. Pitocin to increase contractions, which didn't work. I knew then that I'd given this mountain my best effort. What mattered now was not that I reached the top, but that Gabriel and I got down safely. The midwife sat in the room, not allowed to say anything to the doctors but there for support. I caught her eye, and she nodded. Jimmy went to get the surgeon.

Settled into my postpartum room, I could finally hold Gabriel—all nine pounds nine ounces of him. That wouldn't have been a big deal if his head hadn't been so huge and he'd been facing the right way. Not only was I too exhausted to be mad, but who could hold a grudge against a head that had such a sweet face (and my nose). He was an angel. All babies are, of course, but C-section babies avoid the smushed look that more cooperative babies have. Also, Gabriel, a name we'd chosen when he was due on December 2, had been born—er, extracted—on Christmas Eve. He was already showing his ironic sense of humor.

What an adventure we'd had. And the thing about adventures is, no matter whether they're what I had in mind or not, I learn something new about my abilities. So what if I didn't reach the summit in the manner I'd planned? It wasn't the first time. I vowed to myself not to play the *what-if* game: *What if I'd tried to labor longer? What if I'd gone to the hospital earlier?* My original approach of "leave it alone" had been adapted at the end because preserving a healthy baby was more important to me than having a natural childbirth. I felt as if I'd practiced good stewardship by reassessing my goals and letting go of my notion of ideal childbirth.

As Jimmy watched from the chair beside me, eyelids heavy, Gabriel started to nurse.

"Look at him. He's a natural," Jimmy declared.

"I don't know about that," I said, "but he's beautiful and he's here."

AGE OF ADVENTURE

Jimmy and I left Reno to move back East when he'd finished his doctorate and our son was eighteen months old. While it'd always been the plan to return to our beloved, geologically well-worn Appalachians, we'd assumed we'd head back South near his family. After Jimmy interviewed with a dozen schools, including several in the Carolinas, we ended up choosing the job at a rural Pennsylvania state university. The salary was high, the cost of living low, and he really liked the faculty in the English Department there. Set on the Allegheny Plateau, it promised trees and hills, but with fewer elevation extremes than in Western North Carolina or Reno. This rural area of Penn's Woods had lots of public land. We'd be near the Pine Creek Gorge, which locals called the Pennsylvania Grand Canyon. Here I wouldn't have to work right away and could spend time with my toddler and explore.

Backpacking pregnant in the Sierras (photo credit: Lorraine Anderson)

I kept busy settling into our big old house and the town of Mansfield, watching HGTV, choosing bold paint colors, and hunting in antique shops for quirky used furniture. I'd never lived in a small town, unless you count the raft guide outpost, and loved how easy it was to meet people. In a town of a few thousand (the university doubled the population when in session), I knew not to expect a lot of cultural options or opportunities and thought I'd be making many trips to Corning or Ithaca about an hour away in New York. But in our two-block downtown, Oswald Cycle Works and Main Street Yoga exceeded our wildest hopes. When I needed adult conversation, I walked around the corner to hang out at Night and Day Coffee Café. Everyone, it seemed, was eager to help us settle in, responding to my questions with advice, recommendations, directions, and even manual labor. Not only were the lattes better than at any chain, but Jess and her staff let Gabe toddle around in bare feet, even behind the counter. At least once a week I'd walk down to locally owned Papa V's for pizza that had terrific homemade crust with roasted eggplant and broccoli as toppings. Within a month I joined a writing group with three profs who worked with Jimmy. I was pretty happy with where we'd landed, except for one thing.

I really missed climbing, and I missed all my female friends I climbed with. I missed Jimmy too, the time I'd spent climbing with him, our conversations on the drives and hikes to crags, our sessions in the rock gym. Suddenly my world had changed from wild to domestic. I was no longer buff. Instead I had a softer, new-mama body. While I'd worked hard to earn this body too, and I appreciated it and what it accomplished even more, my sense of identity was going through some geologic shifts.

I knew there were trails in the hills around me, hills that reminded me of down South. Someone in the coffee shop would tell me about a hike and I'd go look, rarely finding it the first time. This land was mostly state forest and game land, and not well marked like the federal land I was used to. The people in Tioga County hunted and fished and had learned where to go from their grandparents. While some people wanted to market the area to outdoor tourists more, most locals seemed happy to keep things the way they were.

State parks were the happy exception. Unlike in national parks, which are meant to be superlative and therefore scarce (especially in the long-settled eastern United States), the primary value of state parks is making natural surroundings and outdoor recreation widely available. Pennsylvania excelled at this, once having a goal to establish a state park within twenty-five miles of every resident. The goal was almost met, and I had several to choose from.

Hills Creek State Park was the closest to us, only eight miles away (once I learned the back roads). When I encountered it for the first time as a mother, my frame of assessment had radically altered. Whereas a couple of years before I might have shrugged it off as scenic but tame, I excitedly called for Gabe to look out his window as we drove by the main pavilions.

"Playground!" he squealed.

These monkey bars were in much better condition than the ones near campus and sported small slides next to the big-kid ones, plenty of low-level obstacles, and two other children playing on the bright blue equipment. In that moment, it was worth a hundred Yosemites. After Gabe wore himself out, we waved goodbye and wandered down the hill to the water. In the warmth of early fall, I stripped his socks, shoes, and pants off, letting him play in the sand at the gentle edge of a lake where he couldn't suddenly tip into it and sink. Here my son had hours of free play fun while I relaxed outdoors. The trails were short enough for me to carry him, and as he grew that year, he walked more and more of their length, learning about maples and hemlocks. And we could come as often as we wanted. There was no entrance fee, unlike in the New York state parks to our north.

The Freedom Machine

Out of necessity, cycling replaced climbing as my central outdoor activity. It'd begun right after Gabe was born because Jimmy had been riding his bike more to get quicker workouts in. I'd had a mountain bike for several years but rarely rode for fun, only to get to school. Truth is, cardio activities never appealed to me as much as strength activities. My heart rate needed to get a workout while I was distracted by other things—the landscape I was hiking through, how hard I could kick a board, the most efficient angle of my kayak to wind and current. But when Jimmy started cycling more and needed to replace his old road bike, I invoked the toy equity clause of our marriage contract. He agreed to sell his pickup truck and we each got road bikes the year before leaving Reno.

Thanks to Oswald Cycle Works in town, we quickly fell into the cycling community in Mansfield. Tom Oswald had cheerfully let Jimmy store our bikes at his shop when we first arrived, so they wouldn't have to stay on the roof of our 4Runner until we could move in. His wife, Sheila, offered to take me on a two-wheel tour of back roads, paved and dirt. Soon we were going on weekly rides, and I knew the area well enough to ride by myself when I could get time away. On weekends Jimmy would put Gabe in the bike trailer and we'd do short rides.

But it was the Wednesday rides with Sheila, when Jimmy would come home early to watch Gabe, that became central to my week and sanity. Anywhere from fifteen to twenty-five hilly miles, during which I learned to ask Sheila about past adventures or ex-boyfriends right before starting a steep section, so she—who could talk while pedaling uphill—would distract me from my huffing. Soon we added Amber, a librarian Sheila worked with, to our group. Amber was younger and even newer to cycling than I was. Watching her experience the thrill of getting faster and faster going down, and eventually faster going up, I remembered my joy as a girl riding my single-speed no-handed around the curves of suburban Maryland hills, the wind whipping my helmetless head, chasing and being chased by neighborhood friends. I'd never had a ten-speed. Getting a road bike in my thirties had been mildly stressful because it seemed everyone else knew what gear to be in but me. But Frances Willard, author of *A Wheel Within a Wheel*, started riding at age fifty-three, when the bicycle craze was at its peak in the 1890s. She claimed that when she determined to take up cycling she suffered from "the impediments that result from the unnatural style of dress" and "the sedentary habits of a lifetime," in addition to the admonishments from those closest to her that she'd get hurt and jeopardize her health. Compared to her, I was neither too old nor out of shape, and I had the full support of my husband, family, and friends.

Willard was president of the Woman's Christian Temperance Union from 1879 to 1898 and worked tirelessly to advocate internationally for women's rights. But her late-in-life relationship with Gladys—the name she gave her bicycle— gave her new energy and insight into the struggle for equality. Bicycles made social mobility more accessible to women, who were less likely to be able to afford to "own, feed, and stable a horse." She immediately saw the advantages the bicycling craze gave to the effort of dress reform, observing that "reform often advances most rapidly by indirection." By linking bloomers with the practical considerations of cycling, she felt those who'd resisted the arguments of dress reformers would be wooed into accepting them first as necessary, and then as fashionable. "An ounce of practice is worth a ton of theory," she wrote. As rock climbing had done for me, learning to ride a bike provided new metaphors and skills for Willard's other endeavors. My favorite of her cycling lessons is "I will not waste my life in friction when it can be turned into momentum."

Very few, if any, women at the tail end of the Victorian era had ridden bikes as girls. But in the 1870s bikes similar to what we use now were designed, increasing stability and accessibility. Women, especially middle-class white women who'd been sheltered at home, gained new strength and mobility, whereas men gained a world changed by women whose growing sense of independence and power manifested itself throughout society. Some men saw this greater equality in a companionable light, but for many it rocked their world (think T. S. Eliot's J. Alfred Prufrock meets Edna St. Vincent Millay). At a time when the women's suffrage movement was also at its peak, Susan B. Anthony told journalist Nellie Bly that bicycling had "done more to emancipate women than anything else in the world."

Though I felt less like a New Woman—the 1890s term for those wearing bloomers, riding bikes, and advocating for the vote—and more like an old mother, cycling was a big help in transitioning into my new place, new role, and new body. It also helped me be less irritated at Jimmy, though the bicycle sure seemed more of a "freedom machine" for him, since he rode more miles and hours per week. It wasn't that I wanted to ride that many hours or miles, but the time he spent with the guys was even more time we didn't have together. In the past, I would've been climbing with them, but on a bike I couldn't keep up and, frankly, didn't want to try. He loved cycling. I enjoyed the hours away from home, roads explored, and calories burned but resented that he had something to fill the void while I stayed home with memories of days on the rocks. When I sometimes joined him and his buddies at the bar after their Wednesday night rides, I never felt fully part of the group.

Even more than I thought I disliked cardio, I thought I disliked racing. Jimmy had gotten into doing local, then regional races, with his buddies. A big barrel-chested man, he prided himself on being the slowest of the fast guys. Talking with Sheila, who projected a serene approach to competing in that she competed only with herself, I began to see the draw in signing up for these small races. They allowed her to set a goal for herself, work toward it, and then give it her all in one endorphin-filled day. It would also help me justify more time on the bike. Amber and I decided to register for the Laurel Flyer, a road race in the next town that June.

All spring we rode, first shaking off the winter lethargy and then adding miles and building endurance. Pennsylvania is very hilly—in fact it has the toughest section of the Appalachian Trail—and we'd been warned there were two doozies on the twenty-four-mile race route. Amber and I rode the route as often as we could, timing ourselves, practicing trading off who took the lead, and pulling while the other drafted close to the leader's wheel, saving energy. Our first goal was to be in shape and not crash. Amber was in her early twenties and I was in my late thirties, different brackets. So we weren't competing with each other, and her company made the training fun.

Cycling helped me with all the changes my body had been going through—losing baby weight and getting back into shape, then adjusting to less activity and maintaining sanity postpartum. I breastfed Gabe exclusively for six months and continued to nurse him as he ate and gained language skills. Once when heading to breakfast at Grammas' Kitchen with Sheila and Amber, both vegetarians, I asked Gabe what he was going to eat, knowing his response.

"Bacon!" he yelled.

Sheila had told me vegetarians tend to miss bacon most of all, so they knew I was taunting them. Being from North Carolina, we had a family allegiance to pork.

"You're a boy made of pig," I told Gabe.

"No," he said back. "I'm a boy made of boob!"

We all laughed at that one. I was pretty proud to have beat out pig for the number one spot.

In addition to the effects of nursing—scrambled brain, always hungry—I was having heavier, crampier periods than ever. I'd never been uncomfortable before, just moody. This was worrying me because the Laurel Flyer would fall right at that time of the month. After doing some reading and talking to other mothers, I thought maybe the changes were caused by my copper IUD. Jimmy and I had recently begun talking about trying for the next and last baby after summer. Because of how long it'd taken me to get pregnant with Gabe, and because I knew I might get relief from monthly pain, I had my IUD taken out. My body quickly settled into familiar patterns, the pain was gone, and I no longer worried how I'd feel on race day.

You know where this is going. I began to suspect over Memorial Day weekend, but when my period didn't come the following week I broke the news to Jimmy that I'd be racing for two. Given our experience with miscarriages, the only other person I told was Amber in case something happened during the race.

Race day dawned clear with perfect weather—chilly high fifties starting out, warming to high sixties. My only real concern had been overheating, which I tend to do even when not pregnant. I made sure I'd drunk lots of water the day before. Rather than race this time, Jimmy was volunteering as a course marshal and cheering me on.

He pinned the number on my jersey and kissed me. "Good luck. Ride hard. Have fun."

I coasted up next to Amber on the runway of the small airport outside Wellsboro. It was a fun start as riders streamed down for takeoff onto Route 660 heading toward the canyon. We let riders zoom past, neither of us comfortable in a pack of more than three. The roads weren't closed to traffic but there were signs alerting drivers.

"Car back," I yelled to Amber ahead. After a couple of minutes I couldn't figure out why it wasn't passing. Then it dawned on me it was what some called a broom wagon, sweeping the race course. I laughed. "We're last," I hollered up.

In the end, I placed third in my gender and age. Apparently there were three women racing in that bracket, because only

Amber and a man in black jean shorts finished behind me. None of that mattered. The endorphin rush added to my burgeoning pregnancy glow.

As with climbing, when I'd broken into a new level of bouldering right when I got pregnant with my son and then lost my edge, my cycling endeavors hit a high right as I got pregnant again. The low came soon after, when we drove back West that summer to visit friends. At two months pregnant I went mountain biking in Boulder, Colorado. After climbing a winding hill, my friends were told the trail we wanted was closed for a race, so we turned around. I was last as we descended and thought how much nicer bumpy downhills felt on my new full-suspension bike. I got overconfident, picked up too much speed, drifted to the outside, and when a curve came clenched the brakes to avoid heading over the drop. In addition to full suspension, this was my first bike with disc brakes, which grab at the slightest pressure. When I sat up, my jersey was torn, my shoulder ached, and my bike was behind me on the ground facing uphill. We'd both done somersaults. I wished my friends had seen what must've been a spectacular crash, but there was no one around. I twisted the brake and gear levers into more-or-less correct positions and rode back. The EMT on-site for the race checked me over and assured me my collarbone wasn't broken. Well cushioned and bean sized, the baby was fine. Still, I decided to ride only paved surfaces after that.

Light Enough to Live

Gloria was born in February, and because of the long, snowy winter and another C-section, my fitness level plummeted again. With a toddler and baby at home, Jimmy at work, and my bike in the garage, the baby blues crept up on me. We lived at a latitude where, regardless of how much I was outdoors in winter, the sun was at an angle where no vitamin D would be delivered, and I didn't yet know I should be taking a supplement. I was ill equipped to cope with cooking, laundry (we used cloth diapers), and many hours of what came to feel like house arrest, let alone face the threat of climate change.

This was 2007, when *An Inconvenient Truth* won the Oscar for best documentary and created a tsunami in mainstream climate awareness. It was a year before 350, the group that began organizing the global climate movement, would be established, but I'd long been aware of the threat formerly known as global warming. I'd heard Bill McKibben speak and had read his books in graduate school. Now in my hormonal sleep-deprived state, I became consumed by anxiety. The crux came when Jimmy, the kids, and I went to an environmental humanities conference that June. With Gloria at my breast, I listened to the new Intergovernmental Panel on Climate Change report and winced as people argued over what could or should be done. An author I loved stood before a packed room and mourned while blaming the audience of academics for talking and doing nothing. Or not enough, at least. I looked down at Gloria sleeping in my arms, the light fuzz of hair with its fleeting reddish tint, and wondered why she'd been born.

I'd heard paddling stories of kayakers getting pinned against rocks, the water's force keeping the boat in place and the kayaker unable to pop the skirt and escape. If there was an air pocket, the paddler could sometimes signal to friends attempting water rescue that he or she was okay. Sometimes rescues were successful, and sometimes the arm that had waved every few minutes stopped breaking the surface. The panic I felt reminded me of those stories. Time was running out.

I went home after that conference to my small town and created an air pocket. I told Jimmy not to talk to me about current events or politics, and to please not listen to NPR where I could hear. I got involved at the grassroots level helping start a local growers market at our church. I made a bigger effort to get outdoors, even if I couldn't be as active as before. Sitting by the creek nursing Gloria while Gabe threw rocks, I concentrated on the sound of water over stones mixing with my toddler's giggles, the starfighter flight of the kingfisher zooming down the river's length, and the pale pink fireworks from mountain laurel on the far bank.

Lying awake at night after Gloria fell back asleep, I ached to be able to talk to my parents about this. Having died before Jimmy and I married, they hadn't been around for the parenting part of my life, and, while I'd missed sharing the joys of raising my children with them, I'd never before wished for their advice. But now I wanted to know what they'd tell me to do, how to raise kids in a time of climate change. I imagined sitting at the kitchen table and asking them, their faces sad and uncertain as I related to them as fellow parents for the first time. I realized they'd be as lost as I was.

We visited my Aunt Gloria in Cape Cod several times in my kids' early years, loving her company and house, her lush gardens, and the bay within an easy stroller stroll. I'd rediscovered this relative when I was young and single, though when I was a child, her sternness had intimidated me. As I grew into a young woman, her frankness and approach to life in advanced age, which combined fearlessness with personal uncertainty, captured my heart. After my parents died, she became my wise elder. Upon hearing we were naming our daughter after her, she commented in her Yankee manner, "I never liked my name. Perhaps this will help me appreciate it."

In the morning light on that eastern tip of the country, Jimmy and I would sit with Aunt Gloria with our sections of the *New York Times* and yogurt with blueberries discussing 9/11, climate change, and celebrities' appallingly bad choices in art and love. Then we'd pack the kids up and head to the bay, the marsh, or the ocean—anywhere Gabe could throw rocks, hunt shells, or get his feet wet.

We swapped recommendations of authors and books, and on the first visit when we brought baby Gloria, my aunt gave me a book of essays by Adam Gopnik, a writer for the *New Yorker*, a magazine stacked in every corner of her house. He wrote of living in New York City with small children post-9/11, and his anxiety over what decisions to make for his family— stay or go? Would any decision make a difference? He was not talking about climate change, but his struggle resonated with me and I grasped onto these words: "The real question that pressed itself upon us as parents was how to let our children live in joy in a time of fear, how to give light enough to live in when what we saw were so many shadows."

Being outdoors was literally and metaphorically where I found light enough at any time. But my usual activities needed some adjusting, at least for the next five to ten years. Not just once, but constantly because kids change so rapidly, with what they can and like to do fluctuating at a speed mathematically impossible to calculate. After Gabe was born we'd packed the baby up into the granite cliffs, handing him off to whomever wasn't climbing. But soon he'd gotten wiggly, and then he'd wanted to crawl, and none of that was a good idea several stories above what might be considered ground. So the climbing outdoors stopped.

We wanted to hike with our children, but Jimmy and I agreed there would be no forced marches, no too-cold outings. So early hikes were short, with few calories burned and few endorphins released. Cycling offered more of a workout. With child number two, I became the one towing the trailer because Gabe rode on the awkward tagalong attached to Jimmy's bike, like a shrunken back half of a tandem. While I often took the trailer and baby out riding when Gabe was in preschool, I stuck close on the paved bike trail.

Friends from Reno, we found out, had ended up in Philadelphia, only four hours away, and now had two kids as well. When John suggested we meet at an equally distant state park for a family camping trip, we packed enthusiastically. We'd gotten a huge Taj Ma-Tent and took the exersaucer for Gloria. I didn't want her on the ground or always on my lap, so the plastic object in bright primary colors sat in the midst of our rustic campsite like a Looney Tunes character swallowing my daughter. Meanwhile, the three older children played and read books to each other, and the parents drank and discussed books and children.

With the kids tucked into tents, Jimmy and I admitted how frazzled we were, something we grinned and glossed over in public but were frustrated and embarrassed by in private. With Gabe, raising a baby had been fairly easy, at least in hindsight. That night our friends made a wonderful, soul-saving admission for which I'll always be grateful. In my mind I see them leaning across the picnic table in the light of the campfire and saying simultaneously: *Having two kids is not just double the work of one child. It gets easier as they get older, but in the beginning all you can do is hunker down and get through it.*

The next day we walked over to the lake. It was Gloria's first time playing in sand. Sitting with her as she laughed at the scratchiness against her feet, at the dogs running by, at her brother and Daddy playing in the water, I vowed to myself that I'd let go of my restless itch to do more of what I used to do and look for new opportunities. One of the aspects of parenting I'd looked forward to most was sharing my love of the outdoors and exploring new places with my children. I couldn't skip over this first stage in their lives and get right to teaching them to belay, no matter how eager we were for our kids to turn into "rope guns"—stronger climbers who'd set the rope for us old farts so we could keep climbing forever.

It wasn't only physical abilities I wanted to teach my kids, but the enjoyment and wonder that the land brings me. Those were life skills as important as looking both ways before crossing the street. No parent ever knows what the future holds, but I could do my best to give my kids a love of the world and ways to entertain themselves that didn't require electricity. If we had to hunker down, we'd hunker outdoors as much as possible.

In Gloria's first few years we spent a lot of time at a friend's farm and garden, where my kids could watch the chickens and cats while learning where food came from. I helped Kathleen England run her co-op at Glenfiddich Farm in exchange for veggies and eggs each week. At first, I looked blankly around at all the green foliage in the area Kathleen had pointed to when she directed me to "dig up some potatoes." Which of these bursts of stems and leaves had potatoes beneath them? My suburban childhood had not prepared me. By the end of the season I could identify everything she grew—even when in other people's gardens. Knowing how to grow and harvest food gave me a different type of connection to the earth. From spring peepers to potatoes, beech trees to butternut squash, my kids knew the earth more intimately than I had at their age.

Jimmy continued to go on several long bike rides a week with his buddies, but I lacked motivation to get into real cycling shape now that my Wednesday afternoon "girls'" rides were no more. Amber had moved to Vermont before Gloria was born, and Sheila had started a new job over three hours away, coming home on weekends. While I had friends who were writers, mothers, and artists who nurtured me in many ways, most of them worked. I didn't have many who'd suggest outdoor activities, and they worked during the day when I was free. I envied the mothers I knew (seemingly almost all of them) with parents or in-laws close who took the kids so they'd get time with their husbands. I enjoyed biking with Jimmy, even though I'd been getting slower as he'd been getting faster, but rides together were rare. He was a new prof focused on publishing and teaching, needed to pedal hard to blow off the stress, and had lots of buddies to go with and lots of races to train for. While one of the benefits of cycling, as opposed to climbing, is it's easy to do by yourself, I never found it that fun alone.

Accidents of Geography

One thing I've realized at midlife is how much my body image is affected by geography. Partially it's because the terrain and outdoor activities available shape certain muscles while ignoring others, and the length of winter affects how often I'm outdoors. But it's also context. When feeling stuck in the house as a young mother, I compared myself to friends out West who climbed, skied, and hiked at high elevations, and I felt out of shape. But most of those friends were like us and put off starting their families until they were in their thirties because of extended studies or adventures, so I felt younger around them. In rural Pennsylvania I suddenly felt old sitting around the table at PTA meetings. Mothers my age had teenagers. People married their high school sweethearts and were grandparents in their forties. The bright side was, in comparison I felt fit and strong.

I try not to compare myself to others but falter regularly. Once I recognized how fickle my perceptions were, it helped me let go of preconceptions. I mean, no matter what shape I'm in I can find comparisons to make me feel better or worse. Back when my kids were toddlers, I was acutely aware of how out of shape I was compared to what I'd been. But now I'd love to be the shape and size I was in those early years of motherhood, have that metabolism back. Yet I'm often more content with my body now than at any previous point in my life. Geography— the land outside and the personal fleshy kind—pushes us to accept what we cannot change. The best way I've found to do that is through play.

In retrospect, while I was focusing on my fitness level or body image when the kids were tiny, the real issue was the lack of women where I lived who would backpack, climb, and paddle with me. (They were there somewhere, I'm sure.) I didn't know anyone in Pennsylvania who'd say, "Let's throw the kids and some sleeping bags in the car and meet at the Asaph campground. You bring the gin and root beer and I'll bring the pizza and doughnuts." The friends who'd say that were in North Carolina and Nevada. Our camping friends near Philly moved out West the next year. It would've been nice if Jimmy had wanted to camp more, but he worked full time, helped with dishes and diapers, and was more interested in training for races in his leisure time.

When Gabe was five, Mike Reed invited us to a cookout. "It's just the family," he said, "but we head a half mile up into the back of our property on a hill where we have a fire ring and I set up a telescope. You guys can camp out if you want." Mike was a father of four and loaned us a kid's backpack that his youngest had outgrown. It was an external frame, and probably still too big for Gabe, but I told Mike we'd hike rather than drive. Jimmy agreed to meet us at the campfire after work and take Gloria home with him so Gabe and I could camp out.

I didn't need to pack much, and Gabe carried only a small sleeping bag (also loaned by Mike) and a few stuffed animals and books he chose. I carried a tarp and ground cloth, sleeping bag and pad, granola bars, water, and Gloria. I held her in the front and followed behind my slow but determined son. Mike found a good walking stick Gabriel's size, and the photos Mike took of us laden and trudging up the hill are some of my most treasured. They capture a day I made the effort and took the time. The campfire was great, and I kissed Gloria goodnight before Jimmy carried her downhill to the car and home. Waking up with Gabe and the sun the next morning, watching spiders walk on dew-tipped grasses and then across the tarp ceiling, peeing in the woods together—these were the experiences I wanted my son to remember. The mother I wanted him to know. The mother I wanted to be.

Soon Mike and his family moved away. I started night hiking with my friend Jackie Schlitzer, who worked at the coffee shop and helped me run the growers market. Night hikes were easy to schedule because the kids were asleep and Jimmy was home then (as long as we didn't go on his bike night). In her, I found a cycling buddy again. Jackie and her husband, Tim, would also invite all of us sledding near their cabin on the edge of the Tioga State Forest. They loved the woods and kids. When Gabe was in preschool I asked whether he had a girlfriend. "Jackie," he'd said.

Jackie liked trail running and did fifty-mile and longer races. I asked whether she'd help me take the kids on the nearby Ives Run Trail Challenge the year Gloria was four and Gabe was seven. I knew he'd want to go faster than his sister. Gloria was upset to learn that Jackie would be with her brother, so Jackie assured her that she'd turn around and come back and find us on the four-mile trail, after she and Gabe crossed the finish line. If there was a scout badge for patience, I earned it that day. So did the volunteers who stayed around so much later than they'd planned while waiting for us. Gloria and I sang to the fairies as we passed fairy homes in the rocks and tree trunks. We made up songs about adventure girls. I promised three more gummy fish once she climbed the next hill. Jackie met us with a mile and a half left, and Gloria took her hand with new energy. Then she took the hand of the last volunteer we saw and towed him along with her for the final loop. It was a fabulous day.

Then Jackie and Tim moved away.

Where I lived I had easy access to woods, trails, lakes, and creeks. So why was it so hard for me to find women to explore outdoors with? I could have tried harder, prioritized it more. Partly I let myself be caught up in what I'd been raised to think should be a mother's focus—cooking, volunteer work, creating a comfy and beautiful home. (Notice I didn't say cleaning.) I could have asked Jimmy to take time to go camping. Packing for a family for a night under the stars seemed like too much work by myself. It was clear Jimmy didn't want to do the things the kids and I could do as much as he wanted to ride his bike with the guys, so I stopped asking. It'd been easy when we were both in shape, had time, and enjoyed the same activities. Now, not so much. A layer of irritation with the world would build up underneath my happy multitasking exterior, an edge that Jimmy got the brunt of when I began feeling cooped up.

I wasn't unusual in this. According to the US Bureau of Labor Statistics in 2005, when Gabe was two years old, women leisured 11 percent less than men and spent only 53 percent as much time as men at recreational sports and exercise. This is not the same as saying women had less free time. Free time can include commuting, taking kids or elderly parents to appointments and activities, volunteer obligations, and other necessary chores that don't fall under subsistence time (economic requirements) or existence time (biological requirements). Leisure time is the part of free time someone spends on voluntary activities they do for sheer enjoyment.

Unemployed mothers in 2003–2006 spent thirty minutes more doing leisure activities than employed fathers. But working mothers spent almost an hour less on leisure than their working husbands, and mothers who worked part time spent 3.4 hours on leisure while their husbands working full time found 3.6 hours to do what they wanted. Every couple's situation is different. Being a stay-at-home mom certainly gave me more free time than Jimmy. Yet my lack of female friends who could recreate while the kids were in preschool (before I had to cook dinner) meant I had to cycle or hike alone. So I didn't do it as much as I could have.

Finding a group to help me connect would've been a place to start. Now, even if there aren't local ones, there are online ones. The Adventure Mamas, a recent nonprofit initiative, is intent on "redefining motherhood" so that outdoor adventure is included. They recognize that many women give up this aspect of themselves when becoming mothers—a time when they may need the wild most of all. They weren't around when I became a mother, but discovering their website now when my kids are old enough to wipe their bottoms and brush their teeth—even toast and butter their own bagels—I still feel a wave of gratitude as I read their mission to "enhance . . . women's health by facilitating adventure. . . . We believe that spending time in wild places is more than a selfish luxury, it should be available to all." Mothers of all backgrounds, including teen moms and those of children with special needs, can get connected to resources and opportunities online.

In an article on their blog about camping during postpartum depression, Mary Beth Burgstahler wrote, "I immediately began to recognize my soul again." This reminded me of the Sam Keen quote that guided my priorities when I was a twenty-something raft guide: "Warning: Be careful what you spend your day touching." Even though I wasn't climbing, paddling, or backpacking regularly—or hiking in the iconic Sierras—I could still touch natural beauty and visit wild places. My peace resurfaced when deep in the Pennsylvania forests, released from walls and a daily schedule, and put me back in my place. Each time it would surprise me that I'd forgotten or denied how essential this was. As essential to me as writing. I blamed my geography—the lack of granite rock faces, limestone boulders, and women I'd known out West—for my lack of outdoor opportunities. In the past I'd lucked into easy access to places and people that fed my soul. It was now important for me to learn how to create such relationships and opportunities when the access wasn't easy.

Some women get right back outdoors after pregnancy, especially those who worked or competed before having children. Mothers who enjoy outdoor adventure and the danger that may accompany it are often judged as selfish or reckless. I was not doing anything labeled extreme by outdoor magazines, but even just going for a three-day tenth-anniversary climbing trip with Jimmy caused strong reactions about the risks involved with a two- and five-year-old at home. To us, the low level at which we were climbing made their concern laughable, but many people unfamiliar with the sport couldn't see that the risks weren't any greater than those of driving a car. Many women who become mothers continue to alpine climb, surf big waves, ski steep remote slopes, fight wildfires, and more. And why shouldn't they?

"If a woman is brilliant in a profession that is dangerous and she becomes a mother, how old do her children have to be before it is acceptable for her to return to work?" asks Josie Barnard in her article about the criticism Alison Hargreaves's husband faced after she died descending the summit of K2. Their children were four and six. Just three months earlier, in 1995, Hargreaves had been widely praised after becoming the first woman to summit Everest without Sherpa support or oxygen tanks. Overnight she went from one of the greatest climbers to a bad mother who left her children. And James Ballard, her grieving husband, became the bad father who let her. "I loved her because she wanted to climb the highest peak," he said. "That's who she was."

According to *Outside* magazine, "the most successful female Everest climber of all time is a housekeeper in Hartford, Connecticut." In May 2017, Lhakpa Sherpa, a native of Nepal, summited Everest for the eighth time. One summit was only eight months after the birth of her first daughter. She climbed Everest again when two months pregnant with her second daughter. Before her seventh summit, Lhakpa hadn't climbed for ten years while she concentrated on getting out of her abusive marriage, learning to drive and read and write, and earning enough to support her children by working as a housekeeper and 7-Eleven cashier. Climbing Everest seems almost easy compared to that.

I can't say exactly how children raised by adventurous women will shape cultural views of motherhood, but I suspect we'll see the effects soon. In a culture that's starting to highlight how nurturing, tenderness, and physical affection aren't parenting traits exclusive to mothers, I look forward to greater awareness that courage, strength, and carefully assessed risk taking aren't behaviors we learn only from our fathers. Devi Lockwood is in her twenties now and remembers missing her mother, who climbed mountains in the Himalayas, and fearing for her safety. In a wonderful piece in the *New York Times*, Lockwood describes how she grew up hating mountains but understood that her mother found healing and solace in climbing. Her mother never made Devi climb mountains, but on Devi's eighteenth birthday her mother surprised her with an urban adventure. They snuck into the Small Dome at MIT, which her mother had attended, and out onto the roof. There her mother clasped her hands to boost Devi onto the dome, to climb to the top as she'd done back in her college years. "I realized that my mother's example has allowed me to be a female adventurer of a different sort," Devi writes. "I didn't become a mountain climber, but for the last two years I have been traveling mostly by bicycle in the United States, Fiji, Tuvalu, New Zealand, Australia, Thailand, Laos and Cambodia. I'm halfway through a project to collect 1,001 stories about water and climate change from people I meet."

As for James Ballard, while the media scolded him for supporting his wife in her mountaineering aspirations, he received letters from mothers whose offspring had grown and left, saying they regretted focusing only on their children and appreciated Alison's ambition and his support of it. He has remained committed to raising his children to be adventurous, as he and Alison had planned to do together.

Off the Couch and into the Classroom

When Gloria was four, I wanted to go back to teaching part time, but the English Department didn't need me. However, the Geography Department had started a concentration in outdoor recreation leadership and needed some classes covered. Though my degrees weren't in this field, my practical experience outdoors and leading trips, combined with my environmental studies background and years of teaching, prompted the chair to offer me the opportunity. Unlike programs in small private schools or large universities, this program wasn't focused around expedition semesters. Our students couldn't have afforded the extra fees for trips and wanted year-round employment after graduation, so we made sure they had a strong geoscience base. Accepting the job meant committing to being outdoors more and rebuilding this part of my identity and self-esteem. This scared me a bit. Was I still that person? Ultimately, the chance to use my experiences and perspective to shape future outdoor leaders motivated me past my insecurities.

Pennsylvania was different from the places I'd done most of my outdoor recreation. In Western North Carolina and Reno, outdoor pursuits like whitewater paddling, rock climbing, and mountain biking were popular and shaped the identity of those places and people. In Pennsylvania, traditional outdoor recreation like hunting and fishing were still top dog. Popular outdoor activities here usually involved motors—off-road vehicles, motorboats, snowmobiles, RVs. This meant the students I had in classes had a much different background than I'd had. They weren't suburban kids out of touch with wild spaces. They had hunting camps they'd grown up going to. They got out of school right after Thanksgiving for the opening day of deer season. My classroom of upper-level students in Leading Outdoor Trips was one-third females—more than I'd expected. They'd shot guns and bows, caught fish, and tromped around the woods in winter. But most hadn't backpacked or pooped outdoors. Same with many of the guys.

The first day in class I looked out at students who wore camouflage instead of fleece, Cabela's instead of Patagonia. Two men were my age. One was an army veteran in the back row who took one look at me and said loud enough for others to hear (but not me), "She can't teach *me* anything." The other man had done adventure races across deserts in several countries. He had a stuff sack full of outdoor experience and could've challenged my authority but never did. Instead, Rolf volunteered stories to illustrate risk assessment scenarios and backed me up on the importance of soft skills (communication, planning and preparation, and teamwork) in addition to hard skills (paddling, route finding, making an emergency shelter). He demonstrated that the best leaders know they can always learn more.

When some guys started squirming in their seats as I addressed how bathroom issues affect female comfort and risk perception outdoors, Rolf nodded. He raised his hand and launched into detailed descriptions of all the eco-friendly menstrual products his wife used, and how she cared for them and herself in the wilderness. Then we tromped out of Belknap

Hall and got in a circle on the grass. I showed them how to squat correctly, feet flat and wide apart, and then they stayed there while I explained why this was the best poop position in general and best pee position for females. They waved as their friends walked or drove by. Dropping all the way down allows the thigh muscles to relax, and it's a position most people can hold more comfortably. Leaning against a rock behind or holding on to a tree in front can help. Fear of splashing them-selves—which can be visible when you return to the group—can keep some females from long hikes or overnights. Freud, I tell my students, had it all wrong. Women don't have penis envy, we have piss envy.

To this day my favorite role-playing scenario is when one male student is told he's taking a group of middle schoolers on an all-day hike. He's the only leader and they've stopped for lunch. One student, playing a kid, says he has to poop. Once the leader has addressed that, another student, a girl, tells him she just got her period. It's her first time. What does she do? The first year I did this the leader panicked, turned bright red, and squealed, "I DON'T KNOW!" Another year the leader put on a brave face and said, "It's my first time too!" When he handed her a tampon from the first aid kit, she asked how to use it. What a beautiful moment it was, watching all the guys in the class realize how much they had to learn.

Unlike the upper-level course, the introductory class met general education requirements and attracted students with all sorts of majors in addition to outdoor recreation leadership. The classes were larger and teaching less interactive, but I especially enjoyed the section on the history of outdoor recreation in America. Few of these students had been out West or had a sense of the vast and various public parks and forests that were technically theirs. I told them the story of how our concept of wilderness started as the endless and terrifying enemy the settlers pitted themselves against (space that was thought of as empty of humans when of course it was not), then became the force that shaped our unique American spirit and rugged individualism, next became the salve that could save our souls corrupted by industrialism, and finally became the natural resources and biodiversity that need conserving lest we run out and find ourselves without a creek, canoe, or paddle. The history of outdoor recreation, I realized in an embarrassingly obvious epiphany, was inextricably entwined with the history of conservation. I drilled this symbiotic relationship into their heads as if I'd known it all my life.

Other than Rachel Carson, individual women weren't mentioned in this section of the textbook, though consideration was given to gender as well as cultural background in the chapter on factors affecting outdoor recreation participation. Good thing I was there to tell them stories of women climbing in the 1800s and thru-hiking the Appalachian Trail in the 1950s. Then one day while discussing why African Americans were the group with the lowest participation rate in outdoor activities, I looked out over the rows of faces in front of me, homing in on the dark ones sprinkled among the white, and thought: what about the stories of people they can relate to? That will inspire them?

Thanks to James Edward Mills, we needed to search only a little to discover many such people: Matthew Henson, who trekked to the North Pole with Robert Peary in 1909; the Buffalo Soldiers, who were the guardians and caretakers of our national parks before there was a park service; Shelton Johnson, who has been a ranger in Yosemite National Park since 1981; and Sophia Danenberg, the first African American to summit Mount Everest. Mills, a black man who has worked in the outdoor industry as a journalist and guide, wrote *The Adventure Gap* in 2014, a book full of historical and contemporary examples of diversity in outdoor adventure. I nodded in agreement over his description of how "the social cues that define the unwritten sets of expectations we have for what people of a certain racial or ethnic background are supposed to do" have created extra barriers for people of color to navigate when recreating outdoors. I wanted to buy this guy a beer and swap stories. His words echoed the ways gender roles and their expectations have made it harder for women, especially women of color and those whose sexual orientation or gender identity does not fit the mainstream notion of what "normal" is.

If the wilderness is, as many historians claim, a key factor in what shaped the American spirit, cultural images have given the impression that only whites have that American spirit—especially straight white males. By going outdoors to engage in activities that challenge and delight us, all of us who aren't straight white males are quietly affirming our place in the land, celebrating the gift of freedom, and asserting that the land and freedom belong to all of us equally. This is not just personal and political empowerment. It is, I hope, a coming together to realize we all depend on the diversity and health of the same biological orb. And we need to work together to face the environmental justice challenges ahead.

In 2010 Oprah Winfrey and Gayle King went camping in Yosemite after being invited by Ranger Shelton Johnson. He wrote, "I need your help spreading the word that the national parks really are America's best idea, and that this beauty belongs to every American, including African-Americans." Rue Mapp, founder of Outdoor Afro, a nonprofit that helps people of color gain access to outdoor recreation, was also thrilled by the media stunt. "Oprah getting out there camping as an African-American woman is showing that it's possible. And that opening is what we need." Mapp emphasizes that mothers of all types need to be encouraged outdoors because they set the leisure-time agendas for their families. If they aren't into it at least a little, then we've lost the next generation of mountain climbers and conservationists. Outdoor Afro holds about sixty-five events a month across the country, each guided by a thoroughly vetted ambassador; twenty-four thousand people attend them annually.

Since long before online communities, the college years have been when people often get their first experience of outdoor recreation. It's when I got a taste of the adventure lying beyond the suburban green spaces or national park parking lots I'd explored as a kid. When I became a professor, it was important for me to get students in contact with the state parks and trail systems. Building on the mountain bikes the university bought for students to use, I encouraged the campus recreation center to buy some tents and other camping gear. I assigned students to go to a new public outdoor area or try a new outdoor recreation activity and write about it. There were those who grumbled the whole way through, but more often they thanked me.

As I was creating opportunities for my students, I recommitted to creating opportunities for my family. But still we rarely camped. I started planning beach camping trips, maybe because in the summer I had the time to pack and unpack all the gear required to rough it or because I grew up going to the shore when school was out. We first went to a state park campground in Delaware, but the sites were too close together and people too loud, too late. The bathhouse was infested with hair dryers and curling irons. The next August we headed to Assateague Island National Seashore in Maryland. The sites were far apart and had no electricity. There was a water spigot, an outdoor shower for rinsing off sand, and a composting outhouse with space to change clothes. Wild ponies clomped through every day, like teenage boys after school looking for something to eat. With the two-room Taj-Ma-Tent still going strong and a new screened tent for over the picnic table, we were comfy critters. If it rained we could go walk the Ocean City boardwalk, look at the shops, and eat out. The one day we did, our son hated it and begged us not to make him go back to those crowds. He and his sister were happiest digging and sculpting sand, finding shells, jumping waves, and chasing ghost crabs in the twilight. They'd each taken to swimming faster than bike riding—the opposite of me. While we never let them in the water without us, they enjoyed a freedom they wouldn't have had at a crowded beach or more developed campground. And Jimmy and I relaxed while the sun burned off the effects of six months of Tioga County winter.

Looking down at my snow-white legs and brown tankini, chosen for coverage and easy peeing, I considered the ways I'd been taught to view my body. I hadn't gone to the beach much since my early twenties in Southern California. Then I'd been fit, though not very curvy, and had overcome the self-consciousness I'd had at thirteen in my first teal-and-purple-striped bikini, the one Mom bought me even though Dad disapproved. That had been on a beach just north of where I now watched my children play. When I was a young girl-turning-woman, beaches had been the epitome of a space where women's bodies were most visible, and comparing them was as much a national pastime as baseball. The *Sports Illustrated* annual swimsuit issue represents the apex of this. Obviously women's bodies were in competition with each other. What other message could I have gotten?

But lying on the beach in my forties, I considered how important it was to our culture and economy that women loathe their bodies and shop until they drop. Like background noise, the message hums that females are never as good as males, that they always need fixing or bettering. Advertising magnifies this, especially when it comes to beauty products. According to a 2013 study, the average woman spends $15,000 on makeup in her lifetime. It's estimated that the global beauty business—worth $382 billion—has a consumer base that's 85 percent women. I'm not saying burn your blusher, but recognize that this industry's bottom line depends on making women feel crappy about themselves.

Ever since well-off white women in Victorian times were granted greater public mobility and were able to venture out to department stores, women have remained the largest consumer group. I went to the mall daily in high school because it was the only place to hang out. Overconsumption is an ecological issue, and so is the way women are taught to hate our bodies. How we treat our bodies is how we treat the land because, hey, humans *are* nature. And it's a political issue because if women are focused on shopping, beautifying ourselves, and comparing ourselves to other women, we have less time and energy to meddle in the male sphere of business and government. And for those women who do enter that sphere, their appearance and age are commented on more than their ideas and policies.

Spending a week at the barrier island, camping with no mirrors, helped me reconnect with the beach as a wild space and forget the cultural connotations it'd always carried. Afterward I was psyched up for another year of teaching and cold weather. I love four seasons and had gone a little nuts every fall in Reno, where all I got were some yellow cottonwoods and aspens. Falls in Pennsylvania were fabulous. But the winters in Mansfield were about two months too long and often very gray. One winter when our oldest had hit double digits, Jimmy surprised me by bringing up something I thought I'd heard the last of when we'd left the Mountain West: ice climbing. Surely our mountaineering attempt on Mount Shasta had satisfied the cold-climbing urge. That type of adventure hadn't been seriously discussed again. Apparently Jimmy had only put it to rest temporarily because of the need to raise little ones and concentrate on progressively harder studies as he earned his doctorate, then tenure. But now the monster with icicle fangs was back. Was that drool or deadly ice melt dripping down?

I knew Jimmy had wanted to try ice climbing back then. It's like rock climbing because you are roped and on belay on steep climbs, but like mountaineering in that it's cold, you wear plastic boots with metal crampons, and since you can't grab with gloved hands you use small ice axes in each hand to hack your way up. When we'd watched videos of Alex Lowe climbing pillars of ice in Colorado, I admit it'd looked technically interesting. But also really, really stupid. I thought then of how my dog Allie had acted when she'd first seen a familiar pond frozen over. She'd stopped abruptly at the edge while her Labrador buddy had run onto it full speed to fetch the stick. I saw the look on Allie's face. That's the way I felt. What fool climbs—not just walks or skates but *climbs*—on something that was once liquid and will be again? Sure there are anchors for the ropes—*in the ice*. To me that seemed like anchoring a boat to a whale. Plus ice climbing is cold.

But dreams don't die easily (unlike people, I reminded Jimmy), and with the plastic boots and crampons from our Shasta venture, Jimmy went out with Ben. He borrowed Ben's ice tools for chopping his way up and came home ruddy cheeked and hooked. As he described it, I realized that ice climbing where they went was nothing like what I'd seen in videos, but shorter and sometimes less than vertical. "Ben will take you out one day while I watch the kids," Jimmy offered. I rolled my eyes and continued making dinner.

A couple of times out was all it took before Jimmy ordered a pair of ice tools. It was like a pointy gauntlet flung at the ice of my resolve. Maybe my spirit of adventure was awakened in its lair, ready to face down the monster with icicle fangs. Or maybe it was offended by this violation of the toy equity clause in our marriage contract. In any case, the next year I announced, "Can you be home with the kids Saturday? I want to go ice climbing with Chris." Chris was the father of our kids' good friends, and our families had been hiking and biking and roasting marshmallows together for a couple of years. A Navajo, Chris was one of the few people I'd let teach Gabe how to shoot. Marilyn was a mother who liked a lot of things I liked (wine, beer, campfires) and who'd take the kids outdoors by herself. Always looking for a chance to go ice climbing when the conditions were right, Chris had been out the weekend before and it'd been perfect. He needed a belayer so he could go again, and Marilyn wasn't into it. On a whim and a prayer I agreed.

When Saturday turned out to be sunny and up in the midthirties, I was thrilled. Hiking in from the road to Colton Point State Park over trailless slopes down to where we couldn't help but meet the creek, I relaxed. I was warm! The little-used road disappeared behind us and I enjoyed the quiet as I hustled to keep up with Chris, our boot crunch the only sound. Sparkles between tree trunks below announced the creek was in sight. Closer in, my breath stuck in my chest. Water flowed under, over, and through ice and roots where they met. Chunks had broken off in the middle of the stream in the widest places, their edges pebbled by the creek, gleaming strings of large pearls. We walked carefully, our plastic boots ready to protect us from a wet step, but more likely to cause one because they were heavy. I kept stopping to look around, feeling the way I did when I'd peek under creek rocks and catch sight of a salamander. These gifts were there if I'd take the time and effort to look.

Chris took his pack off at the top of the waterfall and set up an anchor using trees. Ah, dependable trees! He rappelled down first. It was only twenty or thirty feet. "Half the waterfall has melted," he called. "Last week it was frozen solid all the way across."

Once I was at the bottom, he showed me the chopping

stroke, and what sound meant good ice, and what meant I should reposition. Trusting the toe points of my crampons and pulling on my ice tools, having faith they wouldn't pop out, reminded me of first learning to climb. So much of success is about belief. I belayed him as he climbed. Though I was chilly standing in one place for a while, it was nothing to the cold I'd felt belaying Jimmy one spring morning on a west-facing wall in Tuolumne Meadows when, standing in the shade, I'd verged on hypothermic. This time I was dressed warmly, protected from the wind, and had thick gloves. When Chris had me on belay from above, I started across and up. Slowly I experimented and soon felt confident in my placement of feet and hands, crampons and ice tools. At the top Chris grinned as if to say "I told you you'd love it." And I did. It wasn't the dumb macho activity I'd thought it was. It brought me to this stunning landscape that was so close to where I lived but had never ventured out to find.

At forty-five, I'd ice climbed for the first time, and the ice climbing wasn't the hard or scary part. Getting off my warm butt was. Here I'd been preaching to my students about new experiences and the benefits of challenging yourself outdoors, and I'd stalled out on trying new activities myself. At midlife, when there's more behind me than ahead, I especially need adventure so I can get out of my comfort zone and into the wonder zone.

I try to look at climate change as an adventure—not just the changes but the challenges we face in accepting our role in it, dealing with the guilt and sadness, and pushing forward into working together to problem solve. Many people have begun doing this. Adventure, I remind my students, is any nonroutine activity that involves the sense of danger. Nothing fills me with more dread than what we've done to the planet. As I march, write, and teach with the aim of raising awareness and demanding action on issues of climate change and social justice, I need the physical challenges, play, and deep peace outdoors to keep me sane and motivated.

One summer when we didn't camp at the beach or road trip out West, I took the kids up to visit my cousin and her family in their Adirondack cabin on Little Moose Lake. We'd been there in the winter, but never in August when the water was warm enough—barely—to swim. The kids were big enough to kayak solo and spent their time paddling, swimming, sleeping, and catching frogs (which they counted and put back). I enjoyed doing all that too, except for the frog hunting, but mostly appreciated having time with Cathy, who is twelve years older and outdoorsy. She'd recently retired and her youngest was starting college. Over wine and blueberry pancakes (at separate times), we discussed what life looked like to her now that she had so many options again. I noticed what she spent her day touching: lake water, paddles, hiking boots, trails, glacier-carved rock, family dog, dishes, laundry, broom. "I make myself swim, paddle, or hike every day, even a little. To not take it for granted because it's always here." The lake might be there every day for years and years, but both of us were increasingly aware of how fleeting health and mobility can be.

One night we kayaked in search of the sunset, hoping we'd find loons. Cathy and Marc's place is tucked in a cove on East Bay, and we paddled out on water smooth as a new Mylar emergency blanket. The fir trees on the far bank stuck out above the rest, comically crooked, revealing the dominant direction the wind blew. We heard a loon cry from Main Bay and headed toward shell-pink sky. Cathy checked the marshy shoreline for the mama and babies she'd seen all summer.

No motors were allowed there. The quiet was underscored by the slow lapping of our paddles. She spotted a dot against the pink, and we headed quickly in that direction. In the faint light from behind it, I could see the contrasting white rings on its black neck, and even the white dots on its back. A lone loon. We stopped and drifted, two mothers alone, and wondered whether it was a male or female, and where those babies were. It'd be time to migrate soon. Surely they were big enough to be on their own.

The loon threw its head back and called, and the echo began before the call finished. I thought over my year, realizing I'd heard more loons in it than in all my years before. I'd had several trips on my own and with friends, mostly to work on writing projects. I heard them on Anne LaBastille's lake as I paddled and wrote by the open window in my room. I watched a loon from the dock at Lapland Lake, where my friend Judith and I went to write, and we watched it dive and come up in unexpected places the way ideas for poems do. I'd only ever heard one loon before that year, when I was in my twenties and paddling on a Vermont lake with my friend Ann. She'd wanted me to hear loons, and we hadn't until we turned around because of storm clouds. The loon's call had seemed a warning then, and thunder the echo.

Listening that night on Little Moose Lake with Cathy, I understood why the call gets described as maniacal laughter, especially watching the loon throw its head back like the Joker in Batman cartoons. But it didn't feel creepy, or crazy, or like a warning. I guess a call is whatever you make it. We have a choice about how we respond. It would've been easy for me to hear it as ominous, a reminder of the threats to wild places. But I decided it was an invitation to engage instead. To dip my hands in the cold water, to swat mosquitoes, to feel my muscles as they propelled me gently across the coves and crannies of a lake in a state-protected, forever-wild park that is proof of what humans can do when we are at our best. I resolved again to work toward greater protection of what's wild in the land and in myself. Celebrating diversity in people and geography, getting out of my comfort zone, and stretching beyond my familiar boundaries would teach me how to adapt well. My excursions to places like Cathy and Marc's cabin weren't about retreating from a civilization that is irredeemable, but a recommitment to bringing the best of myself to meet the best of others.

Cathy and I followed the loon, which had grown quiet, back to East Bay. The pink had left. With its every dive, we searched the water ahead and to the sides, moving in the direction it reappeared, paddling slowly without talking. Twice more the loon called, the echo not as pronounced as before. A few lights shone like animal eyes where we knew cabins to be across the bay.

There was a line between the darkness of the lake and the darkness of the land. Then there was the line, not of light, but of an even lighter darkness, one filled with stars that looked tiny and fragile but didn't need anything from us. We turned away from the loon to paddle toward the little shore we laid claim to, the one that held our loves and responsibilities. It wasn't light, but there was light enough.

FIRE IN PARADISE
Privilege

Water drips onto my arms and neck from the car trunk hatch. I reach in for small split pieces of firewood donated by a friend who lives near the state park where I've come for a two-day reprieve. Nothing major, just from social and family obligations. I value them all, so when I start resenting them, I know it's time to retreat. My being comfortable in crowds, even in front of crowds, leads people to think I'm an extrovert. But without quiet and solitude I lose my center fast. I don't know whether that makes me a closet introvert, but I don't need a label. I need space and time outdoors.

I place the wood, careful of the slivers, on my camp chair. It rained all night and morning, so the picnic table, ground, and twigs kindly stacked by the last camper are all wet. I should've brought them inside the yurt last night. I'm camping in luxury, which brings the luxury of being careless. I have a car and a secure canvas roof and walls with a skylight through which I can watch the lightning. I arrange my torn cereal boxes and crumpled newspapers around the slimmest pieces of wood, ones with the best edges for catching quick.

It took a long time to learn how to make a proper fire, one that could be counted on. The year I was in Girl Scouts, I watched the suburban moms, who'd started us off with cooking and sewing badges, try to follow directions in the guide for the log cabin and tepee styles. In my memory, a bunch of little girls in skirts huddle in the church parking lot, stacking sticks that keep falling over. The leaders refer to the book as I watch paper pages flutter back and forth thinking, *give me the book and matches and I'll show you how to make a fire.* Our sample fires are tiny, and I don't recall any ever being lit.

My lighter catches the newspaper. Orange flame jumps to the edges of the cardboard and begins seducing the wood. The secret is to start small and coax—not force—the larger pieces to join in. Do whatever you have to do to keep the air flowing. Soon three pieces are blazing steadily, and I sit back in my dry chair, ready to feed more wood into my completely unnecessary campfire. It's not dark or cold or buggy. There is heat in the yurt if I want it. This fire is decadent, something I never used to have when camping alone.

Campfires are a small example of my privilege. Concentrating so much on how women have been left out of wilderness stories, I run the risk of not noticing that as a straight white woman, I have a great deal of privilege in my otherness. When outdoors with my husband, I benefit from all the access his white-maleness bestows on him. Even by myself I carry a certain assumption of my entitlement to the American landscape that I've come to realize many others do not feel.

My first steps into understanding this came through Barry Lopez's story "The Negro in the Kitchen," where a middle-class black man walking from Connecticut shows up in a white man's rural California kitchen one morning, uninvited. The interaction is relayed through the white man's point of view, and though he is sure he's color-blind the title suggests otherwise. This story always stuck with me because of the black man's explanation that his walk across America was going back to his roots. He had always thought that because America belonged to the white man who hated him, the land felt the same way, and he wanted to reconnect with what he'd lost. What if I'd felt this way growing up instead of seeing national parks and iconic wilderness as my birthright? Though I'd spent years trying to feel safe enough in those places, I'd always felt that the land itself welcomed me.

Of course Lopez is white. And even if some people of color feel that way about the land, it's not true of all. bell hooks writes of how even when blacks were slaves or indentured farmers, they "were indeed a people of the earth," undoubtedly closer to the natural cycles of plants and animals than most landowners. Harriet Tubman's knowledge of weather patterns and signs was key to her success at leading so many to freedom. "Even when that land was owned by white oppressors," states bell hooks, "it was the earth itself that protected exploited black folks."

Yet I don't run into many people of color outdoors. Yesterday, walking the trail around the lake, I was surprised and pleased to see a black man taking a fishing rod from his car. After we spoke and I was entering the woods again, I thought of the *Funny or Die* video featuring actor and director Blair Underwood. "Black Hiker" satirizes the reactions people of color often get when outdoors in public lands. Hiking through what looks like California hills, Underwood meets, among others, a middle-aged white couple amazed that he knows which plants are edible, and two eager park rangers tracking him so they can get him to sign the registry (as if his name would prove a black person had visited). But the encounter that stands out to me is when he comes around a bend and surprises a young white woman jogging. It's staged, of course, but she stops—shocked. Then her culturally conditioned fear triggers and she takes off the way she came. It's clear from the video that a white man in her path wouldn't have elicited this reaction. She'd expect to see white males—they are the biggest participant group. For those of us who think public lands such as national parks and forests are refuges and sanctuaries, we need to honestly ask ourselves what or who we are hoping is kept out. As Latria Graham writes in *Outside* magazine, "many [national parks] were created as an escape from urban sprawl, at a time when *urban* was shorthand for blacks and immigrants."

For many, including members of the LGBT+ community, what makes outdoor spaces a sanctuary is the lack of *all* types of people. If your sexuality or identity is constantly being criticized, then the peace of being left alone is a big part of the call of the wild. If I felt this when trying to escape gender constraints, then how much more would gay and lesbian couples feel it when they could drop their defenses and freely show affection? Of course, fewer people doesn't mean none. Claudia Brenner, whose girlfriend Rebecca Wight was murdered when they were camping on the Appalachian Trail, says, "We were playing by the rules. We were in the middle of the woods. We weren't flaunting [our relationship]." As I've written elsewhere, there is a trend in true and fictional accounts of gay couples seeking a type of "retreat to a safe place for unsanctioned companionship rather than for isolation." This narrative, which I call the Brokeback pastoral after the short story by Annie Proulx, twists the hetero-normative male pastoral retreat—a classic trope of American literature, which is a big reason the wild is considered a special place reserved for special people. Claiming a role in these stories is as important as claiming the right to access the places the stories depict. It's a spark at least.

Security

Water hits the firepit, instantly transforming into steam. Either it's starting to sprinkle or it's leaf drip. I look around at the trees close by on one side. They aren't ideally located, but I could rig a tarp from them over the fire, held up on the far side by two of the longer, sturdy branches lying wet on the ground. I don't need to—if it rained again I'd just go inside and cook on the stove—but knowing I could brings an intense satisfaction. When did I change into this confident camper? When did I start feeling I belong?

Knowing how to adapt to shifting conditions has something to do with it, as does the gradual lowering of my fear radar. My radar's not gone, but I've grown to trust that it will operate when I'm relaxed yet in tune with my surroundings (not artificially relaxed or wearing speakers in my ears). Actually, I think it operates better then, or maybe I read the signals better. Perhaps what I've thought of as the feeling of safety I crave in wild spaces is really a feeling of security. The feeling of being tucked close to a fire in a ring or hearth. Is this the reason many of the fire-building styles are named after shelters? As a girl, I was pretty intimidated by the power of fire and the responsibility of controlling it. I heard only cautions, not instructions about how to work with it. But its force, and those who could shape it, compelled me. Men like those in Jack London's Yukon adventure tales were what I thought I had to be to belong outdoors. They use their guts, woodcraft, and the power of fire to ward off death in the form of freezing or wolves. If they can make a fire they can make a safe space. But only temporarily. Even men get so cold they can't light a match. Even men get so old the wolves aren't afraid of them. Hmmm. Security, not safety. No guarantees out here for anyone, no matter how self-assured they are.

Despite how much less dangerous the outdoors far from a trailhead is statistically, danger exists, and some is aimed at specific people. My white skin protects me from the additional risks blacks encounter on the trail, but as a lone female in androgynous clothing I can easily be labeled a "dyke," as I often was in the years before marriage. Two women hiking or backpacking together can be a different kind of target than a woman solo, as Claudia Brenner discovered in 1988 when her girlfriend was killed. Brenner was shot five times and left for dead when a mountain man and drifter stumbled upon them making love and "experienced uncontrollable rage," according to his lawyer. Julianne Williams and Lollie Winans were hiking in Shenandoah National Park in 1996 when a man singled them out, tied their hands, and slit their throats. The man was convicted and received an enhanced sentence for hate crimes, having "implicated himself by statements that he 'hates gays' and preys on women 'because they are more vulnerable than men.'" I came of age hearing these stories and more on the news, recognizing the name of the national park where my father took me camping.

The smoke from my small fire floats up about six feet before seeming to disappear against the overcast sky. This makes me think of all the Louis L'Amour novels (or were they Harlequin novels?) where the cowboys and the woman with them had to skip a fire or make do with a small one because they were being followed. As comforting as a campfire is, anything that calls attention to oneself can quickly become the opposite of security. The only thing those women who were killed backpacking did wrong was be seen. Yet how can you feel you belong somewhere if your safety is linked to your invisibility?

Latria Graham understands the imperative not to be seen

and the dilemma that creates for an outdoor adventurer. She cautions that just because we don't see black people outdoors doesn't mean they aren't there. She grew up outdoors with family on her grandmother's fifteen acres of farmland in South Carolina. This is where she learned "sustenance and survival," including crafting herbal medicines, tending hogs, building fences, and picking okra. She was a Girl Scout, a more successful one than I was, no doubt. Talking about the family compound in Newberry County, part of a town of fewer than two hundred with street signs swallowed by kudzu, she declares: "We're impossible to find if you don't know where to look. We don't mind."

Nonwhite campers, according to the KOA *2017 North American Camping Report*, now make up a quarter of all campers, having doubled since 2012. "We're at the lake, at private campgrounds close to home, and state parks," explains Graham. I think of the man I saw at the lake here at my local state park, and my black students who say fishing with grandparents has been their primary outdoor activity. Graham's family, like the majority of black Americans, stayed away from national parks. There aren't that many in the South, after all. She cites the 2010 census, which shows that 55 percent of blacks live in the South, where there are only nine main national parks. Eight southern states don't have any national parks, though several have national seashores. Geography is a big reason blacks aren't visible in the iconic spaces featured in magazines and tourism ads. Security is another. Graham's father was raised in the Jim Crow South, and although by 2013 segregation was legally a thing of the past, he was very nervous when they traveled to Everglades National Park. He couldn't shake memories of how an innocent action could be twisted into an infraction or insult. The kind that got black folks killed and crosses burned. A far cry from the fire that brings comfort and belonging.

Desire

The sky is brightening above the white pines and hemlocks, and my fire is blazing. It will rain again later but the blue jays, chipmunks, squirrels, and bullfrogs are raising their voices, telling me I still have time. And there's one more I'm trying to place, sort of howl-like in the distance but not a coyote. When I recognize it, I laugh. It's a rooster. I'd been going down a list of wild animals, yet this state park is ten minutes from my house and closer yet to others'. How easily my brain is fooled into seeing distinctions such as domestic and wild as rigid and clear-cut. Where I am right now is not iconic, and definitely not wilderness, but it's beautiful and for me, today, ideal. You could call it paradise.

As a pastor's daughter who grew up to be an outdoor enthusiast, I often think how screwy it is that the garden was considered paradise and the fall resulted in wilderness, and yet today wilderness is often the epitome of paradise. Not that I read Genesis as a literal account of events, but even metaphorically this is whacked-out. The God I worship is the God of *all* creation—wild, domestic, gay, straight, black, white—oh hellfire, here come the binaries marching in again. Truth is, if we treated all the earth as a paradise, maybe it would be. Unless one of the qualifications to becoming a paradise is that it not be accessible to all. Maybe Eden became one only after Adam and Eve were forbidden to return. If so, then I want no part of it.

After years of studying why women aren't as prevalent outdoors in America, I've come to the same conclusion Graham has about the dearth of blacks outdoors: "The reasons for this are really more about history than desire." Women are in the garden, in the parks with children, on jogging and biking trails, and—if alone or with a female lover in more remote areas—are often keeping a low profile. The majority of people of color outdoors are with their families wherever they have access and wherever they feel safe. And the lack of diversity represented in images and stories comes from the fact that many locations and expeditions do not conform to the basic white-boy nature narrative. That narrative says choosing to put oneself in an unpredictable and potentially dangerous environment is what brings the thrill of achievement. For people whose otherness has them feeling some level of fear on a daily basis, that's the worst way to lure them outdoors.

One day I read an internet forum where a black person described camping as "playing homeless," and it clicked what some students had been trying to tell me. The things I enjoy doing outside and describe as euphoric are the opposite of escape for them; they are a regression. When you or your family has struggled to establish a safe place within walls in a country where violence against people who look or act like you is not uncommon, then voluntarily leaving those walls to sleep on the ground can seem nuts.

Luckily, the rise of the internet has allowed underrepresented people to use digital platforms to showcase the outdoor adventures they pursue on their own terms. Outdoor Afro, Latino Outdoors, OUT There Adventures, Brown Girls Climb, Brothers of Climbing, Flash Foxy, NativesOutdoors, and A Quick Brown Fox are some of the places online where people can share stories about bike riding, climbing, and hiking. More—they have led to festivals, guided trips, and all sorts of real connections between people and the outdoors through recreation. "One of our sayings," explains Elyse Rylander, founder of OUT There Adventures, which gets queer kids into outdoor adventure sports, "is 'There's nothing straight about nature.'" If you don't know what she means, Google "the sex life of slugs."

Desire is often equated with want, the opposite of necessity. While I don't think we need everything we desire, I do think people need desire in their lives to make them meaningful. It's the fire feeding what we do. Too much and it's a disaster, too little and there's no warmth or purpose to our time here. The low voice of the fire beside me surges and pops as if in agreement. And desire isn't always selfish. We're sensory creatures meant to feel pleasure, destined to feel pain. Len Necefer, founder and CEO of NativesOutdoors, argues that getting more Native Americans into outdoor sports will benefit the land because they'll bring their "values of stewardship" with them, slowly diluting the approach of conquering with one of caring. "I'm an advocate for recreation as a vehicle to learn about the land and carry on our traditions," he states. These groups are also training outdoor leaders who bring new ideas to their diverse communities. With a fresh connection to the outdoors and greater leadership skills, underrepresented people are starting to insist on a place at the table where conservation and local land decisions are being made.

I don't think everyone needs to desire outdoor adventure as much as I do, or in the ways I do. But I feel called to help those who've never experienced it get a small dose and decide whether they want another. Sometimes exposure is all it takes—a friend wonders why she never thought she'd like rock climbing. Sometimes it's harder, as in helping kids find vegetables they like. You give little bites, trying different kinds until you find the right one. Black females from the city taking my Intro to Outdoor Recreation class for gen ed credit have told me they loved the outdoors when young but lost touch when being girly became important. Now in college, they find they're scared of bugs and sounds in the green beside the trail. They don't remember sweating when they were little but now hate the sensation. They like our class hikes but were initially worried they'd be out of shape or the weakest in the group. They didn't want to get their shoes dirty. Still, they write about how important it is to them to take their future kids outdoors.

Their desire to not give up their connection to the earth. "Being able to unwind and look at a fire while listening to the sound of the woods is so soothing," writes a young woman from Philly, whose favorite outdoor activities are bonfires and bike rides. She makes me think of Kenny, a black student who wanted to go camping, so some of his classmates and I took him. He'd never roasted marshmallows over a fire before. You should have seen the rapture on his face as he leaned into the light, tasting his first one.

Becoming comfortable outdoors is like building a fire, I tell them. The secret is to start small. Coax—don't force—your friends and children to join in. Breathe. Relax. Do whatever you have to do to keep the air flowing. Soon you'll have a fire circle to invite others into.

Gloria, City of Rocks, Idaho

Going Home

TWENTY-FIRST-CENTURY ROAD TRIP

June 2015. We pulled into the Sheep Lakes information area in Rocky Mountain National Park at 10:00 a.m. as the ranger began her bighorn talk. Other than hikes off the Blue Ridge Parkway when visiting family, Gabe and Gloria had never been to a national park. At eight and eleven, they were old enough to deal with the road trip from Pennsylvania and to appreciate their introduction to the American West. And they were old enough that Jimmy, who hadn't been raised on family treks cross-country to visit parks, could be convinced the trip would be more wonderful than whiny. We'd been hiking with friends in Colorado for several days, and the kids were tired. Exploring the park by car seemed a nice break.

The drive to Estes Park from Boulder had been full of wide-open meadows snug below peaks I hadn't seen since I was twenty-one. On that solo road trip, the Bighorn Mountains to the Tetons had been a favorite stretch. With the open spaces and variety of land formations, my physical experience of the world deepened. The effect was like a sliver of something sharp and beautiful lodging under my skin. Whatever that sliver was—awe, restlessness, or topophilia—it was still there.

The wind whipped Gloria's berry-colored hair, an end-of-school-year treat, as she and I hurried over to where kids of all ages sat around the ranger and her box of horns, hooves, pelts, and skulls. Gloria slid onto an open place on the blanket. I squatted behind her to hear better but not block the view of others sitting on rocks farther back. Not to be hurried, Gabe hung at the edge, a swath of purple bangs masking one eye.

To the left, several shallow lakes were cupped by bright green meadow. Two ewes grazed the knee-high grass in front of the Mummy Range with its white snow on gray scree. The Sheep Lakes, the ranger was saying, aren't true lakes that drain into a river and ocean. Created by glaciers, they hold snowmelt and rain like sinks, the mineral deposits building up rather than running off. These minerals draw the sheep here.

What drew me here? I wanted to do something significant, give my children a taste of epic American wild beauty. But even as I admired the stunning views, a part of me felt as if I was intruding on the wilderness—or what would be wilderness if all of us and the parking lot and roads weren't there. Was I raising my kids to see this land as only a resource to renew their adventurous spirit? Wasn't I compounding the problems of traffic and pollution by driving more than 1,500 miles to be here? Theodore Roosevelt believed that in addition to refuges for wildlife, wilderness was both school and hospital—at least for males. But what's good for the gander is good for the goose, and I agree that wild areas have great potential to teach us and heal us from the wounds of civilization. I also think prioritizing the curative value can be problematic, as if exceptional places preserved for those with the ability to visit means the rest of nature and humanity can just stay sick.

The ranger lifted a large skull that had two short horns—a female's—and described how the ewes raise all the lambs themselves. When they come into the open as a group, one ewe takes watch in each direction. Their eyes are set wide apart on the sides of their head and can see better than we can through our best binoculars. Inside the sanctuary the ewes make, new lambs learn to play. The ranger passed a hoof among the children to show how the split allowed for better gripping. I leaned over the blanket and small heads to see, wishing one of the kids would think to pass it to me.

Lambs spend their time eating, jumping, and butting. "Playing," the ranger said, "teaches them how much force is necessary to properly perch and land. When they get too wild, the ewes gently butt them back into the circle where they won't bother the grown-ups." I nodded knowingly, along with several other mothers.

Waving her arms one minute and making funny faces the next, the ranger told stories that were science. I leaned in even closer, almost tipping onto Gloria, as enthralled as the kids. Perhaps more, I thought, glancing back at Gabe with his eleven-year-old boy's studied detachment. Her presentation skills were excellent, and I wished my outdoor recreation students could see this. But most of them hadn't been out of Pennsylvania.

🌲🌲🌲

After I took a photo of Gloria holding a seven-pound ram horn, the ranger walked us back to her booth to get a booklet we'd seen other kids with: *Rocky Mountain National Park Official Junior Ranger Activities.*

"How much?"

"They're free," she said. Danielle signed the page for ranger programs. "You need to fill in some things you learned, and do the other activities. Then turn these in at a visitor center to get your badge."

"That's so cool," I said, trying to get a better look, but neither kid wanted to share with Mom yet. More than a bit jealous—we didn't have these when I was their age—I waited my turn.

Honestly, I'd been preparing to rein myself in from making everything a teachable moment. I knew that'd kill any interest my kids had. But now the Junior Ranger booklets became the source of questions and prompts to see what they'd learned. And in this way the kids became the experts when I wanted to know what I was seeing.

We continued toward Trail Ridge Road, in search of higher

elevations, snow, and more critters, stopping at Hidden Valley picnic area for a bathroom break. The kids and I stood on the rustic bridge behind the restrooms and stared into the shallow water, wanting to spot a fish so Gabe could check it off on one of his pages. We didn't, but then we noticed the mule deer in the shadows. As it moved into the light, they whispered about how much larger it was than our white-tailed deer. We watched it watch us watching it. I made unconscious noises of appreciation like folks do at fireworks.

On the way to the car Gabe fell back with his dad, and Jimmy started laughing. "Gabe said that you at a national park is like him at a comic-con," he told me.

I had to laugh too. I wouldn't have compared Rocky Mountain National Park to a comics convention where people dress up as favorite superheroes and villains, but I could see his point. Maybe I *was* acting like a kid, but Gabe seemed to enjoy that I was having fun.

Sheep Lakes had been a little over eight thousand feet elevation, and the Trail Ridge Road would take us to just over twelve thousand feet. In the back seat both kids worked on their activities, marking off the deer and bighorn they'd seen, looking out when one side dropped away and they could stare thousands of feet down, or craning their necks to see as far up the steep scree slope as possible.

"I need to find a flower," Gloria said.

"There. Yellow by the side of the road."

Gloria looked where Jimmy pointed. "Got it!" Then her face crumpled. "But I can't remember anything I learned about bighorns and I have to write some down."

"That's easy," Gabe said, busy writing what he recalled, complete with a labeled sketch. He just *looks* like he's bored and not paying attention.

Being a little sister myself, I hushed him up. To Gloria I

said, "What do you remember about their teeth?" I knew she'd
held the jawbone while Danielle discussed this.

"Um, that their back teeth are sharper than ours?"

"Good, write that." There wasn't much space and her young
script took up a lot of room.

"I need another fact," she said when done.

"What about the horns?"

"Oh yeah!" And she started writing without even running it
by me.

Later I looked at their booklets. She'd put, "Female horns
grow strat up and are not much use but the male horns go
cerved and are really importait." Writing in a moving car is
hard. Gabe's said, "Horns can weigh 7 pounds each. The prize
of winning a fight is mating." Then there was an arrow to his
drawing below titled "After a Fight" that showed the common
results: a broken horn, broken ribs, and broken nose. I wondered whether he thought mating was worth it.

Soon we were on top of the ridge, watching the subalpine
firs shrink before us. The higher we went, the more brown
lumps we saw on the tundra. Jimmy and I weren't sure from
that far away if they were mule deer or elk.

"Check your books. What has white bottoms?" I asked the
kids.

"White people!" Gabe shot back.

He'd noticed that was the main type of visitor we'd seen in
the park. Not that we could see their bottoms.

Until recently, very few of Rocky Mountain National Park's
almost 266,000 acres were designated wilderness, a layer of
protection even greater than its status as a national park. But in
2009 under President Obama, nearly 250,000 acres of the park
were declared wilderness—pretty much all but the roads and

heavy-use areas around the visitor centers. So the road we were on wasn't officially in wilderness, but all the land we'd been gazing at was now protected from further road developments, mining, and motorized recreation. By the legal definition, we were looking at more wilderness now than when Rocky Mountain National Park was established. Turns out, as I discovered in the Beaver Meadows Visitor Center where signs announced the park's centennial, that had happened exactly one hundred years ago.

First, we sat in a dark room to view the interpretive video *The Spirit of the Mountains*, which described the magnificent animals and geology. Also how white settlers displaced the Utes, almost wiped out the bighorn, and *did* wipe out the elk and wolves here before we started caring. At least we started caring about spectacular scenery and charismatic megafauna (I made sure I taught Gabe that term). But the reintroduced elk were now doing well and the bighorn herds were holding steady.

As Gabe and Gloria filled in the last few pages of their activity books, I wandered around exhibits, thinking about how long it took Americans to appreciate the importance of preserving some land in as natural a state as possible. And in most cases we were way ahead of other nations, though our reasons for doing so are still evolving. We really got started during Theodore Roosevelt's time, right after the US census declared the end of the frontier in 1890. Roosevelt preached that "every believer in manliness and therefore, in manly sport, and every lover of nature" should join forces and protect our "resources"—wildlife and its habitat. He was a hunter above all.

The tug-of-war between conservation and preservation in the Hetch Hetchy Valley in Yosemite brought the questions of who needs wilderness and why to national attention. Gifford Pinchot (who championed wise use) and John Muir (who didn't give an ouzel's ass about utilitarian values) played key roles in that debate, which turned good friends against each other and which Muir lost when the dam was approved in 1913. Though they were never reunited, their philosophies and approaches came together in the next generation through the work of Aldo Leopold.

A hunter and conservationist trained in the Yale School of Forestry, which was endowed by Pinchot, Leopold eventually grew to understand the role of preservation within a comprehensive management plan. More than a few wolves had to die by his hand before he came to this realization, what he called "thinking like a mountain." In 1924 he helped establish the first wilderness area in the Gila National Forest in New Mexico, when he was a forester. He claimed if we did not set aside some land to study and observe, while interfering as little as possible, it would be like destroying textbooks we did not yet understand. He was an ecologist who, like Muir, learned not to presume that value lay exclusively in what good the land and wildlife did for humans. But he realized this only through decades of close contact with wild places and an ethic of care. Without direct contact, can such an ethic survive? I'm worried we'll find out the hard way.

The Wilderness Act wouldn't be signed until 1964, creating the National Wilderness Preservation System and a means by which more wilderness could be designated. The act declares that such land, "in contrast with those areas where man and his own works dominate the landscape, is hereby recognized as an area where the earth and its community of life are untrammeled by man, where man himself is a visitor who does not remain." All that damn *man* language again. It's as if we're stuck linguistically in Teddy Roosevelt's time.

Gloria shoved something in my hand, finally getting my attention. It was her Junior Ranger booklet. I barely managed to halt her before she charged into the gift shop. "If you're done, you need to take it to a ranger." I pointed to the counter where Gabe was heading.

I stood back as first Gabe, then Gloria held up their right hand and repeated the Junior Ranger oath, swearing to keep wildlife wild by not feeding animals, protect plants by not picking them, place trash in recycling bins or trash cans, and enjoy nature safely and be a good example to others. They will never know how hard it was for me not to cheer when the ranger pinned on their plastic badges.

I let them go into the gift shop after that. Gloria and I were locked in a heated taxonomic debate about whether puppets counted as stuffies. I'd said no stuffed animals, but she thought she'd found a way around it. The puppets were, of course, stuffed and plush. Gabe came up with an olive-green Junior Ranger vest. Happy he was getting into the spirit of the mountains, I agreed, though it wasn't cheap. The vest had mesh sides and fourteen pockets—Gabe had counted them.

"That will be great for hiking," I said.

"And for holding my ammo during Nerf gun battles," he said, heading out of the shop to find his dad.

Gloria held out a small finger puppet, her face pleading. It was a skunk. "But we have plenty of these in Pennsylvania," I said, trying to at least interest her in the bighorn. Nope, she was not beguiled by rare charismatic megafauna, and more power to her. I looked at the price—less than half of the vest's cost—and added the skunk to the pile.

🌲🌲🌲

Driving back to Boulder, I was preoccupied with my thoughts while Gabe listened to his iPod and Gloria played with her skunk. I recalled how Gabe had stayed on the outskirts of the group as Danielle explained that young rams left the ewes after two years. I thought about Roosevelt's insistence that boys about Gabe's age be taken from the moral, civilizing influence of their Victorian mother and be brought to the wilderness to develop that vigorous manliness no American boy should lack. For all his good intentions, this attitude was the clubhouse sign saying "No Girls Allowed" (especially moms). My family hadn't exactly immersed ourselves in wild nature that day. But it wasn't because of me, and it wasn't because of Gloria. We could have, and at times we do.

But if we don't, well, that's okay too. Humans can appreciate wilderness from afar or a car as well. Animals and plants are often better off when we do. But we can't forget we are animals too, and we are nature, so this legal definition that prohibits men from settling wild lands, and assumes women wouldn't even want to visit, bothers me even as I support such designations. And if Roosevelt connected with wilderness through his love of big game animals (though, yeah, he shot them), I guess it's okay if I need it for big games. For rock climbing and whitewater paddling, activities that teach me to interact with the natural world without conquering it. "Places to play in and pray in," as John Muir wrote, two survival skills based on interaction rather than self-reliance.

♣♣♣

"What does it look like?" Gabe asked, as we drove into City of Rocks National Reserve.

"You'll know it when you see it," Jimmy and I said almost in unison.

We were bouncing along a dirt road out of Almo, Idaho, scanning the sagebrush hills and washes of the Basin and Range geography, seeking our first view of the geologic sculptures. Well, the kids' first view, and Jimmy's and my first view since we'd had kids.

Light gray humps and spires appeared amid the dusky green ahead. We all watched as they grew, and we named them as we would cloud shapes—a lion, a castle, a tepee, Swiss cheese. As the kids talked about what our campsite would be like, I was anxious. I'd wanted to reserve one of the sites Jimmy and I had stayed in long ago, but they'd been renumbered. We couldn't tell anything from the map and memory. When I finally got around to calling, there was only one site available for the three nights we'd be there. Number 33 was listed as "rock, main road, no shade." It was also far from a privy. Not ideal, but at least we knew we had a place to camp.

When we pulled off at sites 33–35, I was pleased to see it wasn't so close to the road that we'd be eating dust. Then Jimmy turned right again. A picnic table and fire ring stood near a single pinyon pine. To the side was a large, flattish space of decomposed granite. Behind, a speckled dome gently rose, almost glowing in the sun.

"Can we play on that?' the kids asked.

"That's what we're here for," I said. We clambered out to explore, laughing and pointing out quartz seams and kid-sized potholes.

At the back, the dome swooped up like a dorsal fin and had a window carved by wind, too small for our kids to squeeze through. Then it dropped straight down six feet to the ground, before pinyon pine and Simpson's hedgehog cactus took over again. The rock's gritty texture was great for scrambling on, especially where it slanted down to a minor wash, dry now. Behind the pine and toward our neighbors in 34, rock loomed much higher, several stories tall, and a separate one sat in a midlevel bowl.

"Look, there's a boulder on a boulder!" Gloria said.

"It must've broken off and fallen," Gabe mused.

"Don't go over there without us," I said. "We don't know how safe it is, and we need to respect their space."

Just then a little girl, maybe three years old, came running over past the tree and onto "our" rock dome. Immediately an older girl came after her, and soon her father. Gloria ran off to make friends and Jimmy went over to talk with the guy while I pitched the tent. Gabe got his new climbing shoes and went to boulder on the back of the dome. Tent up, I walked over and Jimmy handed me a beer. He, the other father, and I watched the girls play house in the potholes, each having claimed her "room." The evening sun slanted, and in silhouette they looked a bit like prairie dogs, popping up, disappearing, and scurrying to another hole. Behind them Gabe sat proud on the prow of the fin looking off into the distance, as if posing for an author photo.

"They love it as much as we do," I said to Jimmy.

"Of course they do. It's a huge playground!"

Later, after a simple dinner, cleanup, and rolling out our beds, we told Gabe and Gloria the next day's plans. Jimmy and I had decided to take the kids to Practice Rock. In Colorado, both had gotten real climbing shoes with sticky rubber. Gabe was starting to embrace the vertical world, while Glo was interested some days, and others not so much.

Before turning in, we girls needed to make one last trek down the main road to the nearest privy. The boys peed in the sagebrush, but with so much cactus around I was less keen to squat in the dark. Gloria held fast to my hand in the deep gray twilight. I thought she was afraid. The rock formations were vague shapes looming outside the small arc of our headlamp, used only when I heard a vehicle.

After a few minutes she said softly, "What beautiful life."

"What do you mean, Honey?"

"This." She said in awe. "Idaho. This."

♣♣♣

Practice Rock was just what the guidebook said—short, accessible, with one main crack to set protection in and many ways to set top ropes on the face. It looked like the back of yet another sleeping dinosaur. In the City there is plenty of granite for nonclimbers to explore at whatever level, and the climbs we were doing were short so someone would always be at the base near Gloria. Jimmy got first crack at the, uh, crack. It was a bit of a sore point with us that we were so out of climbing shape and practice. It wasn't a problem of age or having kids as much as it was a problem of geography. If we'd still lived in Reno we'd have been in decent shape. At least that's what we told ourselves.

One positive aspect of our not climbing hard was that it suited us to stick to climbs at a good level for the kids to try. I belayed as Jimmy led, working his way up slowly—"sewing it up," as we say when a lot of gear is placed close together so the rope going through the carabiners looks like stiches of thread. It's the leader's job to place the gear well and protect the climb, and Jimmy excels at this. It's the belayer's job to be patient and vigilant. I'm better at being vigilant than patient.

When Jimmy finished making an anchor on top, I got my turn to climb. It went much faster for me, even stopping to clean the gear, as it usually does for the second. Regardless of how long or tall a climb is, my focus narrows and sharpens. It's like what I suspect meditation is for others: a complete awareness of myself in relation to the world. Not bigger than, not less than, but *of* the world. Enmeshed. Inseparable. Every slight movement of air, the temperature of the rock as well as its sharp edges, gritty texture. The sage and dust smells. The way muscles I don't know the names of move in sync with each other to adjust for the angle of stone, the size of the hold.

Is this play? On one hand, play is considered anything done for enjoyment and recreation. If so, climbing counts. It renews me, primarily when I do it outdoors in wild places. On the other hand, play is the antonym of serious. I certainly don't mean it this way. I think play should be taken very seriously.

Not just the equipment and risk-management aspects that climbing demands, but as a necessity in our lives at all ages, no matter what kind of responsible play we indulge in. I don't think it takes much effort to come up with ways to recreate that can benefit the planet.

"Nice job," Jimmy said as I lowered down. Beside him, Gabe waited like a dog about to be let off its leash.

I wandered over to Gloria and her dolls. Ariel (yes, the mermaid) was teaching beach-boy Ken how to boulder. To his credit, he didn't seem to mind taking climbing tips from a female, even one with fins, not feet. We may be domestic animals, I thought, but we still learn through play. And through play, we were reconnecting with nature and each other. I hoped that somewhere John Muir and my ancestor Will Colby, his coleader on the first Sierra Club outings, were watching.

That evening, we went to Bath Rock, the formation near our campsite we'd watched change shape and color with the sun's moods. Dots of people ascended spider-fine ropes on the eastern side. We circled around back and scrambled up the reddish-brown patinaed surface to a large pocked saddle. A church youth group swarmed over the nontechnical climbing route for hikers that had rebar rungs up the steep section. Gabe wanted to go to the top of the two-hundred-foot rock, so I waited with Gloria below, listening to the teens teasing and encouraging each other.

Gloria, who had never met a stranger, started conversing with one of the adult leaders who'd come down. White, middle aged, and easy to talk to, the man obviously loved Idaho. He spoke of where we should go, and places he'd hunted.

"I hope you don't hunt wolves!" Gloria broke in.

"I haven't," he said. Then to me, as if she couldn't hear, he admitted it was the one animal that had eluded him and the one he most wanted to get before he died.

Gloria was indignant. "Wolves don't hurt humans!" She couldn't believe she knew more about wolves than he did.

"But they're hell on baby calves," he said, smiling at her precociousness.

"Only because we've made it hard for them to find food. Promise me you'll never kill a wolf." Gloria looked at him fiercely, putting her hands on her hips. "*Promise*," she said again as he hesitated.

So of course he promised. Liar. If he doesn't end up shooting one it won't be because of that conversation, but maybe he'll remember the girl with pink hair who spoke for the wolves. My brave little Lorax.

"What do *you* want to do?" Jimmy asked, jolting me out of thoughts of what would be new and exciting for the kids. Hunkering out of the sun at midday, we were eating sandwiches after a morning of hiking and climbing. What do I want to do? What a concept.

"I'd like to lead some routes," I admitted. A mother I'd met had told me about an area nearby where there were easy bolted routes in afternoon shade. Great for kids, she'd said, but they also sounded great for me. "Let's check out Castle Rocks State Park. We've never been there."

We found the cluster of spires and slots that's part of the same geology as City of Rocks, a crossroads where ecosystems come together and overlap at their edges, creating more diversity. In these overlaps, plants and animals from the Great Basin and Rocky Mountains mingle, and scientists can more easily observe ecological changes. After all, they didn't make it a reserve to protect a playground for people, although I'm not sure that's an entirely bad idea. What if more humans saw places as playmates? Not playthings to be used, but as entities to interact with for joy and renewal? Not as resources but as friends?

The routes weren't very tall, maybe sixty feet. Squinting in the sun, I spotted the silver bolts where they hid like chameleons on the gray granite. Having been assured that the anchors were in good shape and easy to find at the top, Jimmy and I checked each other's equipment.

"Climbing," I said, putting my hands against the rock and looking over my shoulder.

"Climb on!" He smiled at me, hands ready on the rope.

And then he disappeared. Or seemed to, which is the sign of a great belayer. He kept the slack so the rope didn't pull and didn't pool, and fed me more when I needed to clip. So I felt alone with the warm rock, the sun on the back of my neck and calves, and the sky wide in welcome. I climbed slowly, not because it was hard but because I wanted to flow with the stone, like a dance when you close your eyes and the music moves your muscles. I hadn't seen anyone do this route; it was my experience alone. Sometimes, when I only follow Jimmy on climbs, removing gear, I feel like the cleanup crew. When I lead, I am in the moment more.

After I left that wilderness and rejoined my family, we tied Gabe in. Gloria happily played in the shade of pinyons, but Gabe gave off a vibe that any climber recognizes (and it had nothing to do with his rank, puberty-funk armpits). This face rose twice as tall as Practice Rock, but he was excited. And this time, he didn't ask to lower before reaching the anchor. This time something clicked. I tilted my head back, watching my son climb into his own wilderness, the rope sliding with care between his father's hands.

A city in the wilderness. A city made of wilderness. A

reservation for nature. A reservation for climbers. And, 125 miles away, a reservation for the Shoshones who once lived here and whose consciousness, as Native American writer Leslie Marmon Silko would say, was still here in the rocks and plants. "The term landscape is misleading," Silko writes. "Viewers are as much a part of the landscape as the boulders they stand on." It's as Americanist Roderick Nash reminds us: "Western civilization created wilderness." Nomadic hunter-gatherer peoples like the Shoshones had no word in their vocabulary for wilderness. There was no concept of controlled versus uncontrolled nature. There was only home.

Unfortunately, the idea of American wilderness has been as much about white privilege as about stewardship. Separating nature from people, especially native and poor peoples, we preserved it for those who could afford to visit as much as for the sake of nature. This cannot be ignored anymore. But I don't want to only criticize. I want to find a way we can honor and protect these wonderful places while blurring their distinctions. To treat even less-majestic ecosystems and watersheds with the same respect as national parks, even as we accept that we can't live without impact.

Two days in Yellowstone National Park didn't seem enough, but we did our best, getting up at 4:00 a.m. to look for wolves. Shannon, a former student of mine working for the Yellowstone Association, kept checking in on her walkie-talkie with the wolf crew, but no sightings yet. The kids were chatting happily in the back seat, maybe because they were sharing it with Shannon, a favorite former babysitter, and maybe because they were allowed Froot Loops for breakfast.

Our first sighting was of a coyote, stealthy but not timid, and soon the bison spilled over the grass like the new sun.

"I can see their babies," Gloria shouted. "And their balls!"

We drove through several valleys but never spied wolves. We did see a cinnamon-colored black bear cub, and—my favorite—a grizzly just behind the tree line off the highway. We had Shannon's high-powered scope so we got a great view from a safe distance.

Outside the visitor center, where we went for Junior Ranger books, a female ranger was giving a wildlife safety talk. She showed how to estimate how far away an animal is. If the bear or wolf is bigger than your thumb when you extend your arm, then you're too close.

"But what if they come up to the road?" someone asked.

"If you are in your car, stay there. That's your habitat. The park is theirs."

How great that our greedy, heedless species has chosen to give other animals priority in national parks. And that within the dual mission, Americans decided preserving nature takes precedence over enjoying nature, realizing the second is not possible without the first. That's a beautiful lesson in what humans are capable of. I hoped the message my kids were getting was that we share this planet with other animals, and their company enriches our lives.

Still looking for wolves, the next day we visited Mammoth Hot Springs, Obsidian Cliff, and the paint pots—nature's fart jokes. The blurping plops that spewed mud globs out of gray-brown puddles cracked Gabe up. Walking back from Grand Prismatic Spring's psychedelic splendor, Gloria and I held hands and got serious. I explained how most kids her age and even Shannon's age had never visited any of our large, spectacular national parks, and many adults didn't understand why government money should go toward them.

"Tell everyone about what you saw," I said. "Tell them so they'll come, and so they'll love them."

"I will," she agreed solemnly. "I want Yellowstone to be here so I can bring my kids to see wolves."

♦♦♦

As we drove east across Wyoming and South Dakota, the kids talked about how empty the plains seemed without the bison that had spread out across the Lamar Valley. How lonely the houses looked, and the dirt roads dotted only with cows and oil derricks. I thought back to that morning as we'd readied to leave the motel, when Gloria told me about her dream.

> Coyote was the boss—the main one who raised me. Also a wolf and some dogs helped. We could understand each other. "Come with me," coyote said. I asked, "Where are we going?" and he said, "To meet some people. Don't ask any more questions." So I went, but I didn't know what he meant by people. I'd only known animals. They were bringing me to my mom. Something had happened to my dad and that's why I was given to the animals, but now my mom could take me back.
>
> The animals brought me to a house. I asked what it was and they said, "It's your home." I said, "Is it like the forest?" "Yes," coyote said, "but it has a door you open and close." They led me up to it and put my hand on the round thing sticking out. Then they told me to turn it. It took a few tries to figure out, then I did and the door opened and I saw my mother, but it wasn't you. Then I woke up.

This was a lot to take in as I stuffed pajamas and toothbrushes into a bag. I studied Gloria's face but couldn't tell anything by her expression.

"Did it make you feel happy? Sad? Confused?" I hadn't known what part of the dream to home in on.

"I felt *awesome*," she said, and then I could see it on her face. "I knew I could have my mother *and* the animals. I could be in the house or forest whenever I wanted. I didn't have to choose just one."

Acknowledgments

I am grateful to those who published the following essays, sometimes in slightly different forms:

"Becoming All Animal" first appeared in *Ragazine.cc: The Online Magazine of Arts, Information & Entertainment* (October 17, 2009).

"Large as Land" first appeared in *Quarterly West* (Spring/Summer 2003): 40–44.

"Outside Expectations" first appeared in *Young Wives' Tales: New Adventures in Love and Partnership*, edited by Jill Corral, Lisa Miya-Jervis, and Bell Hooks (Seattle: Seal Press, an imprint of Hachette Book Group, 2001), 248–57.

"Risking Play" first appeared in *Whole Terrain: Reflective Environmental Practice* 9 (2000/2001): 37–42.

"To Reach Green before Dark" first appeared in *Waymaking: An Anthology of Women's Adventure Writing, Poetry and Art*, edited by Helen Mort, Claire Carter, Heather Dawe, and Camilla Barnard (Sheffield, UK: Vertebrate Publishing, 2018).

I spent a year and a half on this book, but it grew out of lots of writing and talking I did when in the literature and environment program at the University of Nevada, Reno. Thanks to everyone there, especially Cheryll Glotfelty, Jane Detweiler, and Paul Starrs. It was a golden era. Thanks to my North Carolina friends who have been a part of so many of my outdoor adventures, then as young badasses and now as old farts: Melanie and John Derry, Sean McKnight, Faith Faw, and Rich Keen. My students and colleagues, especially at the Outdoor Academy of the Southern Appalachians and Mansfield University, have helped me explore the ideas set forth here.

My writing group in Pennsylvania put up with many drafts of these essays, especially Judith Sornberger. She and Ann

Turkle have gone on frequent adventures with me on and off the page, and their feedback has been invaluable. I have benefited from our writing retreats together, as well as a spring break spent with Jen Westerman at her parents' mountain oasis. Thanks for your help. Sorry you got the flu. An Anne LaBastille Memorial Writers Residency from the Adirondack Center for Writing gave me two weeks of the quiet and community I needed. It came with loons, kayaks, and great people. Rafia Zakaria, you helped me find my voice. Though I couldn't figure out how to get them to sponsor me, I'm grateful to Hills Creek State Park, ten minutes away. The affordable yurts and cabins helped me "disappear" for several days at a time when I needed to make a deadline. I've worked through many a writing dilemma on those trails.

I've had adventures with lots of wonderful people in my fifty years, but these are some whose companionship, guidance, and love of the outdoors have helped shape this book: Lorraine Anderson, Betty Ann, Jessica Birbeck, Jim Bishop, Susie Caldwell, Michael and Valerie Cohen, Ross Cowan, John Elder, Terry Gifford, Windy Gordon, John "Lightnin'" Griffith, Alan Hamilton, Carol Hayes, Jackie Hueftle, Sheila Kasperek, Bill Kelly, Sue Long, Donna Obrecht, Kirk Peterson, Christine Putman (POOTEY!), Jackie Schlitzer, Dave Schulenburg, Kathy Thorne, Anna Wales, and Kristi Walters. Camping, hiking, biking, climbing, and drinking beer around campfires with the York, Nez, Schaefle-Cates, and Eliason families helped sustain me when the kids were young.

My family has supported my outdoor inclinations, starting before I was born with William E. Colby (Grampa's Uncle Will). Thank you for decades of work preserving public lands. Writing this book made me realize how much I owe my father, who never, that I recall, put restrictions on me because of my gender. Wish you could have read this, Dad. And I'm grateful my mother trusted his judgment even when it scared her. I've enjoyed hikes and paddles with my brothers, Tom and Steve, and cousins Cathy and Marc Meacham. LuAnn Guignard and Anna Ward, my aunt and my cousin by marriage, are great women to adventure with whether digging in the garden or traversing Grandfather Mountain.

Finally, thanks to the man who is my partner at home and beyond the walls. Jimmy, your patience, caring, meat grilling, and smart-ass remarks make getting older a blast. And those kids we made, dang, they're fun. Let's keep the wild times coming. So glad I get to tie in to the same rope as y'all.

References

ONLINE COMMUNITIES AND RESOURCES

Adventure Mamas Initiative
  Redefining motherhood
  PO Box 854
  Heber, UT 84032
  hello@adventuremamas.org
  adventuremamas.org

Black Girls Do Bike
  Growing and supporting a community of women of color who
  share a passion for cycling
  blackgirlsdobike@gmail.com
  blackgirlsdobike.com

Brown Girls Climb
  Promoting and increasing visibility of diversity in climbing by
  establishing a community of climbers of color
  Denver, CO, and Washington, DC
  browngirlsclimb.com

Flash Foxy
  Celebrating and encouraging women climbing with women
  flashfoxy.com

Girl Trek
  Pioneering a health movement for African American women and
  girls grounded in civil rights history and principles through walking
  campaigns
  1800 Wyoming Avenue NW Floor 2
  Washington, DC 20009
  202-808-8419
  info@girltrek.org
  girltrek.org

Hike Like a Woman
Online blog, magazine, and podcast sharing experiences of real outdoor women (of all backgrounds, shapes, and abilities) on and off the trails
hikelikeawoman@gmail.com
hikelikeawoman.net

Latino Outdoors
Bringing *cultura* into the outdoor narrative and connecting Latino communities and leadership with nature and outdoor experiences
latinooutdoors.org

Natives Outdoors
Working with indigenous artists and athletes to create gear that supports outdoor recreation on tribal lands
natives-outdoors.org

Outdoor Afro: Where Black People and Nature Meet
Inspiring African American connections and leadership in nature, and changing the face of conservation
2530 San Pablo Avenue, Suite G
Berkeley, CA 94702
510-306-2376
engage@outdoorafro.com
outdoorafro.com

Outdoor Women's Alliance (OWA)
Promoting women through outdoor adventure
info@outdoorwomensalliance.com
outdoorwomensalliance.com

OUT There Adventures
Empowering queer young people through their connection to the natural world
608-772-2883
General Inquiries: info@outthereadventures.org
Programmatic Inquiries: elyse@outthereadventures.org
outthereadventures.com

Queer Nature

   Cultivating earth-based queer community through traditional skill
   building
   queernature.info@gmail.com
   queernature.org

Tough Love: Dating and Relationships in the Outdoors

   Column by Blair Braverman
   Advice on such topics as staying safe as a queer person while camping, gear-obsessed boyfriends, and when your partner isn't as into
   the outdoors as you
   https://www.outsideonline.com/2164616/tough-love-volume-one-
   dating-advice

Women Hunters

   Educating and promoting women and youth in the hunting traditions while instilling ethics, responsibility, and sportsmanship
   wh-info@womenhunters.com
   womenhunters.com

Women Outdoors

   Providing a supportive environment where all women can have fun
   and challenge themselves in a community of women who love the
   outdoors while respecting the Earth
   PO Box 158
   Northampton, MA 01061
   info@womenoutdoors.org
   womenoutdoors.org

Women's Wilderness

   Strengthening the courage, confidence, and leadership qualities of
   girls and women through group wilderness and community based
   experiences
   2845 Wilderness Place, Suite 211
   Boulder, CO 80301
   303-938-9191
   info@womenswilderness.org
   womenswilderness.org

Women Who Cycle
Blog and online cycling community encouraging women around the
world with stories, product reviews, and social media connections
nicola@womenwhocycle.com
womenwhocycle.com

BIBLIOGRAPHY

Recommended outdoor narrative and creative works are
preceded by asterisks.

*Ackerman, Diane. *Deep Play*. New York: Random House, 1999.

Alaimo, Stacy. *Undomesticated Ground: Recasting Nature as Feminist
Space*. Ithaca, NY: Cornell University Press, 2000.

*Anderson, Lorraine, ed. *Sisters of the Earth: Women's Prose and Poetry
about Nature*. New York: Vintage Books, 1991. Reprint, 2003.

*Anderson, Lorraine, and Thomas S. Edwards, eds. *At Home on This
Earth: Two Centuries of U.S. Women's Nature Writing*. Lebanon, NH:
University Press of New England, 2002.

Associated Press. "In Rock Climbing, Women Find Their Own Path
to the Top." *New York Times*, May 22, 2010. http://www.nytimes.
com/2010/05/23/sports/23guides.html.

Barnard, Josie. "I Loved Her Because She Wanted to Climb the Highest Peak. That's Who She Was." *The Guardian*, August 28, 2002.
https://www.theguardian.com/world/2002/aug/28/gender.familyan-
drelationships.

Baym, Nina. "Melodramas of Beset Manhood: How Theories of American Fiction Exclude Women Authors." *American Quarterly* 33
(1981): 123–39.

*Bird, Isabella L. *A Lady's Life in the Rocky Mountains*. New York: Put-
nam's Sons, 1879. Reprint, Norman: University of Oklahoma Press,
1960.

*Blum, Arlene. *Annapurna: A Woman's Place*. Berkeley, CA: Counter-
point, 2015.

*———. *Breaking Trail: A Climbing Life*. New York: Houghton Mifflin
Harcourt, 2007.

Bly, Nellie. "Champion of Her Sex." *New York Sunday World*, February
2, 1896, 10.

Bouchard, Jay. "Lhakpa Sherpa Breaks Female Everest Record with 8 Summits." *Outsideonline*, May 15, 2017. https://www.outsideonline.com/2185096/lhakpa-sherpa-breaks-female-everest-record-8-summits.

Bradley, Wendy. "One Climber's Opinion in Response to: When Feminism Goes Too Far by Davita Gurian." *ClimbfindHeroes* (blog archive), January 20, 2017. https://web.archive.org/web/20170929155820/http://heroes.climbfind.com/post/156131446237/one-climbers-opinion.

*Braverman, Blair. *Welcome to the Goddamn Ice Cube: Chasing Fear and Finding Home in the Great White North*. New York: HarperCollins, 2016.

Brown, Rebecca A. *Women on High: Pioneers of Mountaineering*. Boston: Appalachian Mountain Club Books, 2003.

Buell, Lawrence. "Pastoral Ideology." In *The Environmental Imagination: Thoreau, Nature Writing, and the Formation of American Culture*, 31–52. Cambridge, MA: Harvard University Press, 1995.

Bureau of Labor Statistics. "Married Parents' Use of Time, 2003–06." Press release, May 8, 2008. Washington, DC: US Department of Labor. http://www.bls.gov/tus/.

Burgstahler, Mary Beth. "To the Mama Who Fought Back Postpartum." *Adventure Mamas Initiative* (blog), May 4, 2016. https://adventuremamas.org/rad/mama-who-fought-back-postpartum/.

Butters, MaryJane. "Author's Note." In *Glamping with MaryJane: Glamour + Camping*. Layton, UT: Gibbs Smith, 2012.

Crooks, Ross. "Splurge vs. Save: Which Beauty Products Are Worth the Extra Cost?" *mintlife* (blog), April 11, 2013. https://blog.mint.com/consumer-iq/splurge-vs-save-which-beauty-products-are-worth-the-extra-cost-0413/.

*Deming, Alison Hawthorne. *Temporary Homelands: Essays on Nature, Spirit and Place*. New York: Picador, 1994.

Domosh, Mona, and Joni Seager. *Putting Women in Place: Feminist Geographers Make Sense of the World*. New York: Guilford Press, 2001.

*Finch, Robert, and John Elder. *The Norton Book of Nature Writing*. New York: Norton, 2002.

Garvey, Megan. "The Target That Shot Back." *Washington Post*, June 17, 1995. https://www.washingtonpost.com/archive/lifestyle/1995/06/17/the-target-that-shot-back/d00ee6f6–679e-4fcf-81de-ec982a5a8f2b/?utm_term=.1e66283b7d59.

Gifford, Terry. "Three Kinds of Pastoral." In *Pastoral*, 1–12. London: Routledge, 1999.

Gilpin, Lyndsey. "How the National Park Service Is Failing Women." *High Country News*, December 12, 2016. http://www.hcn.org/issues/48.21/how-the-park-service-is-failing-women.

Glotfelty, Cheryll. "Femininity in the Wilderness: Reading Gender in Women's Guides to Backpacking." *Women's Studies* 25, no. 5 (July 1996): 439–56.

Gopnik, Adam. "Through the Children's Gate: Of a Home in New York." In *Through the Children's Gate: A Home in New York*, 3–22. New York: Knopf, 2006.

Graham, Latria. "We're Out Here. You Just Don't See Us." *Outside* (May 2018): 72–77.

Greenfeld, Karl Taro. "Life on the Edge." *Time* (September 6, 1999): 29–36.

Guignard, Lilace Mellin. "Private Land and Public Fears: Reclaiming Outdoor Spaces in Gretchen Legler's *Sportswoman's Notebook*." In *Inside Out: Women Negotiating, Subverting, Appropriating Public and Private Space*, edited by Teresa Gómez Reus and Aranzazu Usandizaga, 297–316. Amsterdam: Rodopi Press, 2008.

Gurian, Davita. "When Feminism Goes Too Far." *Evening Sends: Inspired Climbing Stories* (blog), January 17, 2017. http://eveningsends.com/when-feminism-goes-too-far.

Hains, Rebecca. "Target Will Stop Selling Toys for Boys or for Girls. Good." *Washington Post*, August 13, 2015. https://www.washingtonpost.com/posteverything/wp/2015/08/13/target-will-stop-selling-toys-for-boys-or-for-girls-good/?utm_term=.2217fef9cfce.

*Harris, Eddy. *Mississippi Solo: A River Quest*. Ontario: Fitzhenry and Whiteside, 1988.

*Hill, Lynn. *Climbing Free: My Life in the Vertical World*. With Greg Child. New York: Norton, 2002.

hooks, bell. "earthbound: on solid ground." In *Colors of Nature: Culture, Identity, and the Natural World*, edited by Alison H. Deming and Lauret E. Savoy, 184–87. Minneapolis: Milkweed, 2011.

*Houston, Pam. *Cowboys Are My Weakness: Stories*. New York: W. W. Norton, 1992.

Hueftle, Jackie. "Beginning Bouldering 101." *Elephant Journal* (blog), September 7, 2009. https://www.elephantjournal.com/2009/09/beginning-bouldering-via-jackie-hueftle/.

Jensen, Clayne R., and Steven P. Guthrie. *Outdoor Recreation in America*. 6th ed. Champaign, IL: Human Kinetics, 2006.

Joyce, Kathryn. "Out Here, No One Can Hear You Scream." *Huffington Post*, March 16, 2016. http://highline.huffingtonpost.com/articles/en/park-rangers/.

Kolodny, Annette. *The Land before Her: Fantasy and Experience of the American Frontiers, 1630–1860*. Chapel Hill: University of North Carolina Press, 2005.

*LaBastille, Anne. *Woodswoman*. New York: Penguin Books, 1976.

*Legler, Gretchen. *All the Powerful, Invisible Things: A Sportswoman's Notebook*. Seattle: Seal Press, 1995.

Leonard, Brendan. "Girly Girls and Manly Men." *Semi-rad: Humor, Essays, Adventure* (blog), July 5, 2012. http://semi-rad.com/2012/07/girly-girls-and-manly-men/.

*Leopold, Aldo. "Thinking like a Mountain." In *A Sand County Almanac*, 129–33. London: Oxford University Press, 1968.

Lockwood, Devi. "Learning to Scale Peaks from My Underprotective Mother." *New York Times*, July 22, 2016. https://well.blogs.nytimes.com/2016/07/22/learning-to-scale-peaks-from-my-underprotective-mother/.

*Lopez, Barry. "The Negro in the Kitchen." In *Field Notes: The Grace Note of the Canyon Wren*, 75–88. Avon Books: New York, 1994.

Lorenz, Konrad. *On Aggression*. New York: MJF Books, 1997.

Marquis, Christopher. "Man Is Charged in 2 Killings That U.S. Calls Hate Crime." *New York Times*, April 11, 2002. https://www.nytimes.com/2002/04/11/us/man-is-charged-in-2-killings-that-us-calls-hate-crime.html.

Marx, Leo. *The Machine in the Garden: Technology and the Pastoral Ideal in America*. Oxford: Oxford University Press, 1964. Reprint, 2000.

*Mazel, David, ed. *Mountaineering Women: Stories by Early Climbers*. College Station: Texas A&M University Press, 1994.

McConnell, Ruby. *A Woman's Guide to the Wild: Your Complete Outdoor Handbook*. Seattle: Sasquatch Books, 2016.

*Mills, James Edward. *The Adventure Gap: Changing the Face of the Outdoors*. Seattle: Mountaineers Books, 2014.

———. "This Is What Adventure Looks Like." *Outside* (May 2018): 56–70.

Mock, Brentin. "How Our Fear of 'Wilding' Colored the Central Park Five Case." *Grist*, July 8, 2014. http://grist.org/cities/how-our-fear-of-wilding-colored-the-central-park-five-case/.

*Mort, Helen. "An Easy Day for a Lady." In *No Map Could Show Them*, 2. London: Chatto and Windus, 2016.

Napora, Joe. "A Newbie on the New." *American Whitewater* (September/October 1999): 107–8.

Nash, Roderick. *Wilderness and the American Mind*. 3rd ed. New Haven, CT: Yale University Press, 1982.

Outdoor Foundation. *Outdoor Recreation Participation Report 2015*. https://outdoorindustry.org/participation/outdoor-foundation-research/reports/archived-outdoor-participation-reports/.

Pohl, Sarah L., William T. Borrie, and Michael Patterson. "Women, Wilderness, and Everyday Life: A Documentation of the Connection between Wilderness Recreation and Women's Everyday Lives." *Journal of Leisure Research* 32, no. 4 (2000): 415–34.

*Roberts, Suzanne. *Almost Somewhere: Twenty-Eight Days on the John Muir Trail*. Lincoln: University of Nebraska Press, 2012.

*Rogers, Susan Fox. *Another Wilderness: New Outdoor Writing by Women*. Seattle: Seal Press, 1994.

Schaffer, Grayson. "The Most Successful Female Everest Climber of All Time Is a Housekeeper in Hartford, Connecticut." *Outsideonline*, May 10, 2016. https://www.outsideonline.com/2078361/most-successful-female-everest-climber-all-time-housekeeper-hartford-connecticut.

"Serena Williams." Post on *Data Lounge*, June 5, 2010. https://www.datalounge.com/thread/9282169-serena-williams.

Shepard, Paul. *The Tender Carnivore and the Sacred Game*. Athens: University of Georgia Press, 1973. Reprint, 1998.

Silko, Leslie Marmon. "Landscape, History, and the Pueblo Imagination." In *The Norton Book of Nature Writing*, edited by Robert Finch and John Elder, 1003–1014. New York: Norton, 2002.

Slovic, Paul. *The Perception of Risk*. New York: Earthscan/Routledge, 2000.

*Solnit, Rebecca. "Walking after Midnight: Women, Sex, and Public Space." In *Wanderlust: A History of Walking*, 232–46. New York: Penguin Books, 2000.

*Strayed, Cheryl. *Wild: From Lost to Found on the Pacific Crest Trail.* New York: Knopf, 2012.

Suprenant, Leslie. "Original Woodswoman: Preserving the Legacy of Anne LaBastille." *New York State Conservationist* (December 2016): 10–13.

Twichell, Chase. "The Pools." In *The Ghost of Eden*, 6–7. Ontario Review Press.com, 1998.

*Underhill, Miriam. *Give Me the Hills.* New York: Ballantine Books, 1973.

Wadewitz, Adrianne, and Peter James. "Women Relax, Men Mountaineer: What Backpacks Reveal about Gendered Marketing." *Huffington Post*, November 27, 2013. https://www.huffingtonpost.com/adrianne-wadewitz-phd/hiking-gendered-marketing_b_4351519.html.

Warren, Karen. "Women's Outdoor Adventures: Myth and Reality." In *Women's Voices in Experiential Education*, 10–17. Dubuque, IA: Kendall Hunt, 1996.

*Willard, Frances Elizabeth. *A Wheel within a Wheel: How I Learned to Ride the Bicycle.* New York: Fleming H. Revell, 1895. Reprint, Carlisle, MA: Applewood Books, 1997.

Worick, Jennifer. *Backcountry Betty: Roughing It in Style.* Seattle: Mountaineers Books, 2007.

Yeoman, Barry. "Murder on the Mountain." November 1, 1996. http://barryyeoman.com/1996/11/murder-on-the-mountain/.

Index